'. . . the candid glance of a man at peace with himself and rather pleased with his new tie'

STEVE RACE

Musician at Large

EYRE METHUEN

First published in 1979
by Eyre Methuen Ltd
11 New Fetter Lane, London EC4P 4EE
© 1979 Steve Race

Set, printed and bound in Great Britain by
Cox & Wyman Ltd,
London, Fakenham and Reading

ISBN 0 413 39740 8

For Gillian Reynolds
who suggested I should
write it, but most of
all for Lonny, who made
sure I did

Contents

IV

Illustrations

The author—

Acknowledgments and thanks are due for permission to reproduce extracts from the following: *Literary Gent* by David Higham (Jonathan Cape Ltd, 1978), *Opportunity Knocked* by Hughie Green (Frederick Muller Ltd, 1965), Langham Diary by Steve Race from *The Listener*, January 1978, *The Letters of Alexander Woollcott* edited by Beatrice Kaufmann & Joseph Hennessey (Cassell Ltd, 1946), *Cautionary Verses* by Hilaire Belloc (Gerald Duckworth & Co Ltd, 12th imp. 1976), *Beecham Stories* by Harold Atkins & Archie Newman (Robson Books, 1978), *J.Y. An Autobiography of Jimmy Young* (W. H. Allen & Co Ltd, 1973), *Ottoline* by Sandra Jobson Darroch (Chatto & Windus Ltd, 1976), *Promise Me You'll Sing Mud!* by Ian Wallace (John Calder Ltd, 1975), and 'The Individual in an Egalitarian Society', an exhibition brochure by John Bratby (National Theatre, 1978).

Acknowledgments and thanks are due to A B C Television for plate 4; to Express Newspapers Ltd for plate 5b; to the B B C for plates 6a, 8a and 8b; to the *Redditch Indicator & Alcester Chronicle* for plate 6b; and to E M I records for plate 7. The frontispiece is by Petrina.

Prelude: Theme and Palpitations

14 April 1965 looked like being a busy day as usual. I had a lunch appointment with a lady advertising executive to discuss composing and recording special music for a commercial television jingle. After that would come a live radio programme from Broadcasting House. To round off the day, there was a concert which I planned to review for a magazine.

I drove into town, left the car near the BBC and took a taxi to Rules Restaurant, in Maiden Lane.

The cab driver proved to be the chatty type, as so many of them are, when they are not surly and embittered. I suppose it must be a lonely life, sitting there at the wheel, shuttling between hither and yon and hither again, with nothing but your contempt for private motorists to keep you going.

'I've seen you before, haven't I?' the cabby began. 'Aren't you on the telly?'

'That's right.'

'Don't tell me your name.' (I wasn't going to.) 'You play the piano, don't you?' In order to make sure that I knew what he meant, he took both hands off the steering wheel and rippled them rapidly to and fro over an imaginary keyboard. 'I'll get your name in a minute. Ross... Rose...' Then triumphantly, 'Sid Rowles!'

'Race, actually.'

'That's it, Sid Race.'

It was hard to hear what he was saying. In order to catch his words over the traffic noise I was sitting so far forward in my seat that I kept slipping off on to the floor. Something had to be done, and I decided the only thing was to kneel on the mat as if in prayer. As bad luck would have it, at that moment he swung into the extreme right lane of traffic, then executed a swift left turn into Glasshouse Street. It is one of the short cuts beloved of taxi drivers – they call them 'back doubles' – though they often involve more snarl-ups than the main roads. I picked myself up and resumed my seat. I was waiting for the Inevitable.

The Inevitable, as any possessor of a television face knows, is the second stage of being recognised. The recogniser has correctly identified you. He is now searching his memory for encounters with other people in your profession, so that he can regale you with a list of their names.

'I had Ray Ellington in the cab once.' (Why is it always Ray Ellington? Does the man never use public transport?) 'One afternoon I took Charlie Drake to the Palladium. Then there was that singer. Irish girl – can't think of her name.'

'Ruby Murray.'

'What? No, that's not it. I know – Ruby Murray. That's who it was. And I had a mate once picked up Danny la Rue ...'

By the time we reached the Restaurant he had happily run through half the entertainment profession and I was pursuing my own thoughts in the back. With relief, I got up off my knees.

The advertising executive I was meeting for lunch was a young woman whom I rather liked. She was quiet and unaffected, indeed for someone in the advertising business she was really quite sane. Confronted with an idea of blinding promise, she did not say, 'Let's run it up the flagpole and see if anyone salutes', whereas most advertising people I had met really did say things like that. She and I had enjoyed some success with a garden tools TV commercial which won an award at the Venice Film Festival. This time we were discussing, I seem to recall, a catfood commercial. Perhaps that is why we both ordered the grilled sole. We also shared a bottle of Montrachet after the sherry. Now I come to think of it, we may have preceded the sole with some pâté, certainly we followed it with a modest portion of trifle. (All right then, just a little cream, waiter.) The camembert was unusually ripe, and the brandy seemed to complement it. Coffee, sir? – Of course.

When Mary left to return to her office, I rose somewhat

heavily to my feet to bid her goodbye. Then I paid the bill, exchanged a few words with the wine waiter, who thought he had seen me before and wasn't I on the telly? He called me, as restauranteurs and waiters so often do, 'Mister Steverace', all in one word.

Out in Bedford Street it was just coming on to rain; heavy, wet drops out of a slate grey sky. I waved at an empty taxi to take me to Broadcasting House. The driver seemed to have acknowledged me, but then just as I was jogging towards him, a man came flying out of Moss Bros with a large box under his arm and took over the taxi, getting in at the opposite door and giving me the firm smile of one accustomed to scorching fags at Rugby. Beginning to feel faintly unwell, I set off to walk towards Oxford Street and Portland Place.

There are two ways of walking when you want a taxi but cannot find one. The best way is to take off with a brisk, jaunty step, like Burlington Bertie sauntering along the Strand. The other way is to trudge on, with one's head screwed miserably round in case a free taxi should come up from the rear. That was my basic posture as I covered the damp mile or more from Rules Restaurant to the B B C headquarters near Oxford Circus. By the time I reached B.H. (as all radio people call Broadcasting House) I was feeling quite poorly. Quite poorly.

Down in studio L 1 on the lower-ground floor the Studio Manager was getting out the mikes and plugging up the equipment. 'I'm not very well,' I told her, in that quaint expression which we English use when we feel we may not last the day. By the time the producer had arrived, and we had begun rehearsing, I had developed two quite marked symptoms of malaise, both of them unfamiliar to me: in my throat was a curious pressure, a welling-up feeling which is hard to describe but unmistakable to experience, while under my left arm I felt as though a bow-string had been drawn tight.

There was a technical hold-up in the rehearsal for some reason. Another producer came in and began to talk to me about a different programme altogether, which I was due to give a week or two later. 'I've just realised that the date we'd fixed for the recording will be Good Friday,' he said. 'Perhaps we could change the date.' We got out our diaries. Mine looked full. I didn't know what to suggest.

And that proved to be the tiny last straw. My body –

protesting at being somewhat overweight and recently over-
fed; protesting at the frustrated taxi-less trudge in the rain;
protesting at my thirty cigarettes a day and slightly erratic
life-style; protesting most of all, perhaps, at my parents having
unwittingly passed on to me a double inheritance of heart
trouble – my body decided it was time to go on strike. I lay
down on the long bench seat at the side of Studio L 1 and had a
heart attack.

I had always been under the impression that a coronary
occlusion, as the doctors call it, involved the patient clutching
his chest in agony and falling insensible to the ground. Instead,
here was I, conscious of feeling more ill than I would have
thought possible, but not exactly in pain. I certainly had no
chest pain. Perhaps the swift arrival of the doctor took care of
that: he gave me an injection. In due course the ambulance
came, I was carried through the interested foyer of Broadcasting House, out into the street and away to the Middlesex
Hospital, the siren warbling a shrill F sharp and A.

Arrived in the Out-patients Department, everything
seemed to come to a halt. I lay on my stretcher fully clothed,
and was sufficiently myself to point out to the nurse where I
kept my money, and would she please look after it? Although
the hold-up might well have been occasioned by the hospital
searching for a spare bed, it occurred to me that equally it
might have been because my heart-beat was too erratic for me
to be moved any further without risk. We certainly hung
about for quite a while in that reception area. Then after half an
hour they moved me to Meyerstein Ward and into bed, wearing one of those crudely starched hospital smocks which were
designed by some nurse who had spent too long on nights, and
which crumple up inexorably under the back and freeze the
legs. Still, it was sheer heaven to be there, thanks to the
injection and the clean white sheets, out of pain, and – who
knows? – perhaps out of danger.

The hectic life of a hospital ward crashed on about me. Then
loved ones came and went, darkness fell, the lamplit night
Sister gave her unintentional imitation of Florence Nightin-
gale. Turning gingerly on to my right side I could see the
oscilloscope which was connected to the leads from my
ankles and wrists. It represented in a very literal sense, The
Story of My Life, second by second. On the blue television

14

screen of the oscilloscope I watched my heartbeats trace their halting way from right to left. 'Ger-bong ... Bliddle ... Ger – Ger-blonk ... Bliddle-dee ...'

Waking in the morning, I looked round a ward in which the customary morning bedlam reigned, different only now in that there was a pervasive smell of mouthwash. I noticed a pair of radio earphones hanging on the rail behind my head. Slowly I reached back for them, put the earphones on, and heard the announcer on the Home Service news bulletin say, 'We have just heard that Steve Race, the pianist and broadcaster, suffered a heart attack in a BBC studio yesterday.'

'Just heard!' – Good old BBC! The studio in which I had distinguished myself sixteen hours before was a mere forty paces from the newsroom. Someone, I thought (recalling an earlier affair with a less happy outcome) had blundered.

But talking of outcomes, what was to be the outcome in my case? I was forty-four years old, a husband and father, well-established and happy in a successful professional life. Was this to be the end of it? Would there be a sudden excruciating flash of pain, and this time darkness, silence? – Hymn-singing?

I glanced over at my new inseparable companion, the oscilloscope. It stared back at me, erratic as ever. I wondered with a very precise curiosity whether I would actually witness the sudden untroubled straight line which signalled my expiry, or whether I would simply blot out, leaving a passing nurse to call out 'Sister, I don't think that new patient's oscilloscope is connected up properly.'

Hasty conference. Then Sister would chide, over my inert body: 'Now come along, Mr Race. We've lost one of our leads.'

But all was well, and after some days had passed my oscilloscope was as regular as a Victor Silvester foxtrot. The *Daily Telegraph* crossword resumed its hold on me. A specialist came to see me on his rounds and found me sitting up in bed with a question of some importance on my lips.

'Doctor,' I asked, 'I've always been fond of swimming. When I get out, will I be able to swim again?'

He regarded me steadily and with the faintest hint of a smile. Then he replied, 'I was wondering when you'd ask. Don't you worry, Mr Race. There's no reason why you shouldn't resume a perfectly normal sex life.'

'I didn't ask that,' I called after him, a little petulantly, but he had moved on to the next bed. Well, I thought, don't excite yourself. Let it go – relax. In any case, good. Get started on that second life. With any luck it will be every bit as good as the one before.

As a matter of fact, I think it has been better.

PART ONE

1. *In which our hero is*

That first life of mine began in a striking setting; the ancient city of Lincoln.

Everyone has an affection for his birthplace and I am fond of Lincoln, though in my day it was very much of a back-water, lying exactly midway on the road to nowhere. It is still on the road to nowhere, unless you count Barton-on-Humber or Irby-in-the-Marsh as somewhere.

The Lincoln of my youth was an oddly unsettled place, trying to find a satisfactory identity somewhere between mediaeval charm and industrial decay. A superb Gothic cathedral greets the tourist, but its towers look out over a sea of sullen nineteenth-century red brick. Moreover Lincoln folk, whether in their workmen's terraces or their stone villas, are not easy to know. They regard the stranger with a wary eye. Friendly at heart but innately cautious, they live in a city with a lost past and an unfound future.

Neither of my parents was Lincoln born. My mother was born in Reading. But her father died when she was five and her mother a year later, leaving her to be sent north to her uncle's house and raised there by a spinster cousin in the stern, deeply religious atmosphere of Victorian Wesleyanism. Having arrived in the city so early, she was ultimately accepted as a Lincolnian, though her speech always bore traces of her native Berkshire, just as mine still occasionally betrays my native Lincolnshire.

My father came from much further afield, having been born in China, the son of a Wesleyan missionary. The local people must have thought him something of a curiosity when he arrived in Lincoln one Edwardian summer, put up a lawyer's brass plate in the Cornhill and waited for his first client to walk through the doorway. Father too overcame the innate Lincolnshire reserve in the end, largely due to the fact that he was a Methodist.

He joined the local chapel on arrival, and promptly fell in love with the girl sitting two rows in front. Under the eagle eye of my mother's guardian they met, went for walks together, exchanged books ('To Miss Hurley, with R.T.R.'s deepest regards'). Finally, on a rowing boat on the river Witham one summer afternoon, father managed to get her alone and proposed marriage. Robina Hurley accepted him – naturally, since she had adored him on sight. She continued to love only him, or his memory, for the rest of her long life.

I was born in 1921, five years after my brother Philip. Within two weeks I sought the spotlight and was desperately ill with pneumonia, until saved by a timely teaspoonful of brandy. They say I licked my lips and rallied on the instant. I still enjoy a teaspoonful from time to time.

Mother's cousin Lena – gaunt, upright, awkwardly fond – figures in my earliest memory. I was sitting up enjoying a bathe in my zinc bath on the kitchen table when Auntie Lena, yielding to a moment of uncharacteristic playfulness, intro-duced me to the story of the little pigs.

> This little piggy went to market,
> This little piggy stayed home ...

At the climax to the story there was a sudden paroxysm of toe-tickling. I did not enjoy it one bit. *Must* one put up a sign reading 'Bath night – No ticklers admitted'? It seems so. At any rate I recall the experience clearly enough not to have inflicted piggy-pinching on any of the children I have met since.

Of my father I remember hardly anything. I cherish a few disconnected whisps of memory; a fleeting vision of a tall man smoking a cigar in the back yard; a grey-suited man, putting on incredibly long button boots and pausing to let me play with the laces; a gentle daddy in a tall forest of fruit bushes, offering me my first delicious raspberry. I remember calling out to him for help when I had accidentally shut myself in the outside lavatory, and his rescuing me as he swung me aloft in his arms, a thousand miles up in the sky, to rest in triumph on his shoulder.

More specifically I remember standing in the front window of our house overlooking the High Street, demanding to know why angry men were marching up the middle of the road towards the city centre. I do not remember my father's answer but I know now that they must have been pickets: it was the General Strike of 1926. Mother swept me away from the window just as I glimpsed out of the corner of my eye a man being jostled and frog-marched along the road by the jeering crowd. I suppose he was a blackleg. Although I saw so little and heard only a hum of voices, the black taste of fear is in my mouth as I recall that May morning.

But the sun was shining happily when three months later we went on holiday to the Yorkshire coast, a family of four laden with buckets, spades, swimsuits and towels, to stay in digs at a house in Crescent Avenue, Whitby. At teatime on the second evening my father announced that he was going for a stroll along the cliffs. A Durham dalesman by upbringing, his 'strolls' tended to be rather taxing, so the rest of us did not go with him.

He was missing for a long time – a very long time indeed. Night fell. Still he had not returned, and my mother, fearful and alone in a strange town, put us boys to bed and walked to the police station to report his disappearance. There the sergeant on duty broke the grim news: that a fisherman on his way to the harbour had come across my father's body in the long grass on the cliffs, at a spot ironically called 'Happy Valley'. Other passers-by had presumably thought he was sleeping, but there was something about the position of the legs which made the young fisherman suspicious. Turning the body over, he realised that he was looking into the eyes of a dead man. My father had suffered a coronary. He was just forty-seven.

The family rallied round as families do in a crisis. An uncle travelled to Whitby to take care of the formalities. We children were shepherded back to Lincoln, Philip ten years old, myself five. And once back there, life seemed to go on very much as before, given the fact that daddy was away 'in hospital'.

It must have been about two months later, in the front bedroom of our house at 6 St Catherines, Lincoln, that I asked my mother the question which had been occupying my mind.

'When is daddy coming out of hospital?' I asked.

I saw her eyes brim with tears. 'I'm afraid,' she said, 'daddy won't be coming back at all. He's gone to live ... He's gone to ...'

But it was a sentence she could never complete. We sat down on the bed together, her arm round me, and as she wept quietly for her lost husband and I for my lost father, a bond was forged between us which nothing ever weakened in all the years that followed. To this day I can hardly bear the sight of tears on a human face, while to sit for more than a moment on the edge of a bed is to bring a sudden dryness to the throat, as memory touches that chord of bereavement and love across more than fifty years.

We never spoke of that evening again, though I know she remembered it, just as I did.

My mother's life must have been appallingly difficult then, financially as well as in the personal sense. During all our growing years she kept scrupulous accounts to the last half-penny, sitting down each evening to balance her tiny budget. It embarrasses me now to think of the money I wasted on toys, magazines and all the transient pleasures that mean so much to a child in those careless years, but cost so much when times are hard. For my mother, bringing up two boys in the 1920s and early 30s must have been a long and lonely struggle. Bitter too, though her gentleness and faith never deserted her.

Magnificently, St Catherines Methodist Church rose to the occasion. In these days of television, bingo, social services and other comforts, it is hard to realise how close-knit and helpful that sort of church community could be fifty years ago. The services at 10.15 and 6 each Sunday marked merely the beginning of a full social week, the chapel premises a constant hive of human activity from Monday to Saturday. There were missionary meetings, prayer meetings, choir meetings and class meetings. The women brought their knitting to the Busy Bees and their needlework to the Sewing Meeting Teas. The men had their cricket team and in the winter their Bright Hour. It seems like another world now, and indeed it was.

We kids were expected to turn up on Thursdays for the Band of Hope, where Mr Butler, earnest, bewhiskered and said to be a hundred years old, would lead us in reciting a solemn oath. Voices raised in enthusiastic unison, we would chant:

'I promise to abstain from all intoxicating liquors as beverages.'

I find it hard now to justify quite tiny children being made to undertake an oath they scarcely understood. Certainly I have felt no compunction in breaking my Band of Hope oath, enjoying 'intoxicating liquors as beverages' with only an occasional feeling that Mr Butler is standing beside me shaking his head sadly.

Mother loved her chapel associations and was grateful for them all her life. She was by no means uncritical, though. Despite her love for many of the old hymns, for instance, she knew well enough that some of them were closer to doggerel than to poetry:

I am so glad that Jesus loves me,
Jesus loves me, Jesus loves me,
I am so glad that Jesus loves me,
Jesus loves even me.

There was high drama in some of the old hymns:

And can I yet delay
My little all to give?
To tear my soul from earth away
For Jesus to receive?
Nay, but I yield, I yield!
I can hold out no more.
I sink, by dying love compelled,
And own Thee conqueror.

Strong stuff, though almost conventional for old-school Methodists who believed – and frequently sang – that redemption could only come through being 'washed in the blood of the lamb'.

Such verbal imagery from earlier centuries still held Methodism in its iron grip. But a lively sense of the ridiculous was the great problem in our pew. My mother suffered both from a sense of humour and from a dangerously catchable eye. She was quite incapable of standing in church between her two sons and singing, with a straight face:

In age and feebleness extreme,
Who shall a helpless worm redeem?

While the splendidly picturesque hymn line which went:

Even a worm shall bend the knee ...

– found her shaking quietly, hymnbook hiding her face.

Mother's sense of humour could be a liability at times, but more often it was the source of great joy. One of the things she loved doing was reading aloud to us. I can see us now: mother resting her arthritic hip on the sofa, Philip and myself in those contorted positions which represent comfort and normality for small boys but would be agony for anyone else. Mother's reading-aloud sessions are among the most treasured of all my memories. To this day I sometimes close a book which has delighted me, with the reflection that it would have made a good choice for the three of us, all those long years ago.

In particular I remember her reading *The House at Pooh Corner*, that charming book (providing one can swallow the somewhat nauseous tea-with-nursie element). Mother was reading the chapter which A. A. Milne had artfully headed 'In which Pooh invents a new game and Eeyore joins in'.

As any Pooh fan knows, the game was called Poohsticks. We had reached page 95 with its Ernest Shepard drawing of Pooh, Piglet, Roo and Rabbit leaning over the bridge waiting for their Poohsticks to float through from the other side. Piglet was very excited because his was the only stick which had been seen, and that meant that he was winning.

At that point mother turned the page and abruptly stopped reading. She had glimpsed Shepard's drawing of whatever it was that had floated under the bridge. As she laughed silently, Philip and I went over to see what could possibly be affecting her in that way, and saw – the reader can check his own copy perhaps – the page 96 illustration of the hapless Eeyore, floating upsidedown with his legs in the air. Eeyore, resigned and mournful to the last. Eeyore, to whom everything happened. Oneself, in fact.

Sunday afternoon was always the great reading-aloud time in our house. But then at six o'clock it was time to go back again to chapel for the evening service; over the Newark Road, past the waterboard offices, past the villas with their old-fashioned names which I find I can still remember.

Our walk took us directly past the brass plate which recorded the memorable professional partnership of two doc-

tors with extraordinary names, Doctors Allcock and Lillicrap.
(One feels that the moment they met they knew their lives
were destined to be interlinked.

'Allcock?'

'Yes?'

'I'm Lillicrap.'

'My dear fellow, I can scarcely believe my good luck. Do
you have a partnership form on you?')

Arrived at the chapel, everything was grey: the stone, the
people, the very air. The hatpegs near the entrance must have
been a foot long, built to accommodate the top hats of an
earlier generation. They smelt of bay rum.

I loved our chapel, but I hated it too. I hated the boredom of
the interminable sermons ('Firstly, brethren ... Secondly ...
Thirdly and lastly ...'). I suffered under the endless extempore
prayers, which were so much a tradition in the Methodist
church but so far beyond the creative powers of most of its
preachers. I revolted against the thunderers and the Bible
thumpers. I caught my brother's eye and giggled uncontroll-
ably as the lay preacher asked 'Shall Satan rule, my friends?'
and then – innocent of the popular song of the day – answered
his own question by proclaiming 'No, no, a thousand times
No!'

I felt the poignancy of a dying evening, as the sun turned to
gold, the shadows lengthened through the stained-glass window behind the altar, and the congregation sang in wavering
unison:

The day-hay thou gay-hay-vest Lor-hord is ended ...

A great sadness filled me then, and I would stand an inch or
two closer to mother so as to feel her comforting presence
against my side. She never failed to put an arm around me in
response. She, too, knew how it felt to be suddenly miserable,
though for her, a widow, there was no protecting arm.

2. All one body we, especially us Methodists

Mother and father had been married in that same church. My brother and I had been christened there. We had every reason to suppose that in due course we would both be married there (though in point of fact neither of us was). In the end we would leave there in our coffins, bound for the cemetery on the Washingborough Road, the last ride.

At quite an early age the awful inevitability of it struck me. A tiny protesting voice told me that I was not prepared for fate to write me off quite so predictably.

Boring and depressing as the church services were, the place had its compensations. For one thing, it bred a circle of genuinely loving friends, in which it was clear that my mother took comfort and pleasure. On a more practical level, we had a splendid organ in the church, quite out of proportion to our local importance, not to mention our musical standing in the city. The interior architecture, too, was pleasing; in fact even now I cannot recall having seen a better looking Methodist Church than St Catherines.

Once inside, there were strange experiences to be enjoyed in our young days. There was the musical pleasure of hearing my Auntie Lena sing what she called 'Seconds', though what she was actually singing was thirds – major, minor or in between – below the tune as printed in the hymnbook. There was old Mr Vinter in the choir, whose son, Gilbert, made a real contribution to the profession of music in later years, but who was the church's sole representative of the bass line. Mr Vinter sang in endless competition with the only audible tenor, Mr Watson, who soared to an occasional top G, with a vibrato which made the font shake. Once I fancied that Mr Watson's vocal fervour

24

was responsible for dislodging a small piece of stained-glass window, but perhaps it was a passing tram.

Annually at the appropriate season the choir would 'render' – always the word used in those days – Stainer's *Crucifixion*. I remember it chiefly for its endless canonic chorus:

Fling wide the/ fling wide the/ fling wide the ...

On those occasions, Mr Mervyn Rees, our organist, would desert his organ bench and conduct the choir, while someone else stood in for him at the console. 'Stood in' was the right expression: during the longer prayers Mr Rees had been known occasionally to stir on his organ bench and depress one of the foot pedals by mistake. A deep, haunting *Hoo–oom* would echo through the church, and the minister would pretend that nothing had happened. It was noticed however that one of them, who was accustomed to thanking the Almighty for 'the gift of music', stopped doing so for a while, no doubt getting back at Mr Rees for upstaging him.

I liked Mr Rees, and I came to realise later what a good organist he was, getting a move on with the hymns at a time when Methodist Hymnody was practically at a standstill. He would vary his tonal registration in a colourful way, and he chose good, tuneful voluntaries to play while the collection was being taken. How many people of my generation can claim to have first encountered in a church the *Intermezzo* from *Cavalleria Rusticana* or the *Praeludium* by Jarnefelt? The cheerful Mr Rees had no illusions about his playing, regarding himself as a journeyman organist. When the time came for us to be favoured with that most bafflingly tedious of all forms of entertainment, the Organ Recital, Mr Rees stepped aside almost gratefully and allowed someone else to take over. Musically-minded though I was from an early age, I could never understand how people could enjoy sitting in a freezing church, looking at nothing and nobody, while an organ boomed its way through some lengthy *Prelude* by Karg-Elert or Steggall. I came to understand later that the organ is like golf, or for that matter sex; the whole point of enjoying it is to do it yourself.

Our pew was at the very back of the church. My brother Philip sat in the corner which had been father's place; mother was between us (a precaution which was sometimes necessary) and next to me sat old Mr Sneath, a kindly old boy with a walrus moustache and a gentle but pervasive smell all his own which for some reason I associate with breadcrumbs: perhaps I could see some lodged in his whiskers. Persuaded that all little boys ever think of is sweets, he would quietly reach for my hand and place in it a large pink gob-stopper. I would smile at him bravely and put the thing in my mouth, parking it on the cheek farthest from his eye while it slowly dissolved, burning the mouth and throat, too awful to move with the tongue. Eventually its core would burst, filling my mouth with a squelchy mixture like the inner contents of a golf ball. At that point my eyes would water and I would concentrate as hard as possible on the scripture reading, which always seemed to be from the book of Isaiah.

Over to the right and two or three pews in front sat old Mr Pye. He was almost totally deaf, and listened to the service through a hearing-aid attached to a long stem. Mr Pye's face, during moments of revivalist fervour, was striking, even beautiful: it was the face of a man in emotional rapture, all the more memorable since so few of us can ever know such heights of spirituality.

So the life of our chapel wore on, month after month, year after year. We ploughed the fields and scattered. We rose with anthems sweet. We wept not for him who onward bears. (I liked to think that the onward bears were related to the she-bear in 'Hark! My Soul, it is the Lord', at the line 'Can a woman's tender care cease toward the child she-bear?' And were they the same family as my friend Gladly, who featured in the line 'Gladly, the cross-eyed bear'?)

Visiting clerics came to star at the Missionary Weekend or the Sunday School Anniversary. On those occasions there was some rivalry, even in-fighting, as to who should 'entertain the visitor'. Sometimes our own house would be dignified by an overnight visit from the Rev. This, B.A. or Dr That, M.A. Then the silver teapot would come out, there would be little square iced cakes for tea, and one would have to remember before plunging in that Mr Rattenbury or Dr Wiseman would expect to Say Grace, with some ceremony and elaboration.

Usually such celebrities stayed with Auntie Lena at Southfield, her tall grey house two minutes' walk away. Southfield had been built in that pseudo-Gothic style one sees

26

so often in Wales. It had a large garden – large by my standards, anyway – with here and there a stone urn full of geraniums, or a metal seat on which mother would sit during the hours of Auntie Lena's all-consuming talk.

Sunday supper at Southfield was a particular form of agony, despite the cream sponge jellies which Auntie Lena bought for us. The talk was always of church functions and church attendance; that tittle-tattle which often passes for concern among church folk. At the end of the evening came the dread moment when Auntie Lena would say, in her hollow contralto voice, 'Now, how about family prayers?' One of us would read 'a portion' from the Bible, and then we would rise from our chairs, turn round, kneel and put our faces where – how to phrase it any other way? – where our bottoms had been. There we would half-close our eyes while Auntie Lena improvised a sombre and lengthy prayer.

But then the worst was over. After that it was get to your feet, turn round, edge towards the door, 'Don't forget to say thank you, Auntie,' and home with mother's hand round mine, perhaps to the drink of cocoa that somehow was never offered at Southfield. Southfield was not a cocoa sort of place.

But Southfield did offer two great joys. The first was to be allowed to drift out into the kitchen; to 'bother Alice', as Auntie Lena put it. Alice wore a lace apron and a lace cap. Alice received, I suppose, ten shillings a week and her keep, in return for something in the region of sixty hours' work. And although these days no red-blooded socialist could bring himself to believe it for a second, Alice was an extremely happy and fulfilled young woman, living in a state of semi-luxury which she would never otherwise have known, occupying an important place in the hierarchy of the chapel by virtue of her position as 'Miss Wallis's maid', walking out (for all I know) with a soldier on her afternoon off, and sleeping between sheets in a warm room with a panoramic view across the South Common.

Alice's kitchen was homely and welcoming. There was always something being baked or some dark dripping to be finished off on a doorstep of bread. There was a huge deal table, on which you could really spread yourself and draw things, while the oval double-portrait of Prince Edward and his bride Alexandra looked down from over the door, and a

27

somnolent old grandfather clock ticked away in a painful 6/8 rhythm. From time to time the coiled spring would quiver on the bell over the door. It was Auntie Lena ringing for something, whereupon Alice would heave to her feet to fetch hot milk or refill the sugar basin with huge rough, glistening sugar-lumps.

The other great joy of Southfield was Timmy. To the very end of the 1920s Auntie Lena managed to maintain a pony and trap. Timmy was her pony. He was looked after by a groom, whose name – in approved Happy Families style – was Mr Spurr. Just 'Groom', Auntie Lena called him, and he did not consider her peremptory because he too was happy to serve Alderman Wallis's daughter. Besides, he had the pleasure of a gentle pony to look after, a lean-to greenhouse to smoke in, and a garden (with geranium urns) to tend. The alternative would have been a routine job in one of Lincoln's heavy engineering works or, more likely in those days, the dole queue. Groom was one of the lucky ones, and he knew it. So was Timmy.

But the late 1920s were the sunset days for Southfield. How different it had all been decades before, when Lena Wallis was a sought-after Liberal speaker; when she was the first lady bicyclist in Lincoln, even something of a suffragette! How lively the Southfield talk had been when Mr Gladstone came to stay, or when General Booth was so rude to the maids that they had to be pacified afterwards by a personal kitchen visit from the master, Alderman Wallis himself.

Thomas Wallis had been a simple farm lad, sent away to work at the age of seven; tied to a wheel in the barn and whipped by his new master to show him once and for all who was boss. Thomas Wallis was the epitome of the Victorian self-made man. Although he never assumed the gold watch-chain or the *embonpoint* of the classic nineteenth-century Alderman, he did woo and win the best-looking girl in the district, 'the beautiful Miss Hewitt' as she was called. Eventually she had a stroke and spent the last decades of her life in an armchair, looking out from the upstairs bay window at the passing scene, her eyes glazed in sadness. But Josephine Wallis's snow white hair was exquisitely groomed to the very last.

Old Tom Wallis was lean as a rake and noted in Lincoln for his generosity with pounds but his meanness with ha'pennies.

He lived on into his eighties, never wearing an overcoat even in that rheumatic city, leaping on and off buses, organising people and anticipating the social reforms which were to come soon after his death in 1931. Wanting to give Lincoln something bright and exciting as a celebratory gift he asked the city fathers what they suggested. 'How about a floating bandstand on Boultham Park lake?' enquired one of them. Grandpa Wallis withered him with a countryman's frank look. 'Waterlogged and worthless within a year,' he said, 'think again.' They did and he finally approved a scheme for a nursery greenhouse in the same park. It is there to this day, with a plaque on the door to commemorate the donor.

I have one recollection of him which I treasure. He owned a sawmill alongside the Pool of Lincoln, and when he was nearing his eighties and I perhaps six years old, he took me to see it. We must have made a rather engaging sight: he lean and spare, like one of Tenniel's old men in *Alice in Wonderland*; myself small and pink, with a Christopher Robin sunhat. I remember him showing me great mountains of planks, stacked almost to heaven but still in the formation of the trees from which they were sawn. I remember his being greeted by the men working there, and without being sentimental it seems to me still that all of them smiled as they met his eye. I remember him putting my hand on the various timbers and moving my palm gently to and fro, so that I could feel the temperature of the wood and sense its character. Then as a final treat, he took me to a long moving conveyor belt two or three feet wide; jumped on it, whisked me up, put me down on the belt as if it were a cakewalk, then whisked me off it again just before we were cut in half by a circular saw. It was an experience I had completely forgotten until many decades later, when I saw the film in which James Bond was almost bisected by a laser, and it came back to me again. I must have been the only male in the cinema who did not wince, but smiled reminiscently instead.

Grandfather Wallis's daughter, Lena, would have been appalled at Bond's drinking habits. 'Shaken, not stirred' indeed! Drink was the curse of the working (and all other) classes and she held firmly to her temperance principles, though in her it was not mere temperance, it was total abstinence. Moreover she had strong views on Sunday observance. When some newsagent was unwise enough to push through her letterbox a sample copy of a Sunday newspaper, Auntie Lena ceremonially fetched the fire tongs, picked up the offending object and deposited it in the middle of the road outside. In vain was it pointed out to her that Monday newspapers caused just as much Sunday labour for journalists as Sunday ones did for the distribution trade. 'There has never been a Sunday paper at Southfield,' she announced, 'and there never will be.' There was no more to be said. Anyway it was her house.

Her views on strong drink would have been entirely a matter for herself had it not been for the fact that she was Chairman of the Brewster Sessions and therefore directly responsible in the area for the granting or withholding of licences to sell liquor. Setting herself resolutely against any encouragement of 'Satan in solution', the devil's own trade, Auntie Lena must have been a formidable opponent for any convivial publican who fancied an hour's extension at a public holiday or local fair.

One of her genuinely kindly acts was to hire a large chauffeur-driven Daimler in which to take mother, Philip and myself out for a Saturday drive in the country. I used to sit in front with the driver, looking avidly for the wild birds which were already a burning hobby with me. Auntie Lena, in the back, would drone away to mother, while keeping an eagle eye on the speedometer. 'You're beginning to go a little too fast, Pearson,' she would call firmly, and Pearson, with a scarcely audible sigh, would drop to 25 m.p.h.

Towards teatime, Pearson would be instructed to call in at some sleepy village inn, where the landlord was no doubt snoozing away after disposing of the mid-day trade, oblivious of the fact that under the law he could be compelled to provide food and drink for any genuine traveller calling at his door at any hour of the day or night. Rap-rap at the door went the brolly as Miss Lena Wallis J.P., explained gently but absolutely firmly to the licensee that we were travellers, and that we would just sit in his parlour for a few minutes while he and his wife prepared tea, bread and butter, jam for the boys here, and perhaps a little cake? Scones or toasted teacakes would be welcome too and something would please be sent out to Pearson, who was sitting outside in the car.

But Pearson was not. Pearson had quietly left the car and

made sympathetic contact with the other members of the publican's family, now arranging for something a little more reviving than 'tea with the hot milk put in first'. Whatever the reviving 'something' might have been, I was aware of it hanging in the air as we drove back into Lincoln. 'You're going a little fast again, Pearson.' 'Shorry, Madam.'

Although Alderman Wallis and his daughter Lena were basically so different – the one so fun-loving and relaxed, the other so erect – they shared a firm religious faith. Once they went for a long walk on the wide, undulating South Common which stretches across almost half the southern rim of the great bowl that forms the city of Lincoln. On returning to Southfield, they found that the front door key had dropped out of Lena's handbag, or in those days I suppose, out of her reticule. What to do? For Thomas Wallis and his daughter it was no problem, for the Lord watches over the just at all times, and especially the Wesleyan just. 'We will go back to the Common,' announced Tom Wallis, 'and we will pray for the key to be restored to us.'

They returned, being instinctively careful to retrace the steps of their earlier walk. (After all, the Lord prefers to help those who help themselves.) Across the Common they went, until at a suitable spot they sank to their knees and requested God's help in finding the errant key. '. . . Amen,' the prayer ended. Lena opened her eyes and, shining there on the turf within arm's length, was a large brass key. Returning home, they let themselves in, and, as Auntie Lena was careful to mention when telling the story afterwards, placed some coins in the Missionary Box by way of a thanks-offering.

There was no excessive piety around my home, where lost keys remained lost. My mother had been brought up in the sanctimonious atmosphere of Southfield, and the chapel did play a large part in our lives – we went as a matter of course to both morning and evening services every Sunday. But otherwise the chapel was a place of recreation, sometimes of downright entertainment. Nothing was done specifically for the younger members – in later years my brother turned it into one of the best Youth Clubs in the country – but in any case during the late 1920s no-one took much interest in what teenagers thought or wanted. Young folk were merely immature citizens who with luck would one day be grown-up enough to have views or wishes that might interest the rest of society. As for children like me, we merely tagged along.

Needless to say, such children tend to lead a secret life of their own. For myself, I had a brother five years older than I, with superior friends and rougher games to play. Their heroes were Sir Henry Seagrave and Sir Alan Cobham; mine tended to be Cherry Kearton and the early radio nature-man Romany (with his dog Raq) who once – miraculous happening! – stayed at our house overnight, though without Raq. Another great thrill of my young life came when mother somehow got hold of a special key to the derelict and overgrown Boultham Park, full of old trees where secret birds nested and with decaying boathouses bordering a neglected lake. We three would let ourselves in on a Saturday afternoon. We had the run of the place, with no one to see us and no interruption other than the screech of a grey heron or the twittering of an agitated black-cap. Once, watching me silently in the deepest wood, I saw there a Golden Oriole . . . Or was it wishful thinking on a small ornithologist's part?

Perhaps I was a solitary little boy, shy and inward-looking. And I still suffered from the loss of my father, when the time came for me to go to the private school a hundred yards down the road from my home.

It was run, gently but in what I now realise was for its day quite a progressive fashion, by a Miss Gertrude Poppleton.

Her school was for little more than babes. I cannot remember much about it beyond the aroma of a girl called Barbara who suffered from what seemed to be hourly bilious attacks. Barbara will be almost sixty now, and I hope she is feeling better. For my part I can only report that to this day if I happen to meet anyone called Barbara I instinctively stand well back.

There are other memories, too, which belong to the growing years of any normal small boy: climbing into the fork of a pollarded willow to picnic on a ha'penny bag of sherbet powder; rescuing (after long persuasion and with the aid of a lassoo) a lost dog which was not lost at all; getting cornered by a threatening ring of gipsy children and having to scramble to safety through a stream; scuffing new shoes, inventing exotic reasons for untouched homework, and chalking STELLA DAVY WEARS RED NICKERS on the railway arch.

My early schooling came at the tail-end of the 'learn by repetition' system but just before the teaching profession got organised on the rather novel idea of engaging the pupil's interest, instead of just demanding his attention. The generation before mine – indeed, all generations before mine, I suppose – learnt its facts parrot-fashion, in chorus: 'two and two are four, four and four are eight ...' like the inchworm in Danny Kaye's song. By a year or so I missed the unison chanting of fact tables. I suppose that is why I have difficulty with my nine-times table and cannot remember which town is on the Oder.

I thought a lot of Miss Poppleton. I remember her as a sensible, kindly person; gentle but practical – a pleasing combination of qualities. She served her pupils well, at what I suppose must be classed as a latter-day Dame School. Whatever her educational standing, it was she who first noticed that I seemed to have some special talent for music.

3. Xylophonia here I come

We had a piano at home. It stood in the front room of our house at 6 St Catherines opposite Hamilton Road: an old Broadwood cottage piano, long on marquetry inlay but short of an octave or so.

In those days if no one in the family performed, then no music was heard. My mother played sometimes; a modest repertoire of three pieces, one of which was called 'Simple Aveu'. As for me, I cannot remember a time when I did not play the piano in some fashion. By the age of five or six I could reproduce at the keyboard any music I heard, in reasonably recognisable form. I know now that I played everything in the natural (if you can call it natural) key of G flat; in other words on the black notes. I shared this characteristic, though no one knew that fact at the time, with Irving Berlin. When I met him some twenty years later I had great difficulty in refraining from telling him so.

Just why the black notes should exercise such an early attraction is hard to say. Their sequence is easier to grasp, in an aural sense, than that of the white notes; perhaps it has something to do with the attraction of the pentatonic scale. I only know that to this day if I think of an old Horatio Nichols song like 'My Inspiration is You', I think of it in the key of G flat. When each year my father's former junior partner Frank Hill (later Sir Francis Hill) would take us as a special treat to the Theatre Royal to see the annual production by the Lincoln Amateur Operatic & Dramatic Society, it was in six flats that I played the tunes from *The Arcadians* or *The Gondoliers* when we got home.

Miss Poppleton encouraged me to experiment on the school piano, which I liked because it had the full range of octaves. At a Speech Day – if one could use so dignified a term for what must have been merely a tea-cup gathering of local mums – she introduced me as a kind of cabaret turn. 'Stephen Race will now play descriptive music at your request.' And as the ladies present suggested the sea, birdsong, march music or whatever, I would oblige with improvised rumble, twitter or rum-ti-tum, as appropriate. I confess that I do not remember this myself, relying on family hearsay. But improvising at the piano was always something I could do without the slightest difficulty, and I still tend to judge the true musicality of youngsters by whether or not they can improvise at the keyboard. The only thing that may have been praiseworthy about that first public engagement of mine was that I gave the whole pianistic performance without being able to reach the pedals. I would hate to have to imitate an angry sea these days without the aid – albeit discreet, I hope – of a little sustaining pedal.

It was clear that I ought to have formal music lessons, and I began at once with a teacher who lived on a steep hill opposite the newly-built Usher Art Gallery. Elsie M. Harrison started me off in the conventional music teacher's method of those days, and I still have the red-covered manual from which I learnt the names of the notes (*Rudiments of Music* by G. Augustus Holmes). Like many of the toys I played with and the clothes I wore, it had been my brother's before me, and I suppose I ought to have returned it to him by now for the use of Debbie, Daniel and Becca in the next generation. But after a lifetime's connection with music it is curious to read, in Miss

34

Harrison's neat pencil hand, that by 17 Feb. I was expected to have learnt that:

Instances will be met with in which irregular numbers of notes are required to be played in the time of one note of larger value, as *five* or *seven* semiquavers, or *nine* demisemiquavers, in the time of a crotchet, and a figure to this effect is accordingly placed over the group of notes ...

It did not seem to occur to anyone in those days that such sentences were not only unreadable but practically incomprehensible to a youngster. Even ten years later I could still feel my mind seizing up when some exam-paper requested that I should 'Supply the correct nomenclature of – ' instead of merely *naming* it.

Miss Harrison thought at first that she had not only a pupil with a good ear but one with outstanding sight-reading abilities as well. In this she was doomed to sudden disappointment, and I to discovery, for I was not reading the new pieces she gave me to play, merely memorising them when she played them over to me. 'How does it go, Miss Harrison?' I would ask, innocently enough, and then as she played it I would find that on the instant I knew it. All I had to do was go home for a week, then come back to her studio and play it to her, whereupon she would adjust a few 'mis-readings', which were in fact notes I had momentarily mis-heard or incorrectly remembered. She told me later that what alerted her to the terrible truth was that she gave me a piece to learn which was in the key of D major. When I came back a week later I played it, perfectly correctly, but in the key of A. (I must have let my mind wander during her initial demonstration.) Since I did not know anything about transposition at the time – nor, I suspect, did she herself know very much about the matter – we were somewhat at cross-purposes for a while.

I look back with much gratitude to Elsie Harrison, who refused to be broken by a combination of constant ill-health and a wayward pupil, soldiering on purposefully with both. She gave me three things: a proper grounding in the conventional techniques of piano-playing, a carefully-chosen repertoire of classics (at a time when a number of rather strange composers were in favour with the teaching fraternity) and, most important of all, something of her own sense of wonder

35

and delight in music itself. I remember one lesson in particular when I was in a bad mood and consequently so was she. I was waving my wrists up and down and generally irritating her. Slowly and with great firmness she closed the keyboard cover on the piano. 'Right,' she said, 'we're going to stop trying to play music and listen to some.' She then wound up a large mahogany gramophone which stood nearby, selected a record and sat beside me as we listened to it.

I was enraptured: there is no other word for it. I believe the singer was Galli-Curci, or was it Tetrazzini? Anyway the soloist sang like a bird, and near the end of the aria was joined by a flute player for one of those glittering cadenzas in thirds. The convention is a well-known one, but it was new to me, and Miss Harrison must surely have seen my shining eyes, because after that she would sometimes play me a record during lesson time: a slightly risky thing to do, if parents had come by unexpectedly and found themselves paying so-much an hour for teacher and pupil to listen to the gramophone.

So I learnt my scales and arpeggios. I played 'Sur la Glace a Sweet Briar', then later the delicious pieces by Gabriel Grovlez that youngsters are still given to play, probably because pupils become teachers and revive their own young days by choosing the same pieces to be learnt. I thundered through Beethoven's Sonata Pathétique, dreamed through Liszt's 'Liebestraum' and stabbed away at Grieg's 'Wedding Day'. I was beginning to attract something of a modest local reputation.

What put the seal on things was the purchase of a xylophone. Since a xylophone is laid out exactly like a piano keyboard any pianist can play it: all he has to do is learn to hit the notes with a stick instead of activating them with flexed fingers. True, there is a slight performance problem, in that the notes do not hold. There is no sustaining pedal on a xylophone. The player of a *legato* piece therefore has to strike the note repeatedly in what is called a 'roll'. This can be tiring for the performer as well as tiresome for the listener and a better idea is to choose for your xylophone repertoire those rapid and agitated selections which do not rely on long notes. They have an added benefit: the music-loving public is deeply impressed by speed, virtuosity and enthusiasm.

Going round Lincoln and district giving my chapel concerts, I soon discovered that it was impossible to play 'The

Wedding of the Painted Doll' at a tempo too fast for the taste of my hearers. Like Nero at the Coliseum, they would clamour for ever more grotesque delights. 'The Flight of the Bumble Bee', dashed off at a speed which prevents any two consecutive notes being correctly struck, could be guaranteed to bring the house down. It still does.

My first instrument served for me to learn on, but it had a tone like a picket fence and I soon outgrew it. Next came a larger, indeed almost professional xylophone. There was scarcely a hall in Lincoln or for some miles around in which I did not appear with my xylophone act during those years around 1930.

To give due credit to my big brother, he was marvellous about that xylophone. I realise now that he was proud of me, though at non-musical moments we did not get on any better than most brothers who are divided by five significant years. We had our rows. Yet I must admit that it was Philip who pressed my ear to a telegraph pole so that I could hear the messages buzzing along the wires; Philip who taught me to throw 'ducks and drakes' on a pond; Philip who drew a seagull for me when I was ill. When a well-meaning adult bought us a glass of fiercely fizzy lemonade (which we both hated) it was Philip who manfully drank most of it in order to spare me.

When I say that Philip was marvellous about my xylophone I mean simply that he carried it for miles in its plywood case, the metal handles cutting painfully into his palms, because he knew that if I carried it myself I would not be able to play when I got to the hall.

There have been a thousand times in my life when I have had reason to be grateful to my brother Philip; this is merely the first of them and being a modest man he will not want them listed. Let me merely say that my affection for him and gratitude to him is boundless. He is the best of brothers and (if the Law Society will permit me to say so) the best of lawyers.

Quite apart from the xylophone appearances as a boy, I had also become a familiar sight in the Mental Hospital at the top of the hill behind our home. Perhaps I should clarify that remark.

It was the practice on Tuesday afternoons for the resident minister at St Catherines Methodist Church to visit the Mental Hospital and take a service in the chapel there. During school holidays, I went along with him to play the organ. It was quite

37

a nice little organ, I recall, complete with foot pedals which I soon learnt to operate after a fashion. The only problem was the particular patient (known then as an 'inmate') whose task it was to pump the organ by hand. He enjoyed the job, I could tell, but he also had strong views about certain hymns, and if the tune did not appeal to him he would flag in his pumping fervour, whereupon my organ and I would grind to a wheezing halt. 'Abide with Me' was his great favourite; he was not so keen on 'The Church's One Foundation'; he was positively anarchistic when it came to 'Come O Thou Traveller unknown'.

There was a reason for this. Charles Wesley, in his infinite poetic wisdom, had written no less than twelve full verses for that endless hymn. No matter how clearly the Rev. G. Cloudesley Shovel announced that we would be singing only Verses One to Five, the little congregation would plough on with the other seven. After an exchange of glances, Mr Shovel and I would give in and join them, until my organ-pumper flagged and the organ petered out around 'withered my nature's strength, from Thee my soul its life and succour brings ...'

I find it hard to believe now, but Lincoln Mental Hospital had a grisly sort of Open Day once a year, when the local folk could wander up and down the narrow wards, goggling and commenting like eighteenth-century rubbernecks at Bedlam. A girl who used to take me out for walks dragged me round there when I was quite small.

I can remember still the lost look of those hopeless inmates; the sudden contortions, the suffering eyes which looked sharply out of the rows of otherwise blank faces. Perhaps it was that Boxing Day afternoon which first gave me my lifelong dread of hospital visiting, though I have had a great deal of it to do and will doubtless have more. I am lost in admiration for the people who staff such places. I simply could not do it myself. But then, I could not draw a tooth or amputate a leg. For humanity's sake, thank goodness there are those who can.

4. Wool-gathering again, Race?

At the age of eight I joined my big brother at what was then called the Grammar School, later simply 'Lincoln School', now the co-educational Christ's Hospital School. The place has improved a good deal, as indeed it should with my brother the present Chairman of the Governors. There was room for improvement.

The school could hardly have been further from where we then lived, the only way to reach it being by double-decker bus, changing in the centre of the town, where (bigger boys graciously permitting) we boarded the bus marked St Giles. With insufficient time to get back at midday, boys from my end of the town stayed for lunch – though of course we called it dinner – leaving finally at 3.30, unless detailed afterwards for compulsory games or detention.

The junior school, known as the 'Prep', occupied a large corrugated-iron hut at the corner of the main playing field, and housed Forms I, II and III. My first form-master was known throughout the school as Stinker. I have my reasons for thinking the name more or less appropriate, though I do not know its precise origin. Stinker rather took to me – I was, I think, quite a likeable little boy. I cannot say that I took to Stinker, though. His eyes glittered a little too sharply, and the first really adult reaction I ever remember having was a resentment on behalf of my classmates – a disgust, almost – that the man was so obviously favouring me above them. I did not want his fond hand on my head, where it rested warm and pulsing.

Stinker had clearly never learnt the Golden Rule of teaching, namely that one should never touch a boy, either in affection or in anger. I appreciate how hard it must be sometimes to resist the latter, but the former requires to be avoided with scrupulous care. Stinker forgot both halves of the rule from time to time. He also had a little ritual, which can hardly have been confined to the one year when I was in his form, whereby he would remind us that we were schoolboys now, just like Tom Brown at Rugby and all those others at Eton and Harrow, and had we read about what life was like in boys' schools? Then, all in great good humour, he would line us up and pass behind us, giving each of us a sharp stroke on the bottom with a ruler. The ritual over, we would go back to our places, chattering and rubbing our rears, while Stinker put away his ruler, glanced once more at the little window in the door, and glittered at his favourite, who happened as usual to be me, though being teacher's pet had not spared me teacher's ruler.

After a year in Form I I jumped a form and hardly saw Stinker again in all the years I was there, other than in the general line-up of masters on special occasions, when they laid aside their black chalk-filled workaday gowns and put on more glamorous attire, even trimmed with fur, which impressed the parents if not the boys. Many years later, in a moment of inspiration, they named the new Swimming Pool after Stinker. He would have liked that.

Mr Marriott, one of the boys told me, had 'sleepy-sickness'. I can see him now, gulping great yawns as we read the afternoon away with Lamb's *Tales from Shakespeare*, or recited *The Inchcape Rock* from our green-covered poetry book *Mount Helicon*. In the gym, compelled by the time-table to supervise a class for what was then still known as 'P.T.', Mr Marriott would stand us at ease, walk to the window, open it wide, and breathe in – out – in – out – in – out for fully two minutes before returning slowly to earth and looking hard and disbelievingly at his watch. A strange man.

He was only one of the noteworthy collection of eccentrics who made up the staff at that school on Wragby Road between 1929 and 1937. One master, for example, emerging from the impenetrable fug of pipe smoke in the staff commonroom, would stride down the corridor suddenly to stop dead in his tracks for a minute or more, like a heron watching a pool. Then off he would trot again, for all the world as if nothing had happened. Perhaps nothing had.

40

Another master sported half-glasses: semicircular lenses which reflected the scene behind him so faithfully that with his back to you, while writing $x(3y)=4z^2$ on the blackboard, he could say 'Race, it is not funny to make faces at Maltby. Kindly desist.' His name was Mr Plant – inevitably he was nicknamed Shrubby – and he at least was not sport-crazed as many of his colleagues were, coming to life only on the sports field or when we returned exhausted from the five-mile and three-mile cross country races. One wonders if any of them heard Bernard Shaw's famous broadcast to sixth forms in 1937, when he told pupils that their schools taught 'notions of physical exercise that will shorten your life by twenty years'. Wise, indiscreet old G.B.S.

The teacher responsible for the spiritual welfare of our 350 boys was known as 'Jazzy' because of his alarming reaction if jazz music was heard, or for that matter even mentioned. Though technically a clergyman, rumour had it that he had been unfrocked for smuggling hashish through the customs. I suspect some exaggeration in that story. However I can truthfully report that in eight years at the school the only thing I learnt about religion was the number of members who constituted the *Sanhedrin*, and that I have forgotten.

Inevitably there were memorable days, moments of interest among the weeks of tedium that lengthened into months and years. One junior French master named Alston took a thick, one-foot square attendance book and hit a schoolmate of mine so hard across the head that we thought the boy was dead. A chemistry master absentmindedly told a boy with a flask to 'pour some water into it', then realising that the flask contained sulphuric acid dashed for the door screaming 'No, don't!' I look at them now, those masters, lined up squarely with all us boys in the annual school photograph. The clock-work panning-device on the camera would worm round the great human arc outside the front cloisters. Arms folded, the staff gazed steadfastly forward; as extraordinary a collection of oddities as one could find outside a Barnum and Bailey road-show. Dooly, who suffered from permanent loss of temper; poor tragic Watty, who some years later could take no more of the cruelty of boys, and went home in despair one afternoon to commit suicide.

The strangest face in the photograph, as befits a leader, is

41

that of the headmaster, C. E. Young, who happened to arrive as I did and left as I did. Arrival and departure were the only things he and I ever had in common. A classics man to the tips of his extraordinarily large ears, he lived in a world of Latin and Greek, lapsing into the former from time to time, presumably to keep in practice, and reading the lesson in his hollow voice at morning prayers as meaningfully as if the words had been in Martian or Esperanto. At the start of each disgusting school meal he would intone a brief grace which my brother told me meant something like 'O Blessed One, Bless Us' but sounded rather like an ingenious classical pun and indeed was. I have seldom loved anyone less than Mr Young. Later in life he took holy orders; perhaps the school's gain was the church's loss.

I did not have personal contact with every master serving at Lincoln School in those days. But of the ones I knew, there were two who I now realise were conscientiously trying to achieve something other than silence inside the classroom and a winning First XI outside it. Mr Williams, known as Weary because of his lethargic manner, was an untidy, likeable Welshman, whose principal job was to teach Geography – the rivers of Peru, jute imports, the world distribution of tundra and scrub – but who alone of the whole staff made some attempt to give us sex tuition.

It was not his idea of fun, indeed it pained him to do it. I can remember the acute embarrassment on his face, though not of course on ours, as he tried to explain the hydraulic principle behind (or rather in front of) a well-known fountain in Brussels and why it was not funny at all but merely interesting in an academic sort of way. 'If any of you boys are puzzled about anything like that,' he said, 'just come and have a word with me afterwards and I'll explain as best I can.' I do not suppose any boy did; the miracle is that in a fully-operational school of 350 boys in the 1930s there was no formal biological instruction of any kind.

I quite liked old Weary. But the master to whom I am most grateful was Jab. The nickname commemorated his initials – he was J. A. Baxter, a small irascible Yorkshireman with spectacles on a little chain, who taught Latin and English, and was the form master of my last year at the school. Jab was 'ratty', as we used to tell one another, but he was fair, as we also noted. His sense of humour was unlike that of most of the other masters because while they were cynical and sneering, adept at putting boys down, he seemed to find fun in incongruity.

He has a personal taste for things of the seventeenth and eighteenth centuries, and thanks partly to his influence, so have I. Whereas in other classes we had been given adventure stories or science fiction to read as our Holiday Task – *The War of the Worlds*, *The Black Arrow*, *Prester John* – Mr Baxter gave us *The Vicar of Wakefield*. Perhaps it was a curious choice for a bunch of fifteen-year-old boys, but at the risk of being thought soft or effeminate I have to say that I loved it, as I still do.

It was a passage in Goldsmith's novel which gave me my first purely aesthetic pleasure outside music. I can remember it quite distinctly. We were reading the book through for the first time in class, each boy standing up to intone a page or so. It was during my turn that I read out loud the Vicar's words to his family, on the subject of his daughter and her suitor:

> 'Heaven grant they may both be the better for it this day three months!' This was one of those observations I usually made to impress my wife with an opinion of my sagacity: for if the girls all succeeded, then it was a pious wish fulfilled; but if anything unfortunate ensued, then it might be looked upon as a prophecy.

I stopped reading for a moment at that point. Jab looked up. 'Why have you stopped?' he asked. 'It's clever, Sir,' I answered, and added lamely something like, 'he's got it both ways, hasn't he?'

Jab, surprised perhaps that a boy reading Goldsmith should notice a felicitous phrase, got me on one side a few days later. 'This book is by the same man,' he said. 'It's two poems. Read them in your own time and see how you like them.'

Later the whole form was given *The Traveller* and *The Deserted Village* to study, but by then I had discovered the essential difference between something you have been told to read and something you have been invited to read. I had also developed the beginnings of a taste for eighteenth century locution and The Age of Elegance in general. For that, and for countless consequent pleasures down the years, I thank the long-departed shade of J. A. Baxter. How appropriate were the words which, thanks to him, I sat up in bed reading:

> Yet he was kind; or if severe in aught,
> The love he bore to learning was in fault.

Jab did love learning, and loved teaching too, though small boys drove him wild with a sudden Yorkshire irritation. How, I wonder, could such a man bear his day-to-day life with the others in that choking staff commonroom?

5. *Two-piece band unexpectedly available*

When Beau Brummell was invited to leave his Mayfair patch in order to dine in Bloomsbury, he enquired politely where he should change his horses. Similarly when in response to an enquiry I tell people that I come from Lincoln, they tend to ask 'Oh really. What part?' Nettled, I point out that if I had meant Lincoln*shire*, I would have said so. I doubt whether the same thing happens to people who say they come from Bedford, York or Northampton. Yet it seems that the very remoteness of the county of Lincolnshire makes people suspicious of the idea that someone might actually hail from there.

Approach Lincoln from the south, and there is the city laid out before you, like a tray of rings in a jeweller's window. About two miles away from the visitor, surmounting the very rim of the opposite hill, stands the magnificent Cathedral, so striking, so perfectly proportioned, that every passing artist for hundreds of years has tried to set it down on canvas. Most of them – including one or two famous ones – have failed. They managed to capture the colour, but somehow missed the exact proportions. Looking over the artists' shoulders at their efforts, generations of Lincolnian rubbernecks have commented bluntly 'You haven't got it, have you?'

When you have been brought up in Lincoln you know the Cathedral from every angle. It watches you while you are shopping; it peers at you through the trees. It leans on you as you climb that last almost vertical stretch of steep hill between the antique shops.

In the afternoons, when we left school, we would wander along towards the Cathedral. Sometimes there were American tourists who were intrigued at the prospect of a schoolboy guide, and we used to take them in tow, pointing out the effigy of the famous Lincoln Imp as he squatted in his stony malevolence high up in the Angel Choir, where only the locals seem able to find him.

On a pinnacle near the northwest tower stands the eleventh-century Swineherd of Stowe, who brought his life savings to help build the original Cathedral. (They say that the stone horn he carries still emits a hollow winding note when the wind is favourable.) If the swineherd had lived in more recent times and within the very city of Lincoln, he would have lived 'downhill', the object of a particular Lincolnian prejudice, the division being between those who live 'uphill', in other words around the Cathedral, as opposed to those who live 'downhill': the site of the factories, the gasworks, my home, and (if there were one) no doubt also the Home for Retired Swineherds. When J. B. Priestley, that perceptive writer, came to Lincoln on his English Journey in the 1930s, he immediately ferreted out our skeleton: our 'uphill/downhill' snobbery. Priestley being Priestley, he poured deserved scorn on us before travelling on.

My 'best friend' lived uphill. I met him under slightly painful circumstances. One morning in Form III, I put up my hand and asked Mr Marriott if I could leave the room. He nodded and looked at his watch, which meant that he wanted me to think he was timing my absence. So I ran down the passage, opened the outside door and sprinted as hard as I could round the corner to the lavatory, alias the 'bog'.

Unfortunately another boy was running just as hard in the opposite direction and he and I ended up in a painful heap on the cinder path. I rather thought my nose was broken, but he said No, not if you can still waggle it without fainting. I waggled it and didn't faint.

His name was Alex Cullen, and we liked each other on sight.

Later that day, in what was left of the dinner hour after we had bolted the shepherd's pie and the spotted dick, we met, to tell each other our amazing life stories. Alex said his mother had just won a consolation prize in a Felix-the-cat Competition in a newspaper, which was extraordinary because my mother had just won a prize in it too. Then Alex told me that he wanted a bike, which was another curious coincidence because so did I. He had a sister, and that was odd too, because I had a brother. But the strangest thing of all was that Alex played the drums. He was going to be a famous drummer one day, and that was fantastic, because I was going to be the most famous pianist the world had ever known.

Alex and I were 'best friends' from that moment on. We met every day during morning break at school. On alternate Wednesday afternoons I went to his house, where we played jazz duets on piano and drums, while his mother cut doorsteps of bread and jam for our tea. Then, on the other Wednesday, Alex brought his drumkit down on the bus to my house, while my mother made the doorsteps of bread and jam and we deafened her for a change. It was a splendid arrangement, and I cannot remember how many years we went on like that. Perhaps the neighbours can.

We must have been about twelve years old when we decided that our music ought to be reaching a wider public. It was all right complimenting one another at the end of each selection from our repertoire, but it would be nicer to hear some applause.

So we became a 'band'. We chose a name for ourselves, The Silver Linings. We got some handbills duplicated and pushed them through half the letterboxes of Lincoln: 'The Silver Linings: two-piece band unexpectedly available'. We even went on a half-day train excursion to Skegsnest, as it was known locally (or just 'Skeg'), talking our way into cafés and restaurants, trying to persuade their astonished owners that every smart teashop requires a resident band of two twelve-year-old schoolboys. They probably thought we had run away from an approved school.

We did actually get one engagement: I believe Alex's sister was behind the invitation. But on that never-to-be-forgotten night at Nettleham Village Hall we were given the bird, well and truly. Like so many artistes before and since, we must

46

have been too good – too advanced for our public. So back we went to the Wednesday afternoon sessions in one another's houses.

But Alex was changing. No doubt about it, he was becoming vague and absent-minded. One Wednesday he arrived to play his drums but realised, when it was pointed out to him, that he had forgotten to bring them. The following week I trailed all the way up to his home in Long Dales Road, only to find that he was building a radio and did not really want to practise 'Bugle Call Rag'. It transpired that his hero was no longer Ambrose's drummer, but a man called Scott Taggart who edited a wireless weekly. Shortly after that Alex's drum career was halted anyway, because one morning when cycling to school and trying at the same time to work out a radio circuit in his head, he inadvertently rode into the back of a milk float and broke his arm. Over the next few weeks he read more wireless magazines than ever before.

The fact was that Alex had 'got science' as other people get Religion or go football-crazy. My ambition was still to be around when Teddy Wilson fell sick and Benny Goodman asked the audience despairingly 'Is there a piano-player in the house?' Alex's ambition was to build an eight-valve superhet.

So we drifted apart. But not before we had spent an unforgettable weekend in London. Our hero at the time was the jazz saxophonist Freddy Gardner. Gardner had made a stunning multi-instrument recording of 'China Boy' and was the star of every London freelance jazz session of note. Even now I have to swallow hard to recollect the cheek of it, but when Alex and I arrived in London, we found Freddy Gardner's address in the telephone book, went round there, rang the bell, asked Mrs Gardner if we could see her husband, and then, when he came to the door, coolly asked this great professional jazz star if he would make a private recording with us.

It makes my blood run cold to think of it. He ought to have kicked us all the way down West End Lane, but he didn't. Perhaps he was impressed by our determination. He said Yes, he would make a record with us on the Monday morning before we went back home to Lincoln. When I asked him what fee he would charge, he said 'Ten shillings ... Or if I enjoy myself, it'll be less'.

47

Alex and I booked the private recording studio, and sure enough, F.G. (as he liked to call himself) duly arrived with his alto sax. We made two sides: 'China Boy' (of course!) and 'Someday Sweetheart'. When it was over I tried to give the great man his princely fee of ten bob but he said No, he'd enjoyed it. Have it on him.

Many years later, working with Freddy on sessions worth rather more than ten bob, I had the opportunity to remind him of his kindness to two admiring fans. As for Alex, I was to see him from time to time during the War which was already beginning to warm up. He had gone into some sort of special branch of the Air Ministry at Farnborough, presumably so that he could build superhet wireless sets when he wasn't cycling into milk floats. Occasionally we met on leave, but he still seemed preoccupied, and later I discovered why. He was busy developing something called 'Radar'. No wonder he seemed abstracted.

Anyone who wants to know about my friend Alex nowadays has merely to look him up in *Who's Who* under 'Cullen, Prof. Alexander, O.B.E.' I understand that many eminent electrical engineers have reason to be grateful to him for introducing them to the disciplines of scientific method and enquiry. I for my part am grateful to him for many years of friendship. He was never quite as good a drummer as Gene Krupa, I admit. But then Gene Krupa had never cycled full tilt into a milk float.

6. *Interview*

Music-struck, broadcast-struck and film-struck, I sat among the rats in the Corn Exchange Kinema one Saturday afternoon, drinking in *The Big Broadcast of 1932*, with Bing Crosby and the Mills Brothers. The place stank of gas-jets, sweat and Flit, but I cared nothing for that. All I knew was that somehow or other, by whatever means and at whatever cost, I was going to be a professional musician. One day *I* was going to rush up to a microphone panting for breath, as Jack Payne did every afternoon at 5.15, and say 'The boys and I will now play a Concert Arrangement ...'

That absolute, total, cast-iron determination to achieve something-or-other is an element in me that has genuinely surprised me at various moments during my life. I am not aware of ever having been a noticeably ambitious person. Certainly I have no wish to exert power over others, nor can I begin to understand what sort of pleasure such power can be thought to bring. Whenever I meet dominant figures in the world of government, business or general administration I search in vain for whatever it may be that attracts them to the giving of orders and the manipulating of men.

All I ever wanted was to be involved in the musical scene, and I do not believe anything in the world could have deterred me. To her great credit my mother recognised the fact, realising that although her elder son was safely on course to follow his father into the legal profession, her younger son seemed more likely to become a member of a dance band. Right, she told herself, let it be the best dance band, and let him be the leader of it. That meant he must study music properly and at the highest level possible.

When I was fifteen she arranged for me to have an audition with the local musical boy who had made good. His name was Frederic Jackson: he had been born in Lincoln and had built himself a modest national reputation as a classical pianist and teacher. Later he became still better known as conductor of the Philharmonic Choir.

I was taken to play for Mr Jackson, and was immediately swept away by the musical enthusiasm, the sheer thrust of a man who was to influence me more than any other musician in my whole life. He was thirty-three years old at the time; an excellent pianist, a particularly skilful accompanist, an arranger, a conductor, a magnificent choir-trainer and a respected vocal coach; a hundred per cent music man with ideas about everything from vegetarianism to the Left Book Club, from vivisection to whether Arsenal would win the Cup.

I sat at the piano and played him various pieces. He

49

listened with a vague impatience. Then he pushed me off the piano stool, and thundered out a piece of mid-nineteenth-century nothing-much. 'What do you think of that?' he demanded. 'Not very much really,' I said. He did not seem displeased.

'How about this?' He played the opening of what I later learnt was a Bax Sonata.

'I like that.'

'What key is it in?'

'G,' I said, 'but then it seemed to go into E for a bit.'

He looked up at me sharply with a glance of appraisal that I got to know well in later years. 'Go and stand over there with your back to the piano,' he said.

'What's the top note of this chord?'

'G,' I said.

'Any idea what the other notes were?'

'Yes. A flat, D flat and C flat.'

'Try this.'

The thing was on my level, and I rattled off the component notes of all the chords he played me as fast as he could fire them. At length he spoke to my mother.

'He's what *I* call a musician,' he told her, 'or he will be if he comes to me at the Royal Academy of Music. Can you manage the money?'

There was the minutest pause. My heart plunged. Then mother said quietly 'Yes, that'll be all right.'

'Good,' said Frederic Jackson. Then turning to me: 'And just in case you get big-headed, young man, you might like to know that I've never heard anybody do a worse job on that Brahms Intermezzo you played. When you come to London we'll tackle that first.'

7. *Young men taken in and done for*

I was not sorry to leave school. But I did have regrets about leaving Lincoln.

For one thing I had become something of a mini-celebrity and in one's early teens that can be a heady experience. From chapel concerts with the xylophone I had graduated to playing at dances with our schoolboy band. The Vita Dance Band, we called ourselves, the leader being the son of a local music dealer, Basil Rose ('Call me Baz, it's not so corny'). The deputy violinist in our band – deputy only because he was two years younger than the rest of us and therefore almost beneath contempt – was a little lad called Neville Marriner. Later, I need hardly add, he left us all at the post as far as musical eminence is concerned, with his Academy of St Martin's-in-the-Fields and his American conductorships. I used to enjoy the way he played 'The Clouds will Soon Roll By'; I like his Vivaldi even more.

The Vita Dance Band was a bunch of musically-minded kids earning an occasional half-crown (and that was for the whole band, not individually). The Lincoln School of Art Orchestra was another matter, however. This was conducted by Mr Hayes, the art master at my school, and consisted of various grown-up string players, together with my friend Alex brushing a discreet cymbal from time to time and myself on that ubiquitous xylophone. Since none of the standard light orchestral favourites were, or are even now, scored for the unlikely combination of strings and xylophone, I had to use my ear and pick up whatever the orchestra was rehearsing: Mozart's *Il Seraglio Overture*, at one time, Rossini's *Barber of Seville* overture or Eric Coates' *London Suite*. I would then join in.

And *how* I joined in! Xylophone hammers flying, I encompassed every note of those complicated scores. There cannot have been a member of the orchestra, from lead violinist to bassist or continuo player, who did not find his part doubled by the small boy rushing from end to end of the xylophone. I dimly remember some sort of pained deputation from the strings to our conductor, who took me aside and suggested that I might choose the best and most xylophonic bits, leaving to other instruments certain passages which especially suited them, such as the cello solo in 'The Swan'. For a while I soft-pedalled (if such a word can be applied to the clatter of a xylophone) but I have an idea that before long I was back on the busy stuff, enthusiastic to a fault.

There will be certain people mentioned in the course of this book to whom I would like to offer unqualified, if belated, apologies. The list is headed by my fellow-members of the Lincoln School of Art Orchestra in the mid-1930s.

Bound at last for a student's life in London, I was especially sorry to leave the Arcadia Dance Orchestra. This was altogether a more professional affair (or semi-professional to use the correct term) with a trumpet, three saxophones, bass, drums, and myself on the piano. The Arcadia was a pretty good band for its day. For its long-suffering members I first tried my hand at orchestration, writing lip-splitting parts for the trumpeter which must have shortened his expectation of life.

We played each Saturday night at St Martin's Hall near the city centre, and I can still hear the sound of smashed beer-mugs which heralded the inevitable 11 pm punch-up between drunken patrons. Like the bandsmen on the *Titanic*, we would carry on playing (though a different tune) while the fight spread like a forest fire throughout the room. In the end protecting oneself gave place to the more urgent matter of protecting one's saxophone or drum kit.

It says a lot for my mother that she let me play at those dances; or perhaps it merely means that I never told her what they were like. She was, then and always, the best of all mothers. From some of her letters to members of the family during those years of adolescent uncertainty, I know now how closely and lovingly she watched me, yet without seeming to me to be watchful at all. In her world – and for that matter in the Lincoln of those days – the very concept of being a professional musician was as strange and remote from everyday life as wanting to be a big-game hunter or a spaceman. Yet she knew that it was what I must do. I must be enrolled at the Royal Academy of Music, whatever the personal cost.

And I wanted to go, with all my passionate determination. So at the age of sixteen I left Lincoln to become a student in London, taking with me a genuine thirst for musical knowledge, plenty of manuscript paper, my best suit and a photograph of my girl friend.

At the rate I was composing music, the manuscript paper did not last long. Nor, now I come to think of it, did the girl friend. We exchanged a few letters, until she ended one of hers with the endearment 'Yours till flies wear socks', at which I terminated the affair, to no great sorrow on either side. When you are sixteen there is no joy in having an absent lover.

I lived in digs in Broadhurst Gardens, Hampstead, tended by an Irish landlady named Norah Savage, who was one of the only half-dozen or so people I have ever known to be genuinely tone-deaf. Music meant nothing to Miss Savage; it was just a jumble of sounds. 'Glad to hear you practising', she would say, as I limbered up for my Haydn Sonata with a quick dash through 'Honky-Tonk Train Blues'. She was tone-deaf and genuinely mystified at her own inability to share in the joy that others so clearly felt.

Thanks to Miss Savage and her large, homely evening meals, I soon lost my homesickness. But as an honest autobiographer I have to add that homesickness was not the only thing I lost during that first year in London. The girl in question was my senior by a year or two – aren't they always? – and if she happens to come across this book she will be relieved (though possibly a trifle piqued too) to know that I have quite forgotten her name. She, perhaps, has also forgotten our brief and untempestuous affair. One shrinks from clinical detail, but for a first encounter in a matter which seems to rule the world, my initiation was remarkably like a non-event. No doubt partly to blame was the fact that I had no very clear idea of what I was supposed to do. Instinct is not always the guide that it is made out to be.

I soon remedied this on a visit to an uncle's house in Golders

Green. In his library was a book called *Modern Marriage and Birth Control*. I was leafing through it goggle-eyed when I heard footsteps approaching. Thrusting the book under my coat, I found I still had it as I left the house that evening for my digs. Put another way, I stole it.

Over at the bus stop in Falloden Way, I stood in a chemist's doorway, read the book and studied the illustrations, while bus after bus went by, until it was too dark to read any more. In the end, slightly drunk with my new-found information, I realised at last something of the techniques that had been lacking in my first real sexual encounter. I determined that next time it would all be different. And so it was.

By one of those strange quirks which life indulges in for the benefit of the biographer, that chemist's doorway in which I first read about the detailed Facts of Life lay only a hundred yards or so from the flat in which my daughter was to live thirty-five years later. That must prove something or other.

8.   *The student prints*

Life as a student at the Royal Academy of Music was not in the least what I expected it to be.

For one thing, it was nothing like a full-time job. I had expected daily lectures interspersed with almost-daily private lessons. But what few lectures there were merely took place in a special week at the end of each term, and even those were far from being compulsory. The week's lessons – in my first study (piano) and second study (organ), together with Aural Training, Harmony and later Composition – could easily be accommodated within two days, leaving the rest of one's time free for practising, writing immensely complicated unperformed symphonies, lounging around, dreaming about girls and generally getting to know London. I did all those things, and now regret only the unperformed symphonies, which bore the mark of a passionate love affair with the music of Delius.

The real love affair for me, though, was simply with The Symphony Orchestra. It is a love which has never abated in all the years that have followed.

It began dramatically when I walked through the gallery doors of the Duke's Hall at the R.A.M. and for the first time in my life heard a full symphony orchestra in the flesh. It was the senior student orchestra, conducted in rehearsal by Sir Henry Wood, and as I entered they happened to be playing the closing pages of Elgar's Cockaigne Overture, with its noble, cumulative theme.

I was bowled over. Never in all the years of loving and seeking out music had I heard anything like it. I slumped down into a seat near the door and simply drank in the rest of the rehearsal, as Sir Henry (together with Olive Zorian, Leonard and Dennis Brain, Noel Cox, Gareth Morris and the rest of my contemporaries there) introduced me to César Franck's 'Le Chasseur Maudit' and then 'Where Corals Lie' from Elgar's *Sea Pictures*.

Three days later I was there again, this time at five minutes to two, and this time I was even moved to surreptitious tears on first hearing the Elgar Violin Concerto. (Sir Henry was certainly giving the students plenty of Elgar that year!) As for Cockaigne, I had been down to the nearby music shop in Marylebone High Street and paid a heart-stopping five shillings – lunches for a week – for a copy of the miniature score.

My head was buried deep in its pages when the Principal came and sat in the row behind, unknown to me. He tapped me on the shoulder. 'Glad to see you studying the score, my boy,' said Sir Stanley Marchant, and I swelled with the double happiness of being singled out for praise and knowing that the final *tutti* was still to come.

After the rehearsal I went straight on to one of my piano lessons with Frederic Jackson. 'What's that in your hand?' he demanded. 'A score? Do you understand about scores? – How they're laid out? Here, give it to me.' I handed it over.

He opened my precious, beautiful, virgin score, reached for a thick pencil, and scrawled all over the inside cover at great speed. 'Woodwind here, you see – treble clefs, all except bassoon – Talk to you about transpositions later – Horns –

dovetailed – remind me to tell you about that – Brass – Kitchen furniture – you can read viola clef? Of course you can't – Well then, you soon will. I'll see to that ...'

I have the score still: it is, as authors like to say, 'before me as I write'. Also safe in my possession I hope is Frederic Jackson's burning enthusiasm for music; not merely for music in its emotion and its power to move, but for the techniques, the skills, the sheer professionalism of truly musical people. Freddie taught me many, many things, but none more important than that music is a profession as well as a calling. There is infinitely more to be done about music than merely to drool over it.

So he sent me chasing across London to play the piano at half-a-crown a time for elderly ladies who resembled (I now realise) Florence Foster Jenkins. He packed me off to join in chamber groups, to accompany at any and every sort of musical concert, with or without expenses paid. He looked seriously at my compositions, though they were scored for forces that made *Belshazzar's Feast* look like a mere snack. Wisely – and for me so importantly – he took me to the BBC's Maida Vale studios when he and his wife, Margot McGibbon, were giving Sonata broadcasts. There I turned over the music pages for him, with the result that when my time came to broadcast I had lost my initial awe of the microphone.

Even on extra-musical matters he was far from idle. He took me to football matches and to political demonstrations, demanded to know what I was reading, whether I was making friends and how my sex life was progressing. ('All right, thank you very much for asking.') He drew me out, guided me, and I think in his brusque way loved me. I certainly loved him, and idolised him to an extent that I never once managed to convey to him and which would have deeply embarrassed him to hear.

When Freddie Jackson died, many years later, it was in a manner which exactly complemented his unremitting love affair with music. One day in 1972 he was in the very act of conducting the Royal Academy of Music students in a performance of the 'Dies Irae' from Verdi's *Requiem* when he died, almost on the instant. He was much too young, just sixty-six, but since he had to go, that was assuredly the way he would have chosen. As a colleague wrote afterwards, 'Freddie

Jackson was a name to inspire love, respect, terror, or sheer astonishment.' Speaking for myself, I shall never forget him. In many musical ways I remain his creation.

My harmony and composition professor was Harry Farjeon, the eldest member of that extraordinarily talented family of which his sister Eleanor wrote so charmingly in her book *A Nursery in the Nineties*. Harry had become almost blind when I knew him, taking his pupils in a specially darkened room on the topmost floor of the R.A.M. building in Marylebone Road. His poor eyes could not cope with strong light, or for that matter with bright manuscript paper. Consequently any student who wished to show him work had to write it out laboriously on specially prepared music sheets which resembled brown wrapping paper of rather inferior quality. Many were the pen nibs that spluttered and died while copying out a score for Harry Farjeon to see, in fact it was his disability more than anything else that cured me of writing long rambling compositions.

Harry regarded his pupils as children, which is very nearly what we were. Once, when I had particularly pleased him with a harmony exercise, he solemnly presented me with an orange that had been reposing on top of his piano, presumably waiting for a worthy recipient. Each Christmas he took the whole lot of us to the Lyceum pantomime, where we occupied two or three rows of the Dress Circle at his expense, laughing at that finest of panto dames, Clarkson Rose, while Harry beamed at us under his dark eye-shade and no doubt recalled the Lyceum in Ellen Terry's days, when the young Harry Farjeon had watched over the still-younger siblings, Eleanor, Herbert and J. Jefferson Farjeon. I knew them all from Eleanor's memoir, so that when I won Harry's special prize for the student who showed the most achievement during the year, and the prize turned out to be a copy of a three-volume Victorian novel written by his father and called *The March of Fate*, I knew already who 'B. L. Farjeon' was.

I cannot pretend that I was a particularly noteworthy R.A.M. student. It was not in my nature to be at my best in viva-voce examinations, though I was good enough at getting my head down in the purposeful silence of a written exam. As for the countless special prizes and scholarships which crop up almost daily at the Academy, there was no hope for any piano playing student in my time because the young Denis Matthews walked off with them all.

The only part of student life which I actively disliked was having lessons on the organ. I am not by nature much of an organ lover. Devotees of that magnificent but highly mechanical instrument can sometimes be like cricket enthusiasts who memorise Wisden but do not always trouble to visit cricket matches. Mention Lincoln Cathedral organ to an organ nut and he will say 'Ah yes, Father Willis 1898, four-manual with three combination couplers and seven reversible pistons.' He may not actually remember any of the music he has heard on it.

My first organ teacher at the Academy was the elderly Reginald Steggall, who cared so little for me that he seemed almost pleased when I was late for lessons. In time I moved on to the famous C. H. Trevor, who liked me even less. But then, his mind was on better pupils and higher things: I was told by a wide-eyed fellow student that Dr Trevor could execute a perfect *crescendo* by suddenly kicking back the swell pedal while simultaneously pulling out successive draw-stops, a feat which I thought less artistically impressive than that of my beloved Frederic Jackson, who by purely intellectual means could produce a *crescendo* on the piano that made you rise in your seat with expectancy. To the pianist, the mechanism of his instrument is a necessary evil to be overcome; to the organist its engineering machinery can be a large part of the instrument's monstrous attraction. Sometimes the music suffers, and even at sixteen I did not believe that such a thing should ever happen. Perhaps Sir Thomas Beecham was not too far from the mark when shown a tombstone which read 'Here lies a fine musician and a great organist'. 'How on earth did they get them both into the same grave?' asked Sir Thomas.

No man is an island, least of all a student for whom life is endlessly interesting and amazingly simple. How easy it is at that age to make up one's mind, not only on musical matters but on everything that affects the human condition! At the age of sixteen or so, political truths seem especially self-evident; social reform is a matter of the greatest simplicity; one stands amazed at the stupidity and obtuseness of the middle-aged and elderly, who find it so difficult to run the world fairly.

And yet – certain views formed at that age are apt to linger on through maturer years. I believed then – and I believe still – in justice and in the rightness of right itself. My instinct is to tell the truth immediately and for its own sake, though I am aware that the habit has cost me the affection of certain people. Although in personal ways I have changed tremendously through the years, I have not changed in that. I can still hardly bear to see a manifest lie go unchallenged, a wrong unrighted.

All this tended to make me a sitting duck for the propagandists of the *New Statesman*. I bought that periodical for something like thirty years, only pausing sometimes when reading the leading article to say to myself 'Something wrong with the reasoning there. Am I being got at?' But the voice was a small one. In any case, 'This England' was so amusing, the weekly competitions so ingenious, that I remained Mr Kingsley Martin's constant reader. Until I had the experience of meeting him, that is. I was in my forties; he, I suppose, in his sixties.

Our one encounter took place in Drury Lane, not far from Mr Martin's famous Xanadu of Great Turnstile. There he was, examining the contents of a shop window, personally unmistakable. I yielded to that curious compulsion everyone has to introduce oneself to a celebrity whom one has recognised. To him I suppose I was merely a man in his forties who had muttered something conventional about enjoying the paper. But I was also an audience.

To my amazement he began to address me as if I were a public meeting, his eyes glued on some distant horizon over my left shoulder, his voice rising in self-assertion as he outlined the paper's policy, reviewed its history and animadverted briefly on its likely future (on which, by the way, he was soon to be proved correct). I stood there transfixed. The impulse which had made me accost him gave place to a wild desire to run away, while still the editor of my political Bible droned on and on. After that the *New Statesman*, like Gershwin's British Museum in the song, had lost its charm.

But all this was in the far future as I sat one morning in 1937 in Finchley Road Public Library, reading the *News Chronicle*. The paper's music critic, the sober and deeply respected Scott Goddard, had decided for some curious reason to review a newly-released record by Joe Loss and his Orchestra. He knocked hell out of the record of course, not because it was a poor performance but because Scott Goddard had no sort of affinity with Joe Loss's kind of music, even at the best of times.

This seemed to me – and incidentally still does – to be outrageously unfair. One might as well have asked Joe Loss to review a record by Scott Goddard, and I wrote to the editor of the *News Chronicle* to tell him so.

'Do not invite a critic to comment on an art-form with which he is out of sympathy,' I wrote pompously, in my best sixteen-year-old hand. I signed the letter 'Worried music-lover'.

The editor did what editors always do: he passed my letter on to the very contributor whom I was criticising with the result that I got a reply from Scott Goddard himself, inviting me to attend a Promenade Concert with him, having joined him first for a spot of dinner and a talk. Was Pagani's all right with me?

Was it? – I didn't know. For one thing I had never had 'a spot of dinner' with anyone, least of all in the evening. Secondly, Scott Goddard was a deeply respected musicologist, critic and broadcaster. Thirdly, what was a Pagani?

Any reader who remembers the gentle and cultivated Scott Goddard will know that I need not have feared him in the least. Arrived at Pagani's Restaurant beside the old Queen's Hall, I introduced myself and saw him start violently when he noted my obvious youth, not to mention my nervous paralysis. Considerately, he ordered for me (liver and bacon), and then called to the wine waiter, 'Luigi, bring me some hock.' It was a line which for me represented the very summit of sophisticated high living. One day, I told myself, I am going to come in here with a girl who looks like Betty Grable and I'll say 'Luigi, bring me some hock.'

In conversation over our hock – was it then that I conceived my taste for wine? – it became clear that the *News Chronicle* music critic had envisaged me as some sort of musical moron whom he could introduce to the splendours of Mandarin music, and I noticed his childlike disappointment when he learnt that I was already a student at the Royal Academy of Music. In case the reader has suspected any less high-principled motive on Goddard's part for befriending a sixteen-year-old boy, I should add that in all my dealings with him there was never the slightest hint of anything venal. He was motivated purely by musical interest and generosity.

And generous he most certainly was. I began to receive through the post press tickets by the handful, admitting me free of charge to concerts and recitals that I could never otherwise have afforded. On special occasions, like the unforgettable Toscanini concerts in 1938, we went together.

After a while, in response to prompting from my quiet but iron-hard ambition, I asked if I might send him brief reviews of some of the recitals he could not attend. He agreed, and after a while he suggested that instead of posting my comments to him I should phone them in to the *News Chronicle*.

So it was that *S.R.* became probably the youngest, and certainly the most inexperienced, critic on any national daily. I well remember trying to lower the youthful tone of my voice when phoning in my copy from the telephone in the hallway of my digs, while the other residents complained that it was nearly midnight and for pity's sake would I please go to bed.

Once bitten by the writing bug, nobody can shake it off, least of all when one's deathless words are being printed. So my next port of call was the offices of the *Melody Maker*, the official (and in those days, only) organ of jazz news and information in Britain. Having volunteered my services as some sort of roving reporter, I managed to pick up a blank press card from the feature editor's desk as I went out, and this, with a suitably forged signature, got me into theatres and even recording studios which otherwise would have been closed to me. It was all, as they say, Experience.

I had a wholehearted belief in my own ability to 'make it' in a profession which was notoriously inhospitable to newcomers. Most of all, I simply believed in Music. I also believed in the equal distribution of wealth, in pacifism, socialism, vegetarianism (which I planned to take up at a later date and would embrace even now if meat were not so very enjoyable) and in the amazing stupidity of people who could not see as I could that all issues were clearly Black or White and therefore readily solvable. In short, I was in my mid-teens. I did not know then that to reduce every millionaire to penury would only provide the workers with another penny a month; that socialists in power act in the end just like conservatives in power since they are confronted by just the same problems in authority. I did not know as I know now that issues, so far from being Black or White, are uniformly Grey in colour and can only be resolved by imposing some sort of grey-scale and hoping one has done the right thing.

Laying aside my Lenin manuals (with some relief, since I could never understand them) I went off to support left-wing demonstrations and even sold the *Daily Worker* briefly at the corner by Baker Street Station. If I had been an American I would have had a rough time at the hands of Senator Joe McCarthy fifteen years later. Even as it was, things did not prove easy on that score.

The climax of my marching days came at the time of Munich. In the morning I walked, sick at heart with apprehension, to the issuing store to pick up my gas-mask. In the afternoon I joined a great anti-Chamberlain march in Trafalgar Square, thousands of us in angry mood at what even then appeared for what it was: a shameful sell-out. From the south side of the Square we converged on what those around me declared must be the German Embassy but was in point of fact the Athenaeum Club. No matter; we stoned it just in case. On we marched towards Victoria, yelling our defiant slogans. But by the time we reached the Army & Navy Stores our battle cry of 'down with Hitler and Chamberlain!' had degenerated into 'Down with Hitler's chambermaid'. At that point I left and having had my pocket picked by a fellow-demonstrator (who like me believed in the distribution of wealth) walked all the way home to West Hampstead. It was my last demo.

By this time I was moonlighting; working in the evenings at what the licensing people call a Day Club, which is a Members Only drinking club where near alcoholics can pretend to themselves that they enjoy good conversation. There were three of us in the band: Chips Henri, the leader on trumpet, myself on piano, and a pretty good drummer who made a great reputation later as a racing motorist and whose name was Les Leston.

It was a hectic life, practising the Tchaikovsky Piano Concerto in the mornings, going for lessons in the afternoons and playing Cole Porter tunes all evening, but I loved it and it brought in some much-needed extra money. Then it all fell apart, when we added a couple of extra players and got the job at a fully-fledged Night Club, the Cuba, run by the black entertainer Ike Hatch who had made a national reputation in the famous Kentucky Minstrels.

I got fired on our very first night. We had played 'Night and Day' for several hours, to the apparent satisfaction of the jogging customers on their tiny postage-stamp of dance floor. Then came the cabaret, which meant a couple of rather sad girl dancers, followed by the Ike Hatch spot.

The formal music for the act was written out in manuscript and I read it with no difficulty. What went wrong for me was that Mr Hatch enjoyed an unusually successful appearance that particular night. Rushing on for his umpteenth bow, he flung over his shoulder at me 'Get out of Town'. It was a song title, not an order.

Now I did not happen to know 'Get Out of Town' and I tried to tell him so. 'Rubbish,' he said (or words to that effect), and plunged into the song. 'Get out of town before it's too late, my love...' he crooned, while I tried a note here, a chord there, in the hope that one or another of them might fit.

Any musician who knows the song will be aware that it is not – in musician's slang – 'buskable'. Like so many of Cole Porter's tunes it wanders gloriously but unpredictably from key to key, from minor to major, ending up in a different key from the one in which it began. I fumbled, Ike Hatch soldiered on, the song ended (unaccompanied), and as he left the stage he hissed at me 'You're fired. ---- off.' So I did.

Came the 1939 summer holidays and I went home to Lincoln to bask in the endless sunshine of that unforgettable year. The morning of Sunday, 3 September, found the family preparing to go to church, with what might well prove to be quite an important broadcast about to be made by the Prime Minister at an hour which in St Catherines Methodist Church chronology I judged to be somewhere between the Children's Address and the Long Prayer. The family agreed to the suggestion that I should stay at home, listen to Chamberlain's broadcast, and then join them in the congregation for the rest of the service.

I duly listened, and learnt that my country was at war with Germany. Anticipating an air-raid at any moment, I ran to the church, to find the minister reading the Notices. 'On Tuesday, the Band of Hope will meet in the schoolroom ...'

His eyes met mine as I slid panting into our back pew. There was such a question in them that I unhesitatingly held up my right fist with the thumb extended Nero-style in the 'down' position.

'I have just learnt,' said the minister, 'that this country is at war. Let us pray.'

And so we did, passionately and – for some – unavailingly. Then the sirens went, and it seemed that life for my generation must be as good as over. It is not an easy thing to accept, when you are eighteen years old, in love with life itself, and burning with unfulfilled ambitions. All I could claim in the way of musical achievement was that I had been personally fired by Ike Hatch.

Well – maybe I would prove to be one of the lucky ones.

9. *Try it on your piano,* *or even underneath*

The war, once declared, stubbornly refused to begin. Apprehensively we waited for the bombs, the fires, the parachutists. We toted our grotesque gas-masks around in their cardboard boxes, trying not to think of the effect which mustard gas raids would have on defenceless babies. We glued strips of brown paper on our windows to reduce the effect of blast, and were told in posters that Our Courage, Our Cheerfulness and Our Resolution would bring Them (whoever 'They' were) victory.

But nothing happened. There were no air-raids, no horrors and there was certainly no victory. So we passed the time by giving our aluminium pots and pans and garden railings to be melted down for guns. When the war ended, six long years later, the piles of railings were still there, thrown on to jagged heaps and overgrown with cow parsley.

That first Christmas of 1939 I fell in love. She and I met at what may as well be described as what it was – a teenage necking party – and it was the first time I had felt the pangs of anything more than a rather impersonal desire to be touching a warm girl. This girl was shapely, unpredictable and intensely pretty, and for me she was the only real person at the party. It happened to be her sixteenth birthday; I was eighteen. The modest necking that went on that evening sent me home with a burning and quite new set of desires, one of which (though not the most potent) was the desire to marry Clair Leng. And eventually I did.

First, though, she had to be wooed. In my case that involved taking her round to an endless succession of band rehearsals in the backrooms of Lincoln's waterside pubs, after which I would walk her home through the allotments, before staggering home myself, obsessed (like Tosca) with Love and Music.

Sometimes when tempted to complain about eighteen-year-olds today, I try to recall the sheer inward confusion of dealing at the same unexpected moment with youth, puberty, adulthood and acne. As if that were not enough, in my case could be added a burning musical ambition. I *had* to become a musician.

As the strange non-war dragged on, I became more and more restless, with no certainty of anything ahead of me other than military service when my time came. In the end I took matters into my own hands. I sat my mother down one day and told her what I had decided.

'I'm going to London tomorrow,' I told her, 'and I shan't come back till I've got a job in a band.'

'All right,' she said gently. 'But if you do get a job, you won't be able to come back will you?'

I had to agree. Nevertheless the next morning I was on the 9.28 train to King's Cross.

On arrival in London I amassed a great pile of pennies and rang up every big-name bandleader I could think of. Mr Payne? – not interested. Mr Hylton was out of town. Messrs Winnick, Lipton, Fox, Stone and Roy were as elusive as Messrs Debroy Somers, Marius B. Winter, Joe Loss and Harry Leader. Wait a moment, though ... Harry Leader had just completed a popular Sunday afternoon radio series, and Yes, his pianist (one Norrie Paramor) was about to leave. Could I be at the offices of Sun Music Ltd at three o'clock tomorrow?

I could. I found Sun Music in Denmark Street off Charing Cross Road. Britain's Tin Pan Alley, even in those wartime days, was thronged with songwriters and song pluggers. Now it is merely seedy, a short cut from nowhere to nowhere. In those days it was the Road to Success.

'Play something,' said Harry Leader. I rattled off my special arrangement of 'Music Maestro Please', which seemed an intelligent choice since it was his signature tune. Then he gave me something to read at sight – it was the standard printed arrangement of 'The Woodpecker Song' – and the interview ended with my being informally hired as the pianist with Harry Leader and his Band. 'See you on Friday morning. The coach leaves at nine o'clock,' he told me. 'Bring your jazz suit, of course.'

I knew that 'jazz suit' meant dinner jacket. (What avid reader of the *Melody Maker* could fail to be aware of that?) Among the many things I did not know was where we would be performing or how much I would get for it. Never mind – details seemed unimportant beside the fact that I was a member of a big-time band. I sent my mother an excited telegram, and with some difficulty refrained from having printed a thousand visiting cards, reading:

STEVE RACE
(pianist and arranger)
Currently with Harry Leader
and his Band

That first one-night stand turned out to be in Oldham, Lancashire, and the wartime coach journey from London was exhausting enough to take the guts out of every member of the band but me. En route I leafed through the piano book. Every single arrangement was in manuscript, specially scored for the Harry Leader Sound. It was a far cry from those turgid printed orchestrations which had been our staple diet with the Arcadia Dance Orchestra at St Martin's Hall, Lincoln.

At Greenacres Ballroom, Oldham, another, lesser band was warming up the dancers for us. What luxury! Then at last we took our places on the platform, the deputy leader gave us 'four in' and as very slowly, broadly and beautifully we played 'Music Maestro Please', Harry Leader himself appeared at the far end of the ballroom, carrying his alto sax under one arm and his clarinet under the other, bowing and smiling to the applauding fans as he made his way to the stand and gave us the cut-off beat.

Its effect on me was, quite literally, physical. Over many later years I can remember something of the same thrill when playing, or even when simply hearing, some broad, superbly-chosen signature-tune. Ted Heath's theme music never failed to give me that *frisson*; even the desperately trivial 'Oh Susannah' that I subsequently played so often with Lew Stone's Band had something of a stardust feel.

Excited and already tired, I do not remember very much else of that first Harry Leader gig. I only know that finally at midnight, after the dance ended, we musicians piled in the coach again and dozed and twitched our way back to north-east London. I finally reached my digs on a morning tube train. I was worn out. But I was also a professional pianist in a name band.

After the weekend it dawned on me that although my new boss had been kind enough to give me a great deal of praise and encouragement, he had not actually given me any money. While praise and encouragement are welcome, they are uncommonly difficult to live on. Accordingly I set out for Archer Street, the musicians' very own back-alley just off Piccadilly Circus, which in those days was blocked each afternoon with casual musicians, half of them looking for work and the other half looking for the bandleaders who owed them money.

'Is Harry Leader around?' I asked someone casually.

'He's usually along about two o'clock,' I was told. 'The best thing to do is trap him in a doorway.'

I would not suggest for one moment that the advice was any more appropriate to Harry Leader than to any other band-leader of his day, but the fact is that he did arrive at two, I did happen to meet him in a shop doorway, and he gave me my money for the five-hour gig and four-hundred-mile round trip. It came to two pounds.

After that I played for Harry at many dances up and down the country, though to my deep disappointment his radio series was finished and I never did a broadcast with him. Harry's travel arrangements tended to be somewhat haphazard. At Ilford Town Hall we were playing for a dance which was due to end at midnight. I was the one who noticed that Harry had wandered off the stand at 11.30 and had not rejoined us when the time came to play 'The King'. We discovered the reason later: the last train had gone at 11.40. Clearly Harry had been on it, all alone with his alto sax.

For the first time in my life, though by no means the last, I found myself unanimously elected to be the Unpopular Spokesman.

'Go on,' said the other musicians, crowding round the now-closed Ilford station. 'Ring him up. He'll be home by now.'

So I did. I got him to agree to reimbursing whatever sum it took to get us all home. He could not really do anything else.

'Good Old Steve,' they said. But it was Good Old Steve who never worked for Harry Leader again.

I went on to a far steadier job which involved working every evening but in less glamorous circumstances than those of a big-name band. The job was at Farr's Academy of Dancing at Dalston. The highfalutin' name of this establishment did not disguise the fact that it was in reality a meretricious dump where girls could be procured for the promise of a drink and a quick tap on the shoulder in a Gentlemen's Excuse-me Quickstep. Still, it was steady work, and I learnt in my first regular nightly job the plain fact that girl-wise the musician sees all, knows all and can take his pick. If the temperature doesn't kill you, the women will.

As a social sink, however, Dalston paled in comparison with the Paramount Salon de Danse in Tottenham Court Road, where life was raw and utterly basic. I joined Ivor Kirchin's Band there just as the London blitz began. Ivor's was a pretty good band for its day. Cramming myself into a silver-lapelled red monkey jacket which had been made for someone else, I sat at the piano (a grand, no less) from 2 pm until 11 pm, every day of the week, as I recall.

By the time the ballroom would normally have closed its doors, the evening air-raid sirens had sounded, and not even the Mecca management was prepared to turn five hundred young folk out into streets filled with falling flak, incendiary bombs and shattered glass. So everybody stayed; girl patrons bedding down as best they could on the right-hand side of the bandstand, men on the left. A pilot light or two was left on to discourage sleepwalking.

But the bandstand was neutral ground and we musicians made the most of it. There was a recess at the side of the stand which our drummer, Cab, made his own. Some of the musicians bunked down in the bandroom, others in the café. I, in my infinite wisdom, slept underneath the grand piano, alone or in company according to the evening's luck.

To choose a pitch immediately underneath half-a-ton of brass, wood and coiled wire, with bombs falling all round and the whole building in imminent danger of collapse, shows a stupidity which I find as foreign to the real me as the recollection of some of the girls I welcomed to my bandstand boudoir.

After a while I grew heartily sick of the whole sordid mode of life. I was, after all, outside the Paramount dance hall for only about three hours in twenty-four. So to break out of the routine I rented a second-floor furnished flat in nearby Bloomsbury, while night after night the bombs rained down during the worst period of the London blitz. Even inside the flat one's life was not too comfortable, since I had taken precautions against loneliness by inviting a somewhat neurotic blonde to share it with me. We were appallingly incompatible.

During that period I did my very first broadcast. It was called 'West Indian Party'. A Trinidadian bandleader named Willie Wilson had invited me to be a member of his calypso band for the broadcast, which was to come from the stage of the Criterion Theatre in Piccadilly Circus. The BBC had taken over the theatre on the wise principle of decentralising its studios. (One such, the old Paris Cinema, still survives as a studio.) The only hope of getting to the Criterion in time for the start of transmission was to take a taxi from the Paramount the moment 'God Save the King' ended, dashing down the then two-way streets of Charing Cross Road and Coventry Street, and hoping for the best.

The sirens normally sounded at about nine o'clock and by the time we reached Leicester Square that night the bombs and general debris were fairly raining down. There seemed to be some total hold-up as we neared the Prince of Wales Theatre, so we took a detour. When finally we reached our 'West Indian

Party' we could tell from the faces of everyone around that something appalling must have happened.

Indeed it had: the Café de Paris had received a direct hit and Britain's favourite West Indian bandleader, Ken Snakehips Johnson, had been killed along with several of his players. The whole purpose of our broadcast, transmitted 'live' to the West Indies, was to show how bright and unconcerned were the London Trinidadians in the face of bombardment. In the event, the Party was more like a Wake, the circumstances so strained but the participants so brave that I have had an instinctive affection and admiration for the people of Trinidad ever since. None of those present will forget that night, certainly not I.

In my final months as a civilian I worked at the Hungaria Restaurant in Lower Regent Street (now the Hunting Lodge) with Oscar Grasso's Band. Oscar was famous as the smoochy-toned violinist with Victor Silvester's Ballroom Orchestra, and he taught me more about the practical commercial side of popular music than anyone else around that period.

When musicians use the word 'commercial' they do not necessarily mean it in the rigidly financial sense. To play 'commercial', especially in those days, meant to give the public exactly what it wanted, irrespective of one's own taste for lush harmonies and ingenious arrangers' tricks, resisting the tendency of every young band musician to launch off into jazz improvisations at the drop of a four-bar intro. Oscar Grasso taught me that when you have played for the dancing customers' benefit a chorus of 'This Can't be Love', what they want to hear next is another chorus of 'This Can't Be Love' played in exactly the same way. They do not care if a third chorus follows the second, provided the tempo is held at precisely forty-eight bars a minute, the tempo at which their legs are now automatically working. Musicians not unnaturally have a tendency to embroider their work on repetition, while such embroidery is absolutely endemic on the part of jazz-minded players. (Not only jazz players, either: something of the same philosophy lay behind the rueful remark of Constant Lambert when he said 'Having played a folk song through, once, there seems to be nothing else to do but play it through again, *forte*.')

70

Oscar Grasso knew his clientele at the Hungaria and in return they trusted him. It was an enjoyable job all round: my first classy place, in fact. The grand piano was the first really good instrument that I had enjoyed in a regular job. However because it took up so much space on the modest bandstand, I found myself squeezed on to the very rim of the rostrum. Behind me, no more than a foot or two away, was a waiter's table bearing a spirit lamp. Whenever any of the diners ordered anything *flambé*, its sudden flame took some of the hairs off the back of my neck. To this day I cannot see a spirit lamp in a restaurant without feeling a sudden hot flush up my back and seeming to smell singed hair.

One evening at the Hungaria we arrived for work to find a set of loudspeakers installed in the restaurant, and in due course Winston Churchill began one of his more memorable broadcasts. I found it curiously moving to be listening to the speech alongside Brigadiers, Colonels and ship's captains; all of us, patrons, waiters and musicians alike, united in still silence, as the living symbol of our resolution outlined in the plainest terms our stern and uninviting future.

The truth was unavoidable: my country was now at war. Conscience told me that less fit men than I were capable of keeping London's bandstands adequately manned. I sent my furious flat-mate back to her own bed-sitter. Then I went down to the recruiting office and volunteered for the Royal Air Force.

PART TWO

10. *How I routed the Hun while only breaking into a light sweat*

Even volunteering for the R.A.F. was not simple. As word got around the kitchen where the band had its meals that I was going for a medical, various spivs buttonholed me and indicated that since they themselves were 100 per cent unfit (and I must say they looked it) it would be the simplest thing in the world for them to borrow my Identity Card for half a day, attend in my place, take the medical examination in my name and get me duly registered as un–call–up–able for the duration of hostilities.

I would have none of it. Optimistic, as I have always been (and hope to continue to be) I was rather looking forward to the possibility of enjoying twelve hours of daylight, regular food, and for the first time in many months a bed to myself.

At the medical examination the R.A.F. doctor looked me keenly in the eyes. 'Is there any insanity in your family?' he demanded, and when I said there wasn't he clearly did not believe me. Perhaps he had heard about my lifestyle.

At Uxbridge I was sworn in, kitted out, and inoculated against a number of exotic ills. Within three days I had turned the colour of grass and was violently sick in the drive of a house about a hundred yards from the camp. They put me in the R.A.F. Hospital, under a sign that read 'vaccinal fever', but forgot to let anyone know where I was. After a week of enquiries my brother Philip (not long in uniform himself) found me, though by now I was out of a coma and even beginning to face the hospital food. Three days later they

73

discharged me – prematurely, as it turned out – and as I staggered out of the camp gates and off towards the tube station I was sick all over again in the very same drive which I had defiled a fortnight before. The house-owner must have thought I had a grudge against him.

There is little point in recounting the minor horrors of R.A.F. life. Others may have richly enjoyed the camaraderie, the sweat, the four-letter words which punctuated all conversation and sometimes almost replaced communication altogether. How manly the wiry blankets, the pease-pudding, the boozy officers, the corrupt N.C.O.s and the ill-designed uniforms! But I hated it all. Especially I hated being a number instead of a name – 1334498. I did not enjoy having to salute for my ten bob at the end of the week. Most of all I hated the stark impossibility of being alone with one's thoughts even for a moment, except in a latrine.

I do not complain: after all there was a war on. Others fared infinitely worse than I. Others never came back, among them some of my schoolfriends whom I remember now dimly but still with affection: Noel Ryder, Ray Holland, Jonathan Rees. They gave all; I merely survived.

Yet it remains to me a total mystery how any organisation as wildly mismanaged as His Majesty's Royal Air Force could remain half a dozen years in business, let alone win a war. One can only assume that the Luftwaffe was run even more capriciously.

'From October 1 greatcoats will be worn.' 'From April 1 greatcoats will *not* be worn.' 'Airmen may not pass in front of the windows of No. 1 Mess unless required to do so by an officer of the rank of Squadron-leader or above.' 'All owners of second forage-caps must be in possession of a signed chit.' The orders were arbitrary, the rules incomprehensible. Only the illiterate could stay out of trouble, because only they were impervious to printed instructions.

On my first Battle of Britain camp in Sussex we had a sudden dusk-till-dawn exercise designed to test the ground defences from surprise attack by those mythical German parachutists who seemed to obsess our superiors. I was in charge of a small body of men in a slit trench in someone's garden not far from Littlehampton. We duly defended it with the utmost efficiency against the dawn chorus, but through an administrative oversight we were never informed that the exercise was at an end. It was only by guesswork and his instinctive sense of leadership that 1334498 Corporal Race S. was able to stand his men down and rejoin the war effort in the cookhouse queue. Given an unquestioning appetite for obeying orders, my brave men and I would have been down that trench yet, submerged in baked-bean cans, like Privates Laurel and Hardy.

Later, when stationed at Marham in Norfolk, I had reached the heights of paid (as opposed to acting unpaid) corporal, and was in charge of a guard picket one night on the south barrier at that godforsaken aerodrome. My men were armed to the teeth with weapons which would have made the defenders of Ladysmith rock with laughter, but our rifles were proving singularly ineffective against the overwhelming problem that evening: an elusive enemy invasion of May-bugs which were flying into everyone's hair and eyes. It was not a pretty sight.

Rising to the occasion, as we decisive types must, I had given some crisp orders to deal with the problem – I cannot now for the life of me recall what my solution was – when the field telephone rang in my hut.

It was the corporal in charge of the picket over at the north barrier. 'Some berk of an officer has just driven up here in a truck,' he reported. 'Know what he did, Steve? He walked up to one of my men and wrestled the rifle out of his hand. Sillisod. Take care of him if he comes up to your place.' He rang off.

I hastily warned my picket that worse things than May-bugs were afoot and we made our preparations. In due course up drove Pilot-officer Prune.

'Everything all right, corporal?' he asked, peering about like a hawk on a telegraph pole. 'Yes, sir,' I replied, with a salute that rattled the teeth.

'I'm not so sure of that!' barked the officer, rounding suddenly on AC2 Bellchambers J. and attempting to wrest the rifle from his grasp.

With a quick wrench, AC2 Bellchambers J. swung the weapon aside and rammed it hard against the officer's neck. For half a second I thought he was going to fire.

'You want to be careful, sir,' he said. 'A little trick like that could get you shot.'

There was nothing P/O Prune could do other than colour

up. Then, remembering his officer training, he came out with the well-known 'you-down-there' cure-all; the remark that has served his type faithfully through more than one war.

'Carry on, corporal,' he told me.

* * *

I was at R.A.F. Ford near Arundel in Sussex when W.A.A.F.s were invented, or at any rate when they became a sudden delightful reality in Fighter Command.

The first consignment of Women's Auxiliary Air Force personnel at our camp consisted of one girl typist, who primped around self-consciously for a month or so, attaching herself to no one airman in particular, but clearly basking in the good-natured wolf whistles coming at her from all sides. After a few weeks she was joined by fifty others and the whole thing took on a sudden importance. We did not just have a girl on the camp, we had *women*.

Mine was a well-formed girl whose tunic was insufficiently generous for her person. She and I got on well from the start, in fact the only difficulty we had was in thinking of things to talk about when we were merely together as opposed to being alone together.

We were billeted at a posh girls' boarding school called Tortington Manor. The place had been requisitioned as it stood, and was rumoured to be the source of the wartime story about dormitory wall-signs which read 'If in need of a mistress, ring the bell'. I did not need a bell.

The school buildings backed on to an infinity of farmland. Late one summer night my W.A.A.F. and I, looking for somewhere to go and not talk, found a barn conveniently lined with hay. Pushing the door open, we went in and made ourselves comfortable on the floor, undisturbed save for the distant hooting of an owl. A.C.W. Someone and I were alone together in the whole world. And very nice too.

At an inopportune moment – though it could just have been worse, I suppose – I heard to my absolute horror the thud-thud of approaching footsteps, then the creak of the barn door being opened.

'Close your eyes, keep them closed and lie absolutely still,' I breathed into the right ear of Aircraftwoman X as we lay there in the hay. 'Pretend to be asleep. It's our only hope.' I followed my own example and held her in an iron grip, eyes closed, heart thudding.

No longer was I, as the song so romantically has it, 'In the Mood for Love'. The footsteps approached ... Stopped a yard or two away ... And then I felt the light of an electric torch fall on my closed eyes. Somehow I managed to keep them shut. We lay there, doggo, as vulnerable as two caterpillars on a leaf.

What would come next? A boot in the rear? A hayfork? A maniacal laugh? – An offer perhaps for Aircraftwoman X?

None of these things, as it transpired. After several hours – or was it really only a few agonised seconds? – the torchlight was abruptly switched off; the footsteps receded and the barn door creaked again comfortingly. Thud-thud on the path outside ... Silence. Aircraftwoman X and I breathed again.

I never heard any more about the episode, nor have I told anyone about it until now. I think it shortened my life by several years. Since that night I have wondered many times who the torch's owner was. A kindly farmer, perhaps, who had known what it was to be in uniform far from home? A tramp seeking shelter? Or was it my Commanding Officer, looking for somewhere to not talk with a W.A.A.F. of his own?

Now I shall never know. But I do know that it ended the affair between Aircraftwoman X and myself; somehow I could never raise sufficient enthusiasm for her again and we drifted apart. Now I come to think of it, I heard that she married a farmer. I wonder ...

* * *

Down there at R.A.F. Ford I had been leading quite a good little band, but the musical gods were not always so kind. Towards the end of my time at R.A.F. Marham the only players available constituted a quartet of trombone, violin, drums and piano, and I defy any musician to make that combination sound other than ludicrous, especially with an ex-army lifer on trombone whose tone sounded like the tearing of calico. Later, at Bridgnorth, I had the occasional luxury of using a Hammond organ. Back temporarily at Uxbridge I was sent out in the evenings to play at the Wings Club for young officers at Hyde Park Corner.

It was there that I met Irving Berlin, who was visiting London to plug his syrupy song 'My British Buddy'. Taking over from me at the upright piano, Berlin rendered several of his compositions in his squeaky voice, rendered squeakier by the fact that he could only play on the black notes. Everything for him had to be in the same key, regardless of its range or (to use the correct expression) its *tessitura*. Any song played and sung by Irving Berlin had to be in key of G flat. I had some sympathy for him, having been a G flat man myself not all that many years before.

'Gee,' he told me, after almost castrating himself with a vocal rendering of 'I've Got my Love to keep me Warm', 'I wish I had my own piano here. I have a gear-lever on it that changes the key for me.'

Talking of celebrities, it was while serving at R.A.F. Marham that I met King George VI. Marham really lies at the back of beyond, the nearest town being King's Lynn. (Where the nearest town to King's Lynn is, I never found out.) As a consequence of its isolation, R.A.F. Marham needed all the entertainment it could get, and one morning the Commanding Officer sent for me and charged me with the responsibility of forming a Station Military Band. 'I'll give you all possible help,' he told me, and I am bound to say he was as good as his word. Excused-duty passes materialised from thin air; euphonium players were given weekend leaves in order to fetch their instruments; a man who mistakenly claimed that he could play the E flat horn was actually let out of gaol to audition for me. (We had to send him back.)

I combed the camp for people who could play wind instruments and succeeded in getting together a Military Band of sorts. Cornet... Clarinet... Big Trombone... It was a bit like the Cornish Floral Dance, but we made a martial sort of noise. We grew in the end to fourteen, and for our key soloist I found one really good youngster who played the cornet.

Unfortunately he was in the Army, not the R.A.F. Nevertheless I used to borrow him for parades and special occasions. I can see us now: a motley crew, all sizes and types and all in Air Force blue except for this young lad in khaki. We used to delight the C.O. by leading Church Parades with our three tunes: A March called 'Sons of the Brave', another called 'The Great Little Army', and a third less reputable march for which we had no music but which everyone knew anyway in those days, Bob Crosby's 'South Rampart Street Parade'.

'I've got some splendid news for you, Corporal,' said the C.O. one day, 'I'm sending you to play for an A.T.C. Cadets' Parade at Sandringham House. Not only will *I* be there, His Majesty the King will take the salute. I want your band at its best, so you have two weeks to get in trim. Sharp's the word.' (He was more right than he knew: we did tend to play sharp.)

With King George VI at the listening end, I naturally wanted the best band I could get. The very last man I could afford to omit was my young army private, the cornettist. But what to do about his khaki-clad figure?

It happened that a friend of mine at Marham was the camp tailor, a sergeant with considerably more service than the rest of us, in fact he must have been fifty years old or more. He was the answer to my problem. I borrowed the tailor's spare uniform and dressed up my army cornettist in it so that we would at least look like an all-R.A.F. band. The two of them were about the same size, even if they were so far apart in age.

Came the day and we set off in our R.A.F. lorry to Sandringham. The King duly inspected the cadets; we played 'The Great Little Army', 'Sons of the Brave' and 'South Rampart Street Parade' – and eventually His Majesty came over to inspect my band. I brought the musicians to attention and saluted my monarch. He asked me a few questions about myself. Then, as he moved down the ranks to talk to some of my musicians, I heard my C.O. hiss at me through his teeth 'You *idiot*!'

It wasn't like him. ('What a performance!' as Sid Field used to say at the time.) I was really mystified; I thought it was all going splendidly. It was only the next day I found out what was worrying the Old Man. He sent for me and was very complimentary about the band. But then his cold eyes homed in on me and he said: 'I was glad His Majesty the king did not elect to speak to that army lad you tell me is so good. That cornettist of yours was wearing the Mons Star!'

I cannot think how long I might have spent languishing in the Tower of London if the King had caught sight of that un-earned medal, he being (as I later discovered) something of an expert on Orders and Medals.

I might add that he also gave signs of being somewhat out of touch with the world of ordinary folk. When he stopped to ask me what I had done in civilian life I told him the truth: that I had played in a dance band.

The king's brown face crumpled up, his shoulders heaved with laughter, and he repeated my comical reply to an aide standing near. For my part I had not thought of it as being in the least funny. But, as Doctor Johnson had said on an earlier occasion, who was I to bandy civilities with my Sovereign, still less argue with him?

Many years later I found that I was not alone in the experience. David Higham, the literary agent, describes a similar experience in his autobiography:

> King George VI, inspecting his troops:
> 'And what were you in civil life?'
> 'A literary agent, sir.'
> The good king laughed and laughed. Later I thought he must have heard 'Literary gent'.

Not so, Mr Higham. It was simply that he found the thought of certain jobs infinitely diverting. Well, there must have been little enough to laugh at in his job at the time.

* * *

Life in the R.A.F., even at my humble level, had its diverting moments. At one camp, summoned to see the Station Warrant-officer about the arrangements for a Sergeants' Mess dance, I found him in the mess bar. As we conversed, I noticed that he was systematically filing down the whisky tot. He saw me notice it, but was untroubled. We both knew that he had power of life and death over any troublesome N.C.O. He must have made a pound a night out of short whisky measures in that hard-drinking Mess.

I was a sergeant by then, sharing a tiny room for a while with the boxer Eric Boon, who, with true R.A.F. logic, had been given a job in charge of gardening, while someone else took care of physical fitness. At the same camp it was noteworthy that one of the sergeant cooks had been a gents' hairdresser in civilian life, whereas the official camp barber had previously been a cook. Nothing in King's Regulations permitted them to switch roles, because they were in different pay groups, so the camp personnel soldiered on as best we could with indifferent haircuts and worse meals.

The author in his garden

*Me, my xylophone, and my
brother's white flannels*

*1334498 Cpl. Race S. with R.A.F. Marham Military Band, by
courtesy of Group-Captain Fred Karno, 1942*

'Congratulations on finding the Lost Chord, Mr Durante.'

'Did you really name it after me?'

Leading a band for an Officers' Mess dance was an experience never to be forgotten, indeed I know one or two musicians who date their conversion to Communism from one single exposure to the Quality with its hair down. The excessive drinking one took for granted; the fact that everyone was pie-eyed almost from the start. Less easy to ignore was the girl-groping which after about 2 am no one troubled to disguise and went on everywhere from staircases to the back of the bandstand. By three or four in the morning the band, tired out, would be playing deliberately slower and slower tempos – more and more somnolent waltz medleys – in the hope of inducing sleep in the few couples remaining vertical. At long last the junior officer who had been put in charge of entertainments and hence condemned to comparative sobriety would indicate to me, the bandleader, that we might as well pack up. We would then launch into 'Auld Lang Syne', to which every dance musician sings (or at the very least, mouths) at the patrons a special set of words, which begin 'Go home, you ————, go home, you ————, go home, you ————, go home.' At long last, dawn breaking over the recumbent couples, we would stagger back to our respective beds, to be awakened an hour or so later by the screams of senior N.C.O.s ushering in a new day.

I already knew a good deal about the Aristocracy at Play from a number of society gigs in my last pre-service year, and from a short spell at an ultra-fashionable Mayfair club called Le Suivi. I had learnt for example how one dealt with requests. The more experienced bandleaders would greet a request for some special tune with the jocular words 'All requests must be written on the back of a five-pound note', and the patron, delightedly entering into the spirit of the joke, would duly fork out a fiver and write his request on it.

Although much play has been made of it in recent years by such people as Benny Green, bright young things really did prance up to the piano in those days and say 'Oh Mister Bandleader, will you play "I Get too Hungry?"', whereupon it was up to me to interpret that what she really wanted to hear was 'The Lady is a Tramp'. A request for 'You Are the One' could be identified as a call for 'Night and Day', while 'Chicks and Ducks' (initially a night club request) became the musicians' own title for 'The Surrey with a Fringe on Top'. One bandleader of my acquaintance even had a request to play 'The Pink Aeroplane', which completely defeated him, until someone pointed out that it was a translation of 'L'Avion Rose'.

There was one dance which was delayed in starting because all the musicians except one were in a car that had broken down. The one player to arrive on time was the drummer, and after half an hour the distraught hostess pointed to her watch, indicated the waiting guests and ordered him to start the music. '*Me*, madam? I'm only the drummer!' But she was adamant.

'Ladies and gentlemen, we begin the evening's dancing with a quickstep,' he announced bravely, and reaching for a pair of wire brushes began to play a quickstep rhythm on his side-drum. The dancers took the floor happily, quite oblivious of the fact that a one-piece band was playing an endless nothing at forty-eight bars a minute.

The drummer, pounding away, cast anguished eyes on the door, but there was no sign of his colleagues. After a few minutes' playing he began to get tired and stopped. The dancers applauded delightedly. It gave him new heart. He reached for the microphone.

'And now, a waltz,' the drummer announced. (1 – 2 – 3, 1 – 2 – 3, 1 – 2 – 3...). Warming to his task, he favoured them with a Palais Glide, and then, greatly daring, a rather complicated Paul Jones.

During the Ladies' Excuse-me Tango which followed, the hostess came over to him beaming with delight. 'Lovely,' she said, 'lovely, Mr Drummer. But will you please play "Jealousy"?'

'Madam,' replied the drummer, 'what else am I playing?'

* * *

The great problem in R.A.F. days, among musicians making a little extra money on the side by playing for the various camp entertainments, was the fact that they were required to provide their own tools, their own instruments. There were problems of damage, of insurance, of sheer wear and tear, not to mention accessories like violin strings, drum heads and saxophone reeds to be provided. In view of this it was not thought funny – at least not at the time – when the Entertainments Officer

greeted a five-piece service band at the start of an Officers'
Mess Dance and read to them from the Group-Captain's
memo. 'These are the C.O's instructions,' he said. 'The first
hour you will play like Andre Kostelanetz. The second hour
you will play like Ambrose. The third hour you will play like
Nat Gonella. And the fourth hour the officers will come up
and play the instruments themselves.'

* * *

During all these diversions a war was being waged, and rather
successfully. The necessary effort was only relaxed, so far as
our camp was concerned, when a big brass-hat officer came
round to see that we were all doing our bit. Then the work of
the whole place would stop for some days while we were lent
new blue uniforms out of store, and the fitters handed in their
spanners and wrenches in exchange for new shiny ones. The
brass-hat would be conducted round the camp like a royal
visitor, repair to the Officers' Mess for drinks and a sumptuous
dinner then be whisked off in his staff car, whereupon we spent
a day or two reclaiming our old uniforms and trying to get
back our favourite spanners. I often wonder whether the
Air-Vice-Marshals of those days ever commented on how
brightly clad everyone seemed during the war years, and how
well the common chaps looked after their tools.

One took such idiocies in one's stride, living merely for
leave, the morning lie-in, the N A A F I break or the night off.
For a while I was engaged to be married to a Flight-sergeant in
the W.A.A.F., a relationship which gave rise to some ribald
and rather obvious jests among my colleagues. After a while –
perhaps it was official R.A.F. policy, who knows? – she was
posted to Downham Market ten miles away. On my ram-
shackle bike I used to cycle in the evenings to a pub a mile or so
out of Downham, where we would meet for a drink and then
go for a walk into the woods, after which I would remount
that bike and cycle the eight miles back to Marham for the
never-to-be-forgotten serviceman's deadline of 23.59. I doubt
if I could contemplate that particular ride now; indeed I would
have to think twice about the woodland walk.

One's stamina, not to mention one's appetites, seemed absolutely boundless in those wartime days, and when I was posted
back to Uxbridge for a while I decided to 'live out'. I took a

bed-sit near Euston Station and began systematically burning the candle at all three ends. It could not last – thank goodness it didn't – and after turning up late for morning parade once too often I was sent to Bridgnorth in Shropshire to reflect, and to some extent to convalesce.

At Bridgnorth I did a sudden about-turn, as youngsters often do, reading for the first time many of the books I now love most, walking endlessly over Clee Hill and Wenlock Edge, playing the piano whenever I could, composing, and even doing some orchestrations which were accepted for broadcasting by the bands of Phil Green and Eric Winstone.

I wrote to the BBC for an audition, and in due course was sent my first individual contract for a fifteen-minute series called *Kings of the Keyboard* – or was it *Keyboard Cavalcade*? – I cannot remember the name. But I do remember taking the train to London on a weekend pass and broadcasting from studio five at Maida Vale the programme of currently popular pieces that I had chosen, The Warsaw Concerto (short version) prominent among them.

Back at camp afterwards I found I was something of a celebrity. Then on top of everything else, a few days later I opened a letter addressed to me c/o R.A.F. Bridgnorth and to my amazement there fluttered out a cheque for two guineas. Another envelope yielded three guineas; altogether there were cheques totalling fourteen pounds. What had I done to deserve such largesse? Had Harry Leader remembered me in his will?

Not so. Unwittingly I had entered the world of the song plugger. In my innocence I had 'programmed the current plug numbers' favoured by certain leading song publishers. The payment of such money was so automatic in those days that the exploitation departments of Messrs Campbell Connelly, Chappell, Feldman and the rest had automatically sent me the going rate for a two-minute piano broadcast of their current plug song. It is interesting to note that my service address could only have been obtained with the active co-operation of the BBC, which was supposed at the time to be fighting song-plugging with great determination.

So it was that I found myself face to face at last not only with the musical profession, but with the music 'business' on which it depends for its existence. It was quite an initiation.

I pondered a moment, surprised, even a little shocked, I suppose. Then I went out and cashed the cheques before any of the publishers could have second thoughts.

Before the war I had become a professional. Now I was a pro.

11. *The hurly-burly of peace*

On a romantic level I cannot claim that I had spent the war years exactly pining away for Clair Leng, but at least I had never missed an opportunity to ask her to marry me. On leave after leave back in Lincoln, regardless of whether she had a current boy-friend or even I a fiancée, I had gone round to see her, taken her out for the evening, and usually ended up proposing marriage. Suddenly in 1944, on one of my weekend visits to Lincoln, I proposed as usual, and this time she accepted me.

Back at camp I was panic-stricken. She had always turned me down before: now I had obviously indulged in the romantic pleasure of a proposal once too often. But then I thought of her face and figure, her sense of humour, and how nice it would be to give up the somewhat overrated joys of male freedom for such a bright and lively possession.

We were married at the Methodist Church on Bridgnorth Hill. Her workmates at A.V. Roe Ltd in Lincoln had a whip round and gave her a bunch of bananas, which, as anyone who remembers the war will testify, was the equivalent of an entire smoked salmon nowadays.

In a moment of patriotic exuberance I had volunteered for training as a pilot; now I hoped they would lose my application form. In the event they never lost sight of it, but the inevitable delays of service paperwork came to my aid and instead of being sent for aircrew training I was suddenly attached to a unit called Tiger Force, with instructions to go out and defeat the Japanese. But even this never quite came off, and the war ended with me back where I started at Uxbridge, checking in for three wasted hours every morning, but able to work in bands at night, notably with a guitarist/bandleader called Howard Lucraft.

Howard remains one of the very few people in the entertainment profession about whom I have never heard anyone utter a critical word. Everyone liked Howard and he had the good sense to start up a small, compact band at the very moment when big bands were being found unwieldy and extravagant. While Lew Stone, Ambrose and their contemporaries slaved away desperately trying to keep a dozen or more musicians together, Howard Lucraft and his Music attracted more and more engagements and broadcasts. In time they made him, and consequently his featured pianist, quite well known in the profession and to some extent with the listening public too.

The day of my demobilisation came. Symbolically it was a great day for anyone who had hated service anonymity as much as I had. In the event the day after was very like the day before demob, except that I had more time in which to pursue my own career. When I came back from the depot, wearing my demob suit for the first and last time, I found that Clair had festooned the house with banners reading 'Welcome home, Steve ... El Alamein ... Sidi Barrani ... Berlin ... The nation is proud of you.' Applied to someone who had never managed to get further afield than Shropshire, it could only mean that I had married a girl with a delicious sense of humour.

Out of uniform at last, I buzzed around everywhere, playing the piano and arranging music, carving out a quick career as a freelance musician, and only making one basic mistake, when I agreed to join the first post-war band of Cyril Stapleton at a Bond Street restaurant called Fischer's (later the Celebrité, and now some sort of belly-dancers' emporium). Cyril was not an easy man to work with, and when I handed in my notice after three months of playing all night and arranging all day, I was sharply reminded of the old truth that no musician ever 'leaves' a bandleader: he only stabs him in the back.

Having innocently 'stabbed' Cyril I took care to spread my

work around spending over half my time doing orchestrations and only the remainder crouched over a hot piano in the small hours.

After one endless night at a country house party in Surrey, I gave up playing for dancing altogether. I had 'flu anyway. The bandleader, seeking to ingratiate himself with the famous press lord for whom we were playing, greeted him with the words 'Good evening, your lordship. Are you having good shooting?' To which his lordship replied 'Hardly this month, Mr ————!' At 3 am the guests were still enjoying themselves hugely; the requests-on-five-pound-notes were simply pouring in, but I was in a state of near collapse. At seven in the morning I was decanted on to my Wembley doorstep with a temperature of 103. 'I'll never do another society gig as long as I live,' I told Clair. And I never have. Since that morning in 1946 no foot has foxtrotted to my music, at least not in my presence. They can dance what they like to my recordings.

On occasional evenings I went to accompany the variety acts at the Stage Door Canteen, or at the similar (though longer lived) Nuffield Centre for the Forces and there I played for Noël Coward, Beatrice Lillie and George Robey, among others. I found that I not only had a gift for accompanying but a real taste for it too. It remains still the only musical ability about which I am confident to the point of conceit: I believe – I *know* – I do it well, and if there is anything these days that could tempt me back to serious keyboard work it would be the prospect of being the really good accompanist that I know I could enjoy being.

Accompanying in the Gerald Moore sense is a fine and important accomplishment, but in the general world of entertainment music it calls for a great deal more than taste, technique and a willingness to be self-effacing. I learnt what all-round accompanying entails when I was made official pianist for the immediately post-war BBC Television Auditions Unit, headed by Mary Cook.

Mary Cook must be one of the great unsung heroines of British show business. Formerly a dancing teacher (Beryl Grey had been one of her pupils from the age of four) Mary spent a good deal of time in Portugal, where she became quite well known as a concert pianist. Back in wartime London, she was summoned by the boss of Chappells, the music publishing firm, to offer assistance to an American songwriter who was holed up in the Dorchester Hotel with a good idea for a song but no means of writing it down. The songwriter proved to be Irving Berlin and the tune he hummed to her as she notated it for him on paper was 'My British Buddy'. She stayed on as Berlin's secretary and personal assistant, moving over in later years to help with the nightly cabaret shows for the forces at the reconstituted Café de Paris (by then the Stage Door Canteen) and at the Nuffield Centre.

Mary, as administrator and one-time performer herself, was the perfect choice to handle the flood of applicants then pouring out of the forces and trying desperately to get their foot in the door of the new and exciting medium of television. Looking back now, it seems extraordinary that the cautious, committee-ridden BBC should have been prepared to place the whole television *yea* or *nay* decision process in the hands of one woman. Nevertheless it was a happy arrangement for the entertainment profession and, as it turned out, for me as well.

We began the auditions in a claustrophobic basement storeroom filled with heating pipes, under what is now the headquarters of the Methodist Missionary Society in Marylebone Road. That first day brought five 'acts', the best of them being a young man who gave his name as Michael Bentine and performed an excruciatingly funny comedy routine using just the top half of a broken chair as a prop. He set a standard which could not possibly be maintained, though within days of Mike's (needless to say successful) audition, we had another very funny man, who did impressions of how different men get shaved in the mornings. His name was Harry Secombe.

On each of our four morning sessions each week the pattern was the same. As the first artist finished his or her brief act, Mary Cook, courteous, sophisticated, cool and very slightly forbidding, would call out to them 'Come and talk to me, darling,' using that term of endearment which was the common form of address in show business, then as now. The secretary would bring in the next auditionee, and I would have three or four minutes in which to sort out whatever music they required.

'Sort out' was sometimes the right expression. The sop-
ranos who brought their copies of (inevitably) 'Love is Where
you Find It' were no problem. The opera singers, who chose
either 'O Mio Babbino Caro' or 'La Donna e Mobile', according to sex, merely needed to be given a calming glass of water
and offered a compliment on their lovely dresses or well-cut
velvet jackets. The comedians, haunted, neurotic and unsure as
members of that profession so often are, asked for eight bars of
'I Want to be Happy' to get them on, then spent the remaining
waiting-time anguishing at the absence of a live audience to
provide a feedback of laughter.

'What's the cue for your play-off?' I would ask them.

'Eh? Oh, when I say "I'm on my way to the asylum accom-
panied by the orchestra," you play a chord in G. Then I say
"Play, professor!" and I sing a chorus of "It's a Lovely Day
Tomorrow" and off. God it's awful without an audience.'

The difficult ones for me were those hopefuls who – incredibly since they were trying for such high stakes – had not
thought to bring along any music at all. They knew what they
wanted to sing or to dance to, but they relied utterly on there
being a pianist present who could manage instantaneous recall
on Liszt's Second Hungarian Rhapsody, 'They Call Me
Mimi', or 'Beat Me Daddy Eight to the Bar', as the case might
be. Giving them whatever they wanted became a matter of
pride for me, as did finding the best key to suit their voices. I
also considered it part of my job to calm their shattered nerves,
insofar as anyone could, until such time as Mary Cook called
down the hall 'Ready, darlings? *Off* you go then!'

Graduating from our Marylebone Road basement, we had a
spell holding auditions in a recording studio off Baker Street,
then settled in at the Nuffield Centre in the Strand. It was there
one morning that we finished a session rather early, only to
discover on checking the list that we had mislaid one of the
auditionees. He was a conjuror, but had grown so nervous
while waiting that he had wandered outside on to the fire
escape to practise his tricks. Once there, the door had firmly
closed behind him and our receptionist had forgotten his existence. But he, like Messrs Bentine and Secombe, duly passed
his audition. His name was David Nixon.

Mary's brief chat with each of the hopefuls was designed to
give them an opportunity to state their professional experience

while at the same time enabling her quietly to judge their personalities and potential. Now and then one of them would bounce into her little sanctum with a jaunty over-confidence, and for them I noticed (just before the door closed on the interview cubicle) that Mary had a special opening line. 'Tell me,' she would ask innocently, 'what it is makes you feel that your act is especially suitable for *television*?' Short of replying 'Because I'm so lovely' the question was more or less unanswerable. Most of the cocky ones realised at that moment that they had met their match, though it made no difference to whether they passed or not: that was a matter of talent.

'That boy,' said a visiting television producer one day, 'has more self-confidence than I've ever seen in anybody. He's *got* to be a star!' – and very soon he was: Max Bygraves. Among those like Max who passed their preliminary audition at the first attempt were Ronnie Corbett, Beryl Grey, Rolf Harris, Alfred Marks, Bob Monkhouse, Frank Muir and Peter Sellers, all of whom arrived in various stages of nervous apprehension but got an eventual thumbs-up at the special stage-two auditions held in front of the cameras at Alexandra Palace or Lime Grove. To the eternal shame of the high-powered TV producers' panel which sat in judgment on them at that stage, only one producer (D. H. Munro) gave a favourable report when we stubbornly brought back Tony Hancock for a third camera audition. 'The man's a genius,' he insisted. 'Can't any of you see it?'

Not all our customers were potential stars. One East European, 'The Strongest Man on Earth' (as he billed himself) loomed heavily over Mary Cook in her small cubicle and tried to borrow money from her. She gave him a penny, which he bit savagely and returned to her with a courtly bow. Another day we had a demonstration of fire-eating by a lady whose breath, as she discussed her musical accompaniment with me, I shall not easily forget. (I say 'she' but must amend the word, since she turned out to be a man.) Occasionally an audition hopeful would have the bright idea of trying to influence matters by ingratiating herself with me, the resident accompanist. One such girl, a torch singer of Sabrina-like proportions, took my hand and placed it firmly over the region of her heart, saying – I remember her words exactly – 'That's how nervous I am, and there's plenty more where that came from.'

So much for my mornings in those immediately post-war days. But if they were taken up with the relatively self-effacing work of audition accompanist, my afternoons and evenings were spent building a career in broadcasting, first of all as a band pianist and then increasingly as a soloist.

I was writing orchestrations by then for Jack Payne and for the Skyrockets, also handling the arrangements for a new young solo recording artist named Dorothy Squires. Dotty, as she has come to be called (not altogether without reason) was married at the time to a leading songwriter, and it was my orchestrations, written in the lush Stordahl/Sinatra style of the day, which launched her smoky, seductive voice in such songs as 'I'll Close my Eyes'.

A trombonist named Ted Heath was trying his luck as a bandleader, and for him I scored the orchestra's very first signature tune, which was his own song 'That Lovely Weekend'. Then there was Phil Green, whose Concert Orchestra enjoyed a constant stream of radio slots, and to whose library I had begun to contribute scores while still serving in the R.A.F. at Bridgnorth. I noticed that the arranger's identity was never mentioned on the air, and discovered that in the studio, after the orchestra had run through one of my earlier manuscripts, one of the musicians had called out 'Whose arrangement is that, Phil?' To which the bandleader replied 'Oh, it's ours.' He was of course technically right: the Phil Green office had indeed paid for it.

In the last year or so of my R.A.F. service I had done several engagements as accompanist to the immensely popular crooner Denny Dennis. Denny was (and is) a charming man; but he will forgive my saying that he represents one of the prime examples in popular music of an innocent bystander unaccountably touched by the fickle finger of fate. For a small man he had an amazing resonance of voice; for a star he had almost too much humility; he was the classic non-showman thrust by sheer gift into show business. His enormous pre-war fame with the Roy Fox Band had led to a curious situation during the war years, for while Denny served at home on a succession of R.A.F. camps, there turned out to be four Denny Dennis impostors appearing simultaneously in different parts

91

of the Middle East and liberated Europe. I was with the real (and speechless) Denny Dennis when he opened a letter from a girl fan writing from some spot he had never visited. He read:

> To Denny Dennis. Dear Sir, If you do not return the gold watch which you stole off me, I shall tell the papers about what happened that night last November. Be warned.
> Yours truly,
> Mavis Throgmorton.

Denny needed a stiff drink after reading that. As far as I know he never managed to pin down any of the phoney Dennises who were cashing in on his fame. In a modest degree in later years I have suffered the same trouble myself; three different 'Steve Races' have appeared in Yorkshire, Lancashire and the Midlands – or are they the same man? – passing themselves off as me, or at any rate not exactly making our different identities as clear as one of us could wish.

I was also accompanist to the delightful and multi-talented Avril Angers, who had made a rapid nationwide reputation as the dumb secretary in radio's *Carroll Levis Show*. With Avril's name printed in huge letters across the top half of the bill, and with 'Steve Race at the piano', in small letters at the foot, we did our joint bit for the dying years of music-hall, then lingering on as Variety, while we toured the Moss Empires and other theatres alongside such acts as the Cairolis and Tom Katz and his Saxophone Six.

I can still hear in my mind those excruciating pit bands, still smell the stale make-up in the filthy dressing-rooms and see the dark empty rows of seats at the dreaded first house Monday night. At Shepherd's Bush Empire (now the BBC's Television Theatre) I shared a dressing-room with a youth who was one of a team of acrobats. At the climax to their act he would balance upside down on top of a human pyramid, his full weight on one single outstretched forefinger.

One evening I was standing in the wings watching this remarkable feat when the young man dashed over to me on the end of a running succession of flipflaps. 'For Pete's sake,' he called, 'go to the dressing-room for me!'

'Why?' I asked innocently.

As he careered back on stage he yelled over his shoulder 'Me finger! Me finger!'

I found it on the table in front of the mirror: a cast-iron forefinger, painted flesh pink, with a hand-grip attached. I threw it to him just as the human pyramid was forming. Later he bought me a well-earned beer.

It was at Chiswick Empire that Avril shared top billing with the veteran comic double-act of Morris and Cowley. The two old men were of indeterminate age but decidedly getting on in years, so perhaps it was a good thing that their act consisted in them sitting side by side on a bench centre-stage, dressed as Beefeaters.

Either Morris or Cowley, I shall never know which, was standing beside me in the wings perfunctorily watching some lesser comedian die a Monday night death.

'It's not like the old days,' remarked Morris (or Cowley). 'Why, at the Gillingham Empire they used to buy fish heads at five for twopence and throw them at comics like us. Had to lower a gauze screen, the management did. Wonderful days.'

'Why?' I enquired, all wide-eyed innocence. 'Why were they such wonderful days if the audience used to throw fish heads at you?'

'The money, boy, the money. Two hundred pounds a week, my partner and me were getting before the First World War. And I'll tell you something else. There was so much work around for the best acts. Do you know that in 1910 we were booking digs for 1920? Mind you, then the war started and spoilt it all ...'

I shall always be grateful to Avril Angers for the fact that I was able to be a small part of that extraordinary, doomed profession before the final blow fell a few years later, thanks to the march of television, and perhaps a little to the sheer tattiness of the Variety Theatre itself.

With her I even made contact with the theatrical West End of London. When she went into a revue at the Duchess Theatre called *Make it a Date*, she sang some of the songs that Sid Colin and I had specially written for her, and shared comedy sketches with Max Wall in his first star billing. Max was not a legend then – perhaps too many ex-servicemen had known his reputation as a drill corporal at R.A.F. Blackpool – but he was clearly destined for the top. The wonder is that it took him so long to get there.

My songwriting partner Sid Colin had been a singer with
the wartime Squadronnaires and was later to establish himself
as one of Britain's major comedy scriptwriters for television
and the cinema. Meanwhile he and I wrote 'special material'
for various cabaret performers, and we even placed a song in a
film. I appeared on the screen myself, playing the role of the
bandleader in a night club where a murder was committed, the
victim being Celia Lipton. The murderer? ... It took Paul
Temple all of eight reels to find that out.

12. Calling Paul Temple and Steve (and Nicola)

In my whole life I have never endured such mind-bending
boredom as the three days at Walton-on-Thames film studios
during which we shot the night-club sequence for *Calling Paul
Temple*. No one outside the business of filming for the cinema
can imagine the hold-ups, the inexplicable hour-long pauses,
the screaming tedium of the movie studio. Though I tell
myself that it must be better now, I still marvel at how film
actors can stand it, still less give a sustained performance, when
so much of their time spent on the studio floor consists of
doing nothing whatever. Endlessly the technicians mutter
about set-ups, tracking lines and fishpole shadows. They
queue up to peer through the camera; after a 'take' they mutter
about 'a hair in the gate'. A day's filming is a day's standing
about.

While we were shooting the song that Sid Colin and I had
written, it became clear that the plot demanded a second song
for Celia Lipton to sing – or more specifically to die while
singing, our film *Calling Paul Temple* being a whodunit, and
quite a good one at that.

I confess it: I ought then and there to have called Sid, told him a further song was needed, and worked through the night with him to create it. Instead I got an idea when driving home that evening, worked out the words and music myself, and sold it to the producer the next morning. I blush now at the thought of what Sid must have felt when eventually he saw the screen credits and discovered the existence of that second song.

The tedious studio work on *Calling Paul Temple* left me with no desire whatever to seek a career in films, even if I had possessed any of the necessary talents. Television though – that was another matter. I did a few appearances from Alexandra Palace in the months following the BBC's resumption of its regular TV service, and became pretty well at ease with the medium, or as easy as any TV performer can ever claim to be. I also played for a quiz show which featured Gilbert Harding in his television debut.

As a freelance pianist and arranger for radio, TV and concerts, I was wildly busy. But then, I had an added incentive to make a success: I was a father. Four months before I left the R.A.F. our daughter Nicola was born. The name we gave her was for those days very unusual: we had found it in a trilogy of novels by Crosbie Garstin called *The Penhales*. Later, following a composition of mine which I called 'Nicola' in her honour, the name became suddenly popular, and I have the authority of the author of *The Guinness Book of Names* for saying that as my song gained in popularity in the 1960s, so did the name Nicola for newly-born girls. It is perhaps my only contribution to British social history.

My contribution to the population figures was born at a maternity home in Bushey, Hertfordshire. When I first saw her at seven hours old, she had a brick-red face, skimpy wisps of black hair and an expression of acute displeasure. In short, she was the most beautiful baby I had ever seen. This book is not about her – it is about her dad – but I must allow myself the luxury of this one paragraph to say that nothing more lovely can happen to any man than having a daughter, especially one as nice as mine. She has been the joy of my life, always near me however far away; closer than words and far beyond their expressing.

While Nicola gained strength (and hair) her father rushed about the country providing for her future. Some of the people

I worked with became great personal friends at that time, among them the lovable Tony Hancock. When Clair and Nicola went on a seaside holiday at an unusually busy time for me, it was Tony who agreed to look after them, though even then poor Tony was far from reliable. My diaries of the period are full of entries which read 'Tony for dinner, didn't come', 'T.H. missed party', or 'Tony overnight unexpectedly'.

One memorable engagement with Howard Lucraft's Band took me to perform at the closing evening of the Henley Royal Regatta. We were to broadcast from a floating raised stage moored in mid-Thames. The structure, I realise now, exactly resembled that in which the Chester Plays were performed in 1594: ' – a high scaffold with two rooms, a higher and a lower. In the lower they apparel themselves and in the higher they play, being all open at the top' – just so. In the higher we duly played, the whole floating edifice being moored opposite the famous Henley finishing post. It was a memorable sight as dusk fell: crowds packed on the hillside, while some dozens of small rowing boats were crammed in between us and the shore.

Our cue to start the broadcast came through a field telephone manned by the announcer/producer, John Ellison. The message received, John duly waved to Howard to indicate that we were on the air, and the music should begin. Half an hour later, another wave from our producer told us that the transmission was at an end.

'O.K.' said Howard. 'We're off the air. Give them "the King".' He pointed at the drummer to start a drum roll.

'No, no, no!' screamed John Ellison. But it was too late. We were well into 'God Save the King' by then. One by one the occupants of the little boats struggled patriotically to their feet; one by one they tottered and fell; one by one they plopped shrieking into the wine-dark Thames. I watched them, fascinated. One man in an Eton blazer I could have sworn was still singing as his head disappeared beneath the water. 'Send him victorious, happy and,' he sang. Maybe it was the spirit which had won us the war. His straw boater floated away between the stoles and the parasols.

Quite a lot of my time was spent in travelling around the country as an adjudicator at *Melody Maker* Dance Band Contests. The paper's chief record critic, organiser of the contests

96

and chairman of the judges, was an extraordinary man called Edgar Jackson. When I knew Edgar he must have been sixty or more, grey and somewhat seedy, a man implacably ill-disposed to all waiters, hotel porters and doormen, indeed to anyone in what must now be laughingly described as the 'service' industries. To put it in a nutshell, Edgar went through life demanding to see the manager.

Arriving by taxi at a hotel in Leicester, he raised an instant and terrible row because two or three cars were parked outside, with the result that he and I had to walk ten yards to the main entrance. No drink could ever be the correct temperature for Edgar; no bedroom faced the right point of the compass; no morning tea arrived on time. He insisted on residents' bars being kept open half the night in case one of us might feel like a drink, and once on a train to Newcastle he reduced the dining-car attendant almost to tears of impotent rage. Myself as well.

These were austerity days. But having gazed distastefully at the menu, Edgar tore it carefully in half. 'This is all rubbish,' he announced. 'My colleague and I' – indicating me – 'will take roast chicken.'

The attendant gave a short laugh. 'There is no chicken,' he said.

'I don't think you heard me, steward. I ordered chicken. My colleague Mr Race is especially fond of chicken and intends to have it.'

'There's no chicken on the train.'

'I do not tolerate insolence, and will have no compunction in reporting you to your superiors, whom I happen to know are based at St Pancras station. With the chicken we will have two portions of roast potatoes and a few carrots.'

'Can't you understand . . .' the waiter began. Then I saw him change visibly, as it dawned on him that anyone so demanding as Edgar Jackson might also prove to be the last of the big spenders.

'I'll see what I can do,' he said, and Edgar's normally ashen face flushed in triumph. 'There you are,' he told me. 'You'll get your chicken, I promise you.'

I, who did not much care for chicken and had never asked for it, was by now too embarrassed to care. Sure enough, though, the steward came back after a while with two plates of chicken, roast potatoes and carrots, which he put down with a flourish, calling Edgar 'Sir' for the first time and going back to fetch some bread, though this was expressly forbidden for anyone who had had soup. 'It was the chef's own lunch, sir,' he said. 'And chef wonders if you would care for some ice cream to follow.'

We would. And when the time came to settle the bill (which in any case was paid for by the *Melody Maker*) I was curious as to what Edgar would add for such spectacular service.

So too was the attendant. Leaning almost on top of Edgar, he watched to see what largesse was coming his way. Edgar, having checked the bill with scrupulous care, opened his purse and produced the exact amount. Then he took out a sixpence and put it on the plate. 'This is for you,' he said.

'What about chef?' the attendant demanded truculently.

Edgar fumbled again and found another sixpence. 'Give this to the chef,' he said. 'And tell him the carrots were hard.'

* * *

The *Melody Maker* had a rival, also weekly, also in those days devoted to popular music but with a strong slant towards Jazz. It was called *Musical Express* and it was founded by a former *Melody Maker* editor who had sworn revenge.

Julien Vedey had originally been a drummer. Following a brief journalistic career he turned in middle-age to film-acting, playing excitable continental head waiters in the British movies of the early thirties, including an appearance as a Pullman-car attendant (if my memory serves me correctly) in Hitchcock's *The Lady Vanishes*.

But all the time he was saving up money and venom against the day when he could beat the hated *Melody Maker* at its own game. At last that day came, he drew out his savings and *Musical Express* was born.

The paper was written, in its entirety, by four people: Julien Vedey, his daughter Georgette, the serious-music critic Malcolm Rayment and me. Every week I would take along copious record reviews, feature articles, even a musical crossword, to the paper's West End office, where Julien would be having one of his turns. Julien's turns consisted in marching round the office shouting at the top of his voice, waving a handful of galley proofs and swearing that this week, as God was his judge, the paper would not come out. Meanwhile his daughter Georgie, who had a vocabulary that would stop a stevedore dead in his tracks, would be screaming on the phone to some bandleader, threatening exposure of his sex life if he did not give her an exclusive news story.

Julien Vedey had one over-riding journalistic principle, which was simply that when a news item could hardly be called news at all, you printed it in the largest possible type, thus turning it into news. So it was that one week, when nothing whatever had happened beyond yet another pathetic attempt on the part of Bert Ambrose to reconstruct his pre-war career, the list of a dozen musicians whom he was rumoured to be thinking of hiring was printed under a screaming page-one banner heading:

AMBROSE RE-FORMS!

The letters were four inches high. When the copy 'hit the streets' (a favourite expression of Julien's) it was seen by some lads in Fleet Street. They sent our editor a telegram, which read:

THIS IS THE SIZE OF TYPE WE HAVE BEEN RESERVING FOR THE END OF THE WORLD.

Julien loved it and proudly showed it to everyone who came in. Not long after that, when the BBC series *Band Parade* came to a temporary end, it was his daughter Georgie who coined the splendid headline:

BAND PARADE MAKES ITS FINAL DEBUT

– inspiring certain readers of my generation to describe any end-of-series, to this day, as a 'final debut'. Somehow it doesn't sound so depressing.

13. *I turn to Stone*

Nothing on the entertainment scene had been more changed by half a dozen years of war than the situation of the big-time bandleaders. The smarter operators among them promptly went into management (Hylton, Payne, Winnick). Ambrose, Harry Roy and Roy Fox tried vainly to keep their big bands going in the face of overwhelming odds. Only the shy, genial Syd Lipton, at Grosvenor House, found post-war life exactly the same as it had been for him pre-war. Two bandleaders who before hostilities began had been top of the Second Division rather than the First now found themselves in a strongly contending position: Lou Preager and Joe Loss. Henry Hall became a radio host; Billy Cotton soldiered on in the variety theatres where his heart lay. Of the once-famous Jack Harris, no one had seen more than a rear view since 1939.

That left Lew Stone. Lew was essentially a musician, a musician moreover who had had leadership thrust upon him, rather than a mere business opportunist in an opportunist's profession. His text book on the technique of dance band arranging had become a standard work in the 1930s although wartime developments in popular music had rendered it somewhat out of date. In short, Lew was a nice man genuinely interested in music.

He was much liked by musicians. More remarkable still, he was even trusted. They were unusual qualifications for a bandleader. But what Lew Stone was not, was a conductor. I became his pianist in 1949 and I soon learnt that instead of Lew conducting the band, it was the band – affectionate and kind, as musicians can be when they feel like it – which was conducting him. I was at the centre of one episode which has passed into musicians' folk lore, so much so that I have heard it told about two or three different conductors.

Our normal Lew Stone dance band combination had been augmented with a string section for a light music broadcast. We were rehearsing a succulent piece called 'The Legend of the Glass Mountain', for which my piano part consisted of rolling arpeggios. Sensing that the basic pulse of the music was somehow shifting I glanced over at Lew for confirmation of the beat. His head was buried deep in the score, while the baton in his conducting arm (the right arm) described a succession of small intricate circles in the air. That was clearly no help at all, so I rolled my arpeggios as vaguely as possible and waited to get back on course when some sort of aural signpost should assert itself. I did not have long to wait.

Suddenly the lead trombonist came in with a magnificent fortissimo entry. 'Yum – tum – TATATATA – TA!' he played. I was dumbfounded with admiration.

Over the tea break I asked the trombonist how he could possibly find so clear a point of entry in the face of Lew's circular beat. 'Oh it's easy,' he replied. 'I always come in at two o'clock.'

One of the staple radio series undertaken by Lew, and for that matter every other bandleader I worked for, was the BBC's *Music While you Work*. The twice-daily half-hour programmes had begun during the war years as an aid to factory production, and any bandleader booked to take part was sent pages of BBC rules and instructions. The general musical style must be bright, enlivening and optimistic, since sentimental tunes tended to slow down production. There must be no vocals, because hearing the words encouraged the industrial worker to desert his lathe in order to listen to them or even try to copy them down. All songs used in the programme must be drawn from an approved list provided by the Corporation in association with the music publishers (that unholy alliance again).

At least two songs were expressly banned from production-line music programmes: 'Deep in the Heart of Texas' and 'Sugarbush', because both of them encouraged the listener to down tools and clap his hands in a repeated rhythmic phrase. Ingenious arrangements were frowned upon too. Key changes were discouraged, since the workers found such things emotionally disturbing.

Artistic censorship of this kind was by no means new to

broadcasters. In 1942 the BBC had issued an order banning the song 'Somebody Else is Taking My Place' in order not to distress servicemen who had been parted from their wives. The Corporation discouraged all 'numbers which are slushy in sentiment', adding for good measure a ban on 'anaemic or debilitated vocal performance by male singers, and any insincere or over-sentimental style of performance by women singers'. There was some internal discussion as to whether 'Blues in the Night' ought to be banned on its title alone.

Even many years later song censorship was still very much alive in the BBC. In deference to a minority's dislike of what used to be called 'jazzing the classics', the Assistant Head of Gramophone Programmes, known in Broadcasting House as A.H.G.P., and supported by a committee, was charged with the difficult task of spotting offending songs as new records were bought into the Gramophone Library or sheet copies submitted by publishers.

The Committee had a hot time, banning 'Stranger in Paradise' one moment (Borodin), 'Till the End of Time' the next (Chopin), no doubt wishing that they had been around early enough to prevent the world from enjoying 'I'm Always Chasing Rainbows', and missing completely several classically-derived pieces such as 'My Love and Devotion' (Wieniawski), much to the glee of Tin Pan Alley songsmiths. To this day many LP records in the BBC Library bear the warning: 'Side 1, Band 4: not to be broadcast without reference to A.H.G.P.', though the present-day holder of the equivalent post would be staggered to be asked whether special permission could be granted for a performance of 'Baubles Bangles and Beads'. As for records which contain downright 'undesirable material' – 'Not to be broadcast, A.H.G.P' – it was noted that the bearer of those initials was always ready with a dubious story in the corridors of the Gramophone Department. No doubt he needed moments of relief from his arduous pursuit of purity.

As a member of Lew Stone's Orchestra I took part in many a *Music While you Work* as well as in ordinary dance band broadcasts. We even did a few stage concerts, though Lew made no real attempt to make the concerts anything other than pleasant musical recitals. Gone indeed were the pre-war days of 'Little Nell', even if we still had the 'heroine' of that saga with us, the bass player Tiny Winters. For one casual broadcast from the BBC's studio in Lower Regent Street Lew brought in as a last-minute replacement a sixteen-year-old guitarist named Julian Bream. I remember giving the lad some quiet professional advice. However he seems to have vanished from the dance-band business.

It was in that same year, 1949, that Lew asked me to attend a morning meeting at the Baker Street flat of Hughie Green. Hughie had been something of a teenage star before the war, in fact my sixteenth birthday treat had been a visit to the Theatre Royal, Leicester, to see 'Hughie Green and his Gang'. Now, after some Hollywood appearances and much experience as a wartime flyer, Hughie was back.

A short series launching the talent show *Opportunity Knocks* had proved a spectacular mismatch. Hughie and the BBC had parted company on the worst of terms, he accusing them of corruption, the Corporation in effect banning him from further broadcasts. (One has to add the words 'in effect', because when I asked a Head of BBC Television Bookings if Hughie Green was banned, he replied 'Not banned, no. But on his card it says "Not to be booked".')

The meeting at Hughie's flat was to lay plans for the transfer of *Opportunity Knocks* to Radio Luxembourg. Lew Stone was to conduct the orchestra; I was to handle all the orchestrations for the series.

It was a colossal job to take on, especially at the rate at which we were recording the programmes. Night and day I sat at my desk scoring those special arrangements, running a shuttle service of cars and taxis over to the house of my copyist, Dennis Sheridan, where he would extract the individual orchestral parts and prepare them for the recording sessions. Finally I would turn up in the studio myself, sit at the piano, and watch Lew trying to conduct my scores.

It is one thing to conduct a dance band playing 'That's a Plenty'. It is quite another to conduct a concert orchestra in the accompaniment to a soprano singing the Bach-Gounod 'Ave Maria', or as duettists stand eyeball-to-eyeball rendering 'O Mimi tu piu non torni' from *La Boheme*. It was simply not among the many things that Lew Stone could manage. After a short series Hughie put his foot firmly down and Lew Stone left.

At Hughie's insistence I stayed on, to be reunited first with my old sparring partner Cyril Stapleton, who had been brought in to conduct the series on the strength of his experience as a fiddle player in the R.A.F. Symphony Orchestra. Cyril fared better, though frankly not a great deal better.

His place was then taken by Roberto Inglez, leader of the Latin-American band at the Savoy Hotel, though he had been better known in his birthplace (Glasgow) as Bert Inglis. Perhaps surprisingly, Roberto managed the conducting side of things better than either of his predecessors. However, after a further series the blunt practicality which is the hallmark of Hughie Green's nature asserted itself. To quote from his autobiography:

> Steve started out as the arranger with the Stone band and after a time I was able to persuade the sponsor to allow him to take over the baton himself. Steve is a man with impeccable taste in music, and his kindness, patience and understanding with the terrified amateur artists had to be seen to be believed.

Well, let me return the compliment. Of all the great showmen I have worked with, Hughie Green remains one of the greatest. However, the truth must be faced: the radio and TV world is littered with producers and technicians who would rather share a prison cell with Clive Jenkins than be scheduled to do another programme with Hughie. Brilliant and demanding, he is far from being an easy man to work with, and for an entirely valid reason: Hughie Green is a perfectionist.

Though I never see him these days I remain one of his admirers. It is a fact that Hughie engenders a kind of desperate affection in his taut colleagues. A good deal of that affection in my case centred in those early days on the fact that nothing – but nothing – was ever too good for one of Hughie Green's Discoveries.

Expensive special orchestrations? – Naturally, if it added to their impact. Glamorous publicity? – Of course, and regardless of cost. Quite a few of today's entertainment stars have reason to be grateful to him for their start in the profession. Though they may not always remember to say so, all of them know how unstintingly he launched them on their show business careers.

As for me, quite apart from the fact that it made sense for the arranger to turn his own scores into sound if he were capable, I enjoyed the act of show conducting, regarding it as a physical extension of the accompanist's art. Such work calls for two specific talents: an infallible 'tempo memory' by which one can reproduce to a hairsbreadth the speed of a piece one rehearsed some hours before, and a gift for that flexibility or 'give' which a singer needs in his accompaniment if he is to *express* a song, rather than merely get through it. I enjoyed conducting as an exciting means of practical music making, though other conductors enjoy it as a direct exercise of power. They are the ones with the flamboyant gestures, and in the main they are the ones the public most enjoys watching. Which type their orchestral musicians prefer to watch, is another matter.

No account of my life would be complete without mention of a young man who wrote to me about this time as a result of a record review and to whom I offered a job as my secretary-cum-personal-assistant. His name was Pip Wedge. Pip and I struck up an immediate understanding and I came to rely on him completely for running the office side of my work. In dealing with musicians and other artists he quickly developed a personality which, coupled with his manifest ability and sustained by his very obvious ambition, set him on the clear road to the top in the entertainment business. After a few years he left with my blessing, worked successively for a record company, an ITV contractor, then for Hughie Green as manager for his TV quiz shows. Pip is now Vice-president and Director of Programming for CTV in Toronto, and I hope the people of Canada realise how lucky they are. I would have him back any time as my personal assistant again, but I cannot afford to pay a million dollars a year. So Pip stays in Toronto: one of my dearest friends, and one who is not too proud to mention who gave him his start in the profession.

14. TV, K.2 and
thank you, Sir Huw

Back to 1950. Four times a week I continued to play for the
BBC Television Auditions, where one of our successes was a
charming man named Michael Westmore. He had arrived
one morning, fresh from the Players Theatre revue the
night before, bringing for my accompaniment a song about
the wax models in Madame Tussauds and how they spring to
life after midnight. It was an ingenious song, as breezy and
extrovert as Michael himself, but it had been written out for
some other singer and was clearly not in the right key for
him.

For his audition I transposed the song down a couple of
keys. Then while waiting for his subsequent interview with
Mary Cook to end, I passed the odd few minutes in writing out
the song for him in a lower key. I handed him the new
manuscript with my compliments, and scarcely another
thought.

But that free arrangement proved to be important: my
version of the thorn which Androcles drew out of the lion's
paw, only to meet the creature at a subsequent engagement.
When Michael Westmore was taken on to the BBC staff as
one of the first producers for Children's Television, he offered
me the job of looking after the music for his first series. It was a
fortnightly magazine programme on Saturday evenings,
called *Whirligig*.

Those were, in television performers' terms, the Golden
Years. Relatively few people had TV sets, but those who
did own them threw their homes open to friends, especially
when children's programmes were on. The result was that

virtually the whole country was watching *Whirligig* on the nation's one-and-only TV channel, at five o'clock on Saturdays.

At first I was merely the accompanist on the show, playing my piano (or as Hank the Cowboy called it, my 'joanna') for our resident puppet characters Hank, Silver King, Mr Turnip and later Sooty. Their human friends and operators were also in attendance: Francis Coudrill, Joy Laurie, Peter Hawkins, Humphrey Lestocq and Harry Corbett.

Francis Coudrill not only made his own 'Hank the Cowboy' glove puppets, he painted their scenic backgrounds and appeared alongside the characters as narrator and ventriloquist. One of the most congenial people I have ever met and certainly a brilliant graphics man, Francis was just about the worst ventriloquist in the history of that curiously introverted art. He made scarcely any attempt to conceal his lip movements, and it was often impossible for the viewer to tell whether Hank, Silver King, Francis himself or one of the other characters was supposed to be speaking, other than from the context of the words. A useful rule of thumb for Hank-watchers was that if the Hank puppet was waggling about, it was probably Hank who was speaking. If Francis's lips were still, it could only be because I was playing a four-bar introduction to one of his songs.

The reason for this strange non-ventriloquism was, I firmly believe, simply that Francis enjoyed it all too much. He adored working, lived for the moments he was on the screen, and – like so many puppeteers before and since – was more than a little in love with his dolls.

I had proof of this one evening in the studio when we had just come off the air and were packing up before wandering off to the pub. Francis had put his puppets away – it was always something of a shock to see Hank folded unceremoniously in half and stuffed into a suitcase – and was reaching for his coat when I passed beside him, and said 'I left my watch at home. What's the time, Francis?'

For a moment I thought he had not heard me. He turned aside, fumbled with his suitcase for several seconds, then finally drew out the Hank puppet. Straightening it, he put it on his right hand and wagged the model's head in the direction of his left wrist.

'Why, Steve ole partner,' he said, in Hank's Western drawl, 'it's a quarter after six.'

'Thank you,' I said. And feeling the words somehow inadequate, I added, 'Thank you, Hank.'

A few months into the run of *Whirligig* I was offered my own spot, and moved into vision as piano-playing compère of 'Steve Race's Music Room'.

For some of the editions I would be able to afford the fee for a guest, and I remember inviting the great horn player Dennis Brain to play 'The Swan' for my young viewers. Cleo Laine was another guest, at a time when she had scarcely met John Dankworth. Julian Bream played guitar solos for me sometimes. Stanley Holloway came, to give (at my request) his monologue 'Per tuppence per person per trip'.

Every now and then I would announce a competition for the young viewers, when I invited them to write a song or submit a painting on a given subject. One fateful week I asked the viewing children of Britain to make up a tune for the recorder.

During the following week the entries came in through the post, over six hundred of them, which was pretty good when one considers that I was asking the contestants to go to the trouble of first composing and then laboriously writing out their musical manuscripts. I chose the three ultimate prizewinners with great care, and the following week hired a guest recorder player to demonstrate them as I read out the winners' names and addresses.

Leaving the Lime Grove studios that evening I was handed a telegram from a viewer which read:

SECOND PRIZEWINNER NOT MARY JANE BIDDLES OF YORKSHIRE BUT WOLFGANG AMADEUS MOZART OF SALZBURG.

(I have changed the little girl's name in order to protect her still, though she must now be in her early forties.)

How well I recall the chill of discovery as I checked my Mozart scores and found an early Minuet (K.2) which that little horror of a girl had copied out and submitted under her own name! Hastily I rearranged the prizewinners' order and got the programme secretary to send the Book Token prizes to the three children who had deserved them, leaving out the one who had not.

I then made my great mistake. On the next available programme I announced that the prize list had been changed
because one of the pieces had proved to be by Mozart instead
of being original, and that the amended prize list was as
follows ...

When the programme ended, a harassed-looking BBC
Press Officer came looking for me. Harassment is not a characteristic one associates with that particular man, since his name
was Huw Wheldon. (Later, as Sir Huw Wheldon, he became
the head of the whole BBC-TV set-up.)

Huw told me that the press had already been on to him, and
that they were about to enjoy a field day at our expense.

'They want to know the name and address of the little girl
who cheated,' asked Huw. 'Are we going to tell them?'

'Certainly not.'

'Good man,' said Huw briskly. 'We'll tell them everything
else they want to know, but we're not going to have that child
branded as a cheat, are we? – Even though she is.'

We stuck to our guns, Huw and I, through a barrage of
national press phone calls. The reporters tried everything they
knew to squeeze out of us the name of the cheating competitor,
including the muckraker's favourite line about 'the public's
right to know', and the Fleet Street sob-story that begins
'Would you gag the freedom of the press ...?' Only later did I
learn that one reporter, smarter than the rest, had rung my
home and said to my wife 'I've just spoken to Steve and he
asked if you would look up the little girl in his files and give me
her name.' She did not oblige.

By now Huw Wheldon was enjoying the whole thing, the
light of battle glittering in his Welsh eyes. He issued a statement which had me goggle-eyed with admiration, in which he
stated that (a) the BBC wished to congratulate Steve Race on
finding Mozart's piece at all among so many entries, even if he
didn't recognise the Master's work; and (b) who was to say
that Penelope Twistlethorpe, the winner of the first prize,
would not one day be regarded by posterity as the equal, nay
even the superior, of the great Mozart whose work she had
relegated to second place? It was quite in vain. The following
morning the Sunday papers came out gleefully with the story,
and typical of them was the *Sunday Express*'s page-one headline, which I so richly deserved:

I learnt several things from that experience. I learnt that if in conscience a broadcaster can somehow or other refrain from apologising, he will save himself a great deal of trouble, since the apology always seems to reach twice as many people as the original offence. I learnt that a reporter nosing out a story is no man's friend: naturally enough, I suppose, when you reflect that journalists have a vested interest in Trouble and are tempted in its absence to manufacture some. I learnt that Huw Wheldon was a good friend in a corner and clearly destined to rise to greater BBC heights than that of Press Officer. And I learnt that when the chips are down, the British Broadcasting Corporation will stand up for its artists in a tight spot. I have not had any reason to change that view.

On the other hand, I have been careful never again to give Mozart *second* prize. You'll always be first in my book, Wolfgang.

15. *Jazz and Judy*

Running television competitions for kids was great fun. Calming down, or in some cases jollying up, terrified *Opportunity Knocks* contestants was an enjoyable challenge. So was the responsibility of giving them the best possible special orchestrations. But my hobby, and to an increasing extent my job, was Jazz.

'Jazz' is a word which means something different to each person. To the musical snob 'jazz' means anything from a Scott Joplin rag to Liberace crooning 'I'll Be Seeing You'. To the authentic New Orleans specialist, genuine jazz virtually ended in the 1930s. To the be-bop addict it more or less began with Charlie Parker in the 1950s.

'Be-bop' – what a word! The whole jargon of jazz is riddled

with awful, demeaning expressions. 'Boogie-woogie', 'blues holler', 'jam session', 'barrelhouse', 'honky-tonk', 'funk', 'scat', even the word 'Jazz' itself – they all have an ugly sound, though to the specialist they carry quite precise meanings.

In about 1950 came the jazz revolution. The modern movement, represented by Charlie Parker, Dizzy Gillespie and their cronies, sought to widen the excessively narrow confines of improvised jazz. So the harmonies became more involved, the rhythms looser, the melodies more wayward. The whole impact of their music – soon to be known simply as 'bop' – was a deliberate challenge to the ultra-simplicity of the old jam session type of jazz, whereby a sixty-year-old New Orleans cornet player could take his instrument into any night club from Tokyo to Tyneside and be sure to find a trio playing 'Sweet Sue' in the key of G.

The critical opposition to the new post-war jazz was quite extraordinarily bitter, even vicious. Only two of the published jazz critics in Britain embraced the new sounds: one (much to his credit in view of his age) was the veteran *Melody Maker* critic Edgar Jackson. The other, a far younger man and therefore more likely to welcome innovation, was me. But the opposition was loud in its condemnation. It is interesting now to recall that among the stiffer reactionaries were such noted later converts as Humphrey Lyttelton and Charles Fox.

The Charlie Parker revolution in small group jazz was accompanied by Stan Kenton's experiments in the big band field, Kenton's efforts in America being mirrored on the European side of the Atlantic by Vic Lewis.

I attended the Hammersmith Palais launching of the large, wild and terrifyingly loud Vic Lewis Progressive Jazz Orchestra. I was with a group of friends which included the Hon. Gerald Lascelles, nephew of the then King George VI and a keen amateur jazz fan. The band – reinforced with no less than ten brass players, I seem to remember – played like dervishes. It was an exciting but shattering evening, and at the end of it my wife and I found ourselves on the dance floor standing next to Gerald and his partner while the last screaming arrangement ended. (No Last Waltz nonsense for Vic Lewis.)

It was closing time, the dancers applauded, and Vic's drummer executed a drum roll of sorts. We stood to attention,

Gerald Lascelles notably erect as befitted a man of his family connections, while Vic Lewis's Progressive Jazz Orchestra played the most extraordinary version of 'God Save the King' ever heard outside a be-boppers' madhouse. I glanced at Gerald, and saw that his lips were moving. Still at attention, I leaned a little towards him, and heard him say under his breath 'Good God! I must tell Uncle George about this.'

That year, to my amazement, I was placed second in the *Melody Maker* Piano Poll, after the brilliant jazz pianist Ralph Sharon. Ralph's reputation as a wit stood almost as high as his reputation within the profession as a player, and he was at his best when telling stories about his own Jewish people. Ralph it was, who was overheard singing a parody of the popular 'Lavender Blue':

Married a Jew, silly-billy
Married a Jew....

I was pleased enough to be voted second to so fine a pianist by the nation's jazz fans. But I can honestly say that the honour did not go to my head and a week or two later I had almost forgotten about it. The profession's own opinion was more valuable.

So it was with some surprise that I wandered into a pub one evening before appearing at the Bedford Jazz Club, to hear the barmaid telling one of the locals in a deeply-charged voice: 'Do you know, we've got the second-best pianist in the world appearing upstairs tonight!' It took me some time to work out the reason for her remark: someone had shown her the *Melody Maker* poll results.

Two years later I had dropped a few places in the Piano section of the poll, but was placed in two of the other sections: Best Arranger, and Musician of the Year. A while after that I came first in the Jazz Journalists Poll. Strange – I felt like the same person, doing the same quality of work.

The fact is of course that anyone in the entertainment profession has to make an early decision as to whether or not he will pay attention to such things as popularity polls, or, for that matter, listener and viewer ratings. (The clinching argument on that subject occurred outside show business. Just after World War II a British airline, concerned for the safety of its

*The Mark-1 Frank Sinatra in 1950, with Georgette Vedey, editress
of the original Musical Express*

Mood Indigo: Duke and commoner

Ken Dodd shows frightful injuries resulting from incautious use of tickling-stick

passengers, placed a slip of paper on each seat which read 'Do you prefer forward- or backward-facing seats?' Forty-eight per cent of the replies read simply 'Yes'. So much for *vox populi*.)

The articles and reviews which I was writing at that time for the old *Musical Express* led to encounters with various American stars who were visiting the London Palladium. One of them was the engagingly shy, hollow-cheeked Frank Sinatra, fresh from his film successes as the sort of young American boy too bashful to kiss a girl, though in private life he was experiencing no such inhibitions. Sinatra won me over completely at a crowded press reception because as he left he remembered my name, though he had heard it only once, and that a good hour earlier. There was also Jimmy Durante, less bashful in manner, with whom I played a ragtime duet. There was that most gentlemanly of performers, Nat King Cole. With Nat I taped an hour-long interview backstage at the Palladium and struck up a *rapport* which will not surprise anyone who knew that charming man.

Nat Cole's opening night on 4 September 1950 led to an extraordinary attack by the *Daily Express* critic John Barber, who called Nat's top-of-the-bill act 'a novelty turn' given by 'a grotesque, gangling sooty vocalist'. How anyone claiming to be civilised could coin such an expression, even in 1950, is beyond my understanding. Nat Cole himself was appalled and hurt. I hurled every adjective I could think of at the (Daily) *Express* man in my infinitely lesser (Musical) *Express*, and there the matter rested, except that I received from Nat Cole a letter of thanks which I still treasure.

When Judy Garland came to the Palladium at the start of a tour including Scotland and Ireland, she needed some new orchestrations which I helped to provide.

Judy had long been one of my heroines and just meeting her, let alone working with her on sorting out routines and keys, was exciting to someone like myself who has always had a capacity for hero and heroine worship. But poor Judy: in a world of neurotic people she was already far gone in excitability and moodiness. She was seriously overweight, a heavy body propped up on matchstick legs. It was obvious to everyone that her marriage to Sid Luft was in the shadows. Her advisers and hangers-on – why must they have so many? –

seemed to be of little help. Admittedly her personal musical director Buddy Pepper was a gentle support, but Judy staggered from day to day, alternately flamboyant, pathetic and defiant in the face of the monstrous life of the superstar.

Musically speaking I have never known a more hardworking or competent professional. Not for Judy was the old pro's trick of 'marking' a performance, whereby one sings under the breath, mumbling lines or indicating stage moves with a descriptive wave of the finger, in order to save oneself for a public performance. Judy Garland, in a rehearsal room or a hotel apartment, sang out as if she were on the stage of the Palace Theatre, Broadway, though in fact her great triumph there was still some time ahead. Eternally eager for perfection, the wide-eyed little girl of 'Over the Rainbow' had become the arranger's dream: a singer of impeccable musicianship, with a huge appetite for exacting work, a perfect pitch-sense, and (despite an off-stage vocabulary of bright blue words) an odd kind of eternal innocence. I shall never forget Judy Garland, or cease to marvel at her shining, tragic talent.

It was exciting to go backstage at the Palladium during those star-studded years, and for two weeks I worked as holiday relief pianist in the Palladium theatre pit, while George Burns and Gracie Allen argued so charmingly in their top-of-the-bill act. Lower down the bill, Ben Blue bored me with his eccentric dancing as eccentric dancing always does, but an astonishing American named Frank Marlowe offered something unusual. He made his entrance by dancing swiftly across the diagonal of the Palladium stage and straight into the orchestra pit, where a special spot was prepared for his landing. No one ever topped Frank Marlowe's entrance and nothing could follow it ... not even Marlowe's own patter act.

I cannot at this stage recall how many performances a week we in the pit orchestra gave, but the show was twice nightly and there were at least two days when we also had to do a matinée. On such treadmill days I found it almost impossible to keep track of time, to remember whether we were playing the second half of the first house, the first half of the second, or possibly the second half of the third. At the end of the evening I only knew that it must be time to go home because one of the trombonists just behind me had his bicycle clips on as we played the finale.

114

Another strangely exhausting engagement was a TV series called *Television Icetime* for which I was musical director and which came direct from the Queen's Ice Rink in Bayswater, following a complete day's rehearsal. The temperature all day long was (not unnaturally) freezing, which suited the skaters but not us musicians. It is not easy to play even a condensed version of the Tchaikovsky Piano Concerto with blue fingers. A further problem concerned our producer, Peter Dimmock, who marched about the ice rink all day, barking orders through a grossly distorting loud-hailer. The stage manager – who is now a top BBC executive himself – took care of that by arriving early one morning and deliberately short-circuiting the loud-hailer's battery, leaving Peter Dimmock exasperated but inaudible for the rest of the day while we got on more calmly with the work in hand.

Much as I fancied myself as an accompanist, I found musical ice work almost impossible. A ballet dancer on a theatre stage executing an *enchainement* necessitates a half-cocked eye on the conductor's part, so as to ensure unanimity of performance. But on ice a skater can travel several yards in a fraction of a second. The result is that a musical chord which was meant to occur when the performer was in front of the conductor, suddenly coincides with a wild leap at the far end of the rink. 'Fast' ice or 'slow' ice can play havoc with dancers on a rink.

Furthermore, the musical tempos required for ice dancing are so unnaturally slow at the best of times that after an hour or so one seems to be part of some strange lethargic slow-motion film. Reactions lengthen, speech becomes affected, the brain numbs with cold ... No, I shall not be doing any more engagements on ice. And I noticed that even the enthusiastic Peter Dimmock gave them up after a while.

16. Boult the Red, Commie Race and the man from M.I.5

It was Sir Adrian Boult on the telephone.

'I am given to understand,' he said, in that splendidly manly but kindly voice, 'that you feel troubled, as several of us are, by the activities of Senator McCarthy and his Un-American Activities Committee.'

How had that got out? But yet, troubled I certainly was. During those early years of the 1950s it was virtually impossible to hold the most basic of liberal humanitarian views without being disgusted at the activities of the Senator for Wisconsin; a demagogue who could reduce a once-successful artist to suicide merely by mentioning his name in the privileged setting of a televised senate hearing. The climate of innuendo and recrimination in America in those days had become a major evil, drawing together good men of all persuasions. McCarthy and his gang prolonged by ten years the instinctive left-wing bias of my *New Statesman*-trained generation. It was a time to stand up and be counted.

'Yes, Sir Adrian, I *am* worried about McCarthy, especially insofar as his techniques might spread here.'

'Exactly. Arthur Benjamin and I are organising a meeting to see whether we cannot combat McCarthyism in Britain to some degree. We do hope you'll come.'

And that was how we formed a committee called The Musicians' Organisation for Peace, born at a meeting in the home of the Australian composer Arthur Benjamin, and supported by an across-the-board list of British professional musicians which ranged from Sir Adrian and the Quaker conductor Frederick Woodhouse, to some quite well-known fellow-travellers in the Communist cause. Equally, our ranks included Sir Robert and Lady Mayer, and no one ever described them as 'dangerously left'. It was indeed this very breadth of members' political affiliations which was intended to be our strength. In the end it caused our downfall, not to mention the professional near-downfall of some very earnest people, myself included.

It is almost impossible now to recall how dangerous it was in those years to associate oneself with the word *Peace*. To speak of peace was to be thought to favour a cowardly retreat in the face of the world-wide red menace. To cherish peace meant giving in to the Commies. The only smart thing to do was not to use the word at all.

For all I know, the fears of our opponents may have been politically justified to some extent. Certainly country after country was falling under the communist heel. I do know, however, that the methods used by some of the red-hunters were as inimical to human freedom and individual justice as the very system which they were opposing. It was in an attempt to prevent the hounding and persecuting of decent, humanitarian members of the musical profession that we formed our Musicians' Organisation for Peace: M.O.P. for short. ('New MOPs sweep clean,' jocularly observed one of our number, Frank Merrick.)

I was one of the least eminent members of the steering committee, and therefore perhaps the only one who had not taken the precaution either of living out of town or of having his London telephone number made ex-directory. (I have since repaired both those omissions.) The result was that at half past one in the morning, following our first press release, I was hauled out of bed by a reporter.

'This is the *Daily* ———,' he announced, with no hint of an apology for the lateness of his call. 'Mr Race, the witch-hunt is on.'

He was right: the witch-hunt was indeed on. Hounded and harangued, we were personally vilified in the press and our homes haunted by seedy *paperazzi* looking for our 'Commie' associates. It was an exercise in sustained pressure which will be recognised by any reader who has had Fleet Street snapping at his heels. Before then I had tended to believe what I read in print. I have not done so since.

After some days the furore died down, but it was weeks before one lost the feeling of being watched; of being willed into making some slip of the tongue, or caught associating with someone whom it might have been wiser not to know. Then one evening John Dankworth came to a party at my house. Dear John – the gentle, talented John – Mister Clean himself.

He came late and was persuaded to stay on after the other guests had drifted off.

'Someone was talking to me about you the other day,' said John mysteriously, adding when pressed: 'It was a Scotland Yard Inspector. He asked me quite a lot of questions about you. In the end I asked why he didn't talk to you himself, and he said "That stage may come later. Your friend Mr Race is a good deal too pink for our liking."'

Pink! I was about as left-wing as Earl Attlee O.M. K.G. P.C. C.H. It was ludicrous. But in my mouth I felt the taste of danger just as surely as if an assassin were in my wardrobe.

The following morning at nine o'clock I was on the phone. *Whitehall 1212* . . . 'Can I speak to Inspector English, please? My name is Race. Steve Race.' A pause – a click.

'Ah, Mr Race. I rather thought we might be hearing from you. I've had conversations with a number of your associates.' (*Associates?*) 'Yes, by all means come and see me.'

Arrived at Scotland Yard, I was shown into a small bare whitewashed room where it was obviously intended that I should cool my heels, perhaps grow increasingly nervous. On the contrary, I was so incensed that I felt no apprehension, only the anger which stems from being falsely accused. I was also indignant that my country – my deeply-loved country – should stoop to the pressures of McCarthyism.

When Inspector English* came in, I found him to be a mild man, quite unlike the black-stubbled Senator of the rasping stateside drawl. After some brief introductory conversation, we came to the point.

'You seem to think I'm a Communist,' I said, 'and what's more you've implied as much to a friend and colleague of mine.'

'Ah yes, Dankworth.'

* It is not quite his name.

118

'I am not, and never have been –' I began, automatically (and to my own fury) slipping into the exact wording so beloved of Senator McCarthy's inquisition. 'It could be very damaging for me in my particular profession to have M.I.5 enquiries made about me,' I went on lamely.

The reference to M.I.5 clearly pained him. We spent a minute or two in ironing out who he was not, though he never told me exactly who he was.

'All right,' said the Inspector after a while. 'So you're not a fellow-traveller or a card-carrier. I'm going to mention a telephone number and ask you what you know about it. I'll just go and get it.'

He went out, leaving me alone in the whitewashed interview room. 'What number is it going to be?' I thought. Then suddenly, I knew. I wrote down *Wembley 9662* on a piece of paper and placed it on the deal table before me.

The Inspector came back and opened a file. 'We found this number,' he told me, 'in reverse on the blotter of someone who has defected to Moscow' (and he gave me the name of the lady in question). 'Beside the number was your name. It's the number of a known Communist cell organiser. Can you explain to me why your name should be written down beside that number?'

I looked across and read *Wembley 9662* on the top sheet of his file. Then I pushed across to him my slip of paper, bearing the same number.

'I don't know anything about the people you tell me are at that number now,' I said, 'but I can tell you who lived there until a couple of years ago. I did. It was the number I gave up when I moved house.'

He looked suddenly deflated, though I suppose one cannot blame him. After all, a crafty bit of Holmesian sleuthing had just expired before his very eyes. The coincidence certainly was extraordinary. My phone number, during the period when the defector lady and I had both been members of our Peace organisation, had subsequently been re-allocated by the Post Office to a person who turned out to have a bank account full of roubles. The Inspector had drawn the obvious deduction. Race was on the Moscow payroll. Elementary, my dear Clouseau.

We parted on affable terms. They might have been almost

cordial if he had not pushed his luck by asking me to snoop around and write him a secret report on a theatrical conductor and a jazz guitarist of my acquaintance, both of whom he suspected of having Russian connections. Though in one case he was probably right, I told him that I disapproved of witch-hunts just as strongly as ever and would have nothing to do with secret dossiers.

After a while the Musicians Organisation for Peace bit the dust, destroyed by the very breadth of support which was its founders' greatest pride. The public was not impressed by Boult's courage in associating with the far left in a proud cause. On the contrary they merely said to one another: 'Just fancy! I didn't realise that Sir Adrian Boult was a Communist.'

Some years later a tiny sequel ended my encounter with Scotland Yard. While planning the first of my American tours, it suddenly struck me that I might have difficulty in getting a visa. I rang *Whitehall 1212, extension XYZ.*

'Inspector, this is Steve Race,' I said, adding nastily, 'formerly of *Wembley 9662*, remember? I'm hoping to go to the U.S.A. next month. Can I expect there to be any trouble over my visa?'

'Not so far as I'm concerned,' he replied. 'I'm retiring next week and I don't really care any more.'

I hope he has enjoyed a happy retirement, free of all cares and secret enquiries. I would have called him to see how he was getting on. Unfortunately I don't have his present number.

PART THREE

17. Man the scuppers,
reef the mainsail,
run tele-cine, roll V.T.R. . . .

The leaders of the British nation, for their several and adequate reasons, had decided that it was time we were given an alternative television channel. So Independent Television was born, though not without labour pains. The new Television Bill had an extremely rocky passage through the House of Lords, where their lordships were concerned about the flood of distasteful advertising which they were sure would be launched into our homes on a tide of liver pills, suspender belts and contraceptives, while it was feared that the actual programmes would set a new low in audience-appeal, thereby provoking the BBC into a lowest-common-denominator ratings chase. The extent to which they were right is an indictment of populist TV planning; the extent to which they have been proved wrong is a testimonial to something imperishable in the BBC ethos.

Wheeler-dealing on the grand scale had led to the first ITV franchises being handed out in 1954. The lucky companies, still staggering under the bludgeoning of the Lords, had had to do some rapid repair work in order to improve their cultural image. Approaches went out from the various contractors to Messrs Sargent, Boult and Beecham. The London weekday company, Associated-Rediffusion, sent an emissary to woo Sir John Barbirolli, who was based in Manchester with his Hallé Orchestra.

No doubt the company thought that someone with his head in the symphonic clouds would be a pushover in return for some artistic flannel and a couple of thousand pounds, but in this they were to be disappointed. Sir John was nobody's fool. He was also advised by the very knowledgeable General Manager of the Hallé, Kenneth Crickmore. Between them they exacted, as the price of Barbirolli's co-operation, a contract for setting up the necessary Television House music department in London, as well as a string of peak-hour televised concerts for his beloved orchestra, together with whatever personal advisory fee Sir John thought appropriate.

The music company was promptly set up, its directors being Barbirolli, Crickmore, an up-and-coming lawyer with show business connections, a friendly Sheffield steel magnate, and myself. The up-and-coming lawyer was then known as Abe Goodman, due later to be ennobled, indeed almost canonised.

My job, as light music adviser for Associated-Rediffusion, was to set up music and record libraries, arrange for instrumental musical purchases such as pianos and percussion stores, while advising on musical programme matters and maintaining liaison with a management which, from noon until 4 pm was usually absent, and from 4 pm onwards frequently incoherent.

At the head of the motley A-R management crew – and, let it be said, the soul of sobriety – was the now legendary Captain Brownrigg R.N., whose fine wartime record in the Mediterranean and in the Far East had naturally fitted him to run a television company. He and I liked one another, insofar as the Captain noticed me at all, but I fell foul of him in the end, when I was doing interviews for an early evening series of general interest programmes. One day we visited a boatyard in Thames Ditton. Having been shown over a moored motor cruiser by its owner, I said (on a stage manager's cue),

'Right, let's go shall we?'

whereupon our little craft did a brief circuit on the Thames and then returned to the quayside.

The viewers found it rather fun, as I did. But at the next programme planning meeting Captain Brownrigg was distinctly peeved.

'Did any of you see that programme Race did on the Thames?' he snorted. 'Disgraceful. Appalling. He said "Let's go". Doesn't he know the expression is "Carst orff?"'

The Captain had expressly announced that he would run the TV company exactly as he had run his naval establishments, and crisp corroboration of this came from the commentator Leslie Mitchell, who observed, on abruptly leaving the company's employ, that 'Brownrigg said he'd run the place like a ship, but I misheard him slightly.'

It had been at an early exploratory meeting attended by various members of our music company that Captain Brownrigg fell momentarily athwart Sir John Barbirolli. The Captain was recounting his experiences in the Med as the war drew to an end, and he made a distinctly audible reference to crowds of Italian prisoners whom he had seen 'cowering in their compounds'; not the happiest allusion when entertaining to dinner the proudly Italian Sir John.

Someone kicked Brownrigg under the table and after a few moments he seemed to decode the signal. Nice man that he was, he immediately set about repairing the damage.

'Well, that's all over now,' he observed gruffly. 'But I'll tell you one thing, Barbirolli,' he went on, 'damned brave, those Eyeties.' Up to a point, Lord Copper.

It will be noticed, I hope, that I liked Captain Brownrigg. For one thing he had a gentle equability. On a Commanding Officer's tour of Television House one day he saw a secretary's small dog tethered to a radiator (she was taking the animal to the vet at lunchtime). 'That's a nice cat you have there,' said the Captain.

The girl was nonplussed. 'It's a dog, sir, not a cat.'

'No,' said the Captain, 'it is a cat. If it were a dog it would not have been allowed inside Television House.'

As for Lord Goodman, that brilliant and entertaining man, I always thought it characteristic of his quiet efficiency that while other elevated folk floundered around trying to find a name that no other peer had used, he calmly chose to be called Baron Goodman of Westminster. As for his attitude towards those extraordinary early ITV years, I remember one of our staff being asked to point out to him, very gently, that he had been addressing the parent company incorrectly.

'They ask if you will kindly remember the hyphen in "Associated-Rediffusion", Mr Goodman.'

'Indeed I must,' he replied affably. 'It is the only thing holding the company together.'

In this he was about right. The prodigal spending of the first year's programming had led to a deficit which so frightened the Associated Newspapers half of the combine (as opposed to the British Traction Company's half) that they pulled out altogether, leaving more determined investors to prove that Lord Thompson's famous 'licence to print money' remark was about to come true.

Meanwhile we, the programme makers, soldiered on, or in Brownrigg parlance sailored on. One or two nights a week I did a programme called *And So to Bed*, consisting of a little harmless piano music and a word or two about the following day's programmes, totalling in all about four minutes.

Such an undemanding production was an ideal skid patch for trying out those L-drivers of television, the trainee directors. My experience of them was always the same. A face would appear round my office door and a timorous trainee would say 'I believe we're doing a programme together', mentioning a date some three months in advance. Over the next few weeks he would reappear constantly, bearing ever more complicated shooting scripts and floorplans, until in the end his debut on *And So to Bed* would come to rival *The Birth of a Nation*, in complexity if not in budget allocation.

It so happens that there are only two ways of photographing a pianist alone in .the studio, and both of them consist in starting on a vase of flowers and gradually pulling back to reveal the performer seated at the keyboard. (The alternative shot is the same thing done rather too quickly.) If the director really wants to make difficulties for himself, he will arrange for the cameraman to 'crab' round the piano in a circular movement, getting his cables caught up in the piano legs, and sometimes severing another camera's cables completely with a nasty blue flash. A fourth alternative begins with a shot of the piano's innermost strings, followed by a panning shot up to the pianist's face. There is even a fifth shot, which involves manhandling Camera 3 on a rope up into the very roof of the studio, from which one can gain a rather startling bird's eye view of the pianist's head before cutting to Camera 1 for his announcements.

All these variants would be described to me in loving detail by the bright-eyed trainee director as he juggled his plans, shooting scripts and dummy viewfinders. Then came the surprise; the all-too-inevitable final visit to my office, two days before the programme.

'I've had a new idea,' he would say, looking slightly pale from the sleepless nights and the constant worry. 'It's a great idea. I'm sure you'll approve. *I'm going to take the whole thing on one camera!*'

* * *

Only highly experienced TV directors were let loose on our most memorable series, *Late Extra*, indeed only a seasoned warrior could have stood one week on the show.

The basic idea for *Late Extra* was a good one. We, alone among television production companies, had an operational studio in the centre of London. When BBC-TV wanted to interview some visiting fireman staying at, say, the Savoy Hotel, they had to send a car to collect him, take him to Shepherd's Bush and then back again to his suite, a procedure which could easily occupy a couple of hours of his life. However, when we wanted, for example, Rodgers and Hammerstein, we picked them up at ten and had them back at the Savoy in thirty minutes. It got us many elusive star guests, some of whom I interviewed, among them the aforementioned Rodgers and Hammerstein, Duke Ellington, Raymond Chandler and John Huston.

The trouble with *Late Extra* was that it tried to be every kind of TV programme known to man. Set in some mythical chromium night club with model girls perched provocatively on barstools, it was dedicated to the well-known media proposition that the best way to glean interesting information is to interview someone.

The truth is quite the reverse. Aubrey Singer, wise BBC official that he is, once said in my hearing that he regarded interviews simply as a means of eliciting information in twice the time it takes to tell, half the time being Questions and only the remaining half Answers. In 1941, long before Singer's time, the American humorist Alexander Woollcott had written to a friend expressing a similar view: 'The interview is the dullest and most fatuous form of journalism. As editor of a department in one or other New York paper for fourteen years I never allowed an interview to be printed. What would you say were the four most successful journalistic ventures of the past twenty years? *Life*? *The New Yorker*? Winchell's column?

Reader's Digest? At least these four have this in common – none of them has ever printed an interview.'

Our *Late Extra* bosses believed passionately in the Interview. More remarkably, they believed that somewhere in the television world there existed a compère or commère who was at once strikingly handsome of face, cultured, well-read, profound, politically balanced to a hairsbreadth, highly experienced in studio work, not too expensive, and free of all other contractual obligations. Our first all-purpose host/compère/interviewer was the film star Edmund Purdom. A number of others were tried, but all proved to be lacking either in looks or profundity. Even the *bon vivant* Fanny Cradock took a turn, dressed for her inaugural week in a *burnous* like the hero of The Desert Song. Yet still the chemistry was somehow lacking.

I was however grateful to Fanny for a personal kindness. I was already suffering from the back trouble which has plagued me all my adult life. The disc in my lower back has defied the ministrations of doctors, physicians, orthopaedic specialists, physiotherapists, chiropractors, osteopaths and – yes, I've tried that too – acupuncturists. All of them were dedicated and concerned. But to quote Hilaire Belloc:

Physicians of the utmost fame
Were called at once; but when they came
They answered, as they took their fees,
'There is no cure for this disease.'

One day in the studio, while we were rehearsing Fanny Cradock in her inaugural *Late Extra*, I was sitting at the piano almost doubled up with disc distress. During one of those breaks in rehearsal which seem to occupy most of any studio's time, I noticed Fanny's eye resting enquiringly on me.

'What is it?' she boomed across the floor. 'Your back?'

'Yes, I'm afraid so.'

'Don't worry.' She strode over to the piano and stood behind me with her finger pressed firmly on the bit where it hurt. And there we remained, a sort of *tableau vivant*, while the Cradock fluence did its work. Then the floor manager called her over to rehearse an interview.

'Johnnie,' she called to her monocled husband and partner, 'Come and take over.'

126

Behind me I could feel the finger of Johnnie Cradock being substituted for Fanny's. 'Thank you,' I said wanly. It seemed inadequate, but I could not think of anything else to say.

We remained, Johnnie and I, united in our healing contact, until a minute or two later, when I noticed Fanny looking apprehensively over in our direction. 'Steady, Johnnie,' she urged, frowning. 'Steady, man. Don't pass out. No need for that.'

I stood up as hastily as I could and turned to look at him. Johnnie Cradock seemed to have entered a minor catalepsy, his eyes heavy-lidded, his famous monocle manifestly insecure. To recall him, I grasped his hand and wrung it forcefully. It seemed to work. Nice man that he is, he enquired politely after my back.

'It's a lot better,' I said. 'You seem to have cured me.' I only wish it could have been true.

Fanny Cradock lasted longer than some of the other anchor-persons in *Late Extra*. Quite apart from my gratitude at the back incident, I genuinely think she was one of the better personalities who were tried out, though I had to admit that she tended to get on better with male guests than with women. Indeed during Fanny's interview with a British film actress newly married to a distinguished stage actor, the actress considered herself so slighted that she could scarcely be persuaded to remain on her bar stool while Fanny wooed her handsome husband.

As things turned out, the briefest tenure as *Late Extra* host went to a fellow musician. My office door opened one morning to admit the show's executive producer, closely followed by the Man with the Golden Mouth, Larry Adler. 'Larry is taking over the compèring,' said my boss.

I could believe it. Within ten minutes our new compère had recast the format of the show, and informed me that he would be playing a solo in the middle of the programme in place of my customary band number. Then he left, rushing back to tell me that he was changing the signature tune of the series, which would in future be his own composition 'Genevieve'.

'Are we calling the show *Larry Adler Rides Again*?' I asked, but the producer said No, the title would be the same as ever. There would be no major changes, he said.

He was mistaken though. Larry's *chutzpah* – which he

would probably define as lovable cheek – saw him safely through the first two hours of rehearsal that night. But just before the live transmission began, I overheard our *chutzpah*-proof executive producer hiss at Larry through gritted teeth, 'It isn't *your* show, it's *our* show. Don't forget that.'

Alas, Larry forgot. Our dynamic new compère, signature-tune composer and shot-in-the-arm whiz kid lasted for just three editions. Then he left. And I was sorry, because I was enjoying the cheerful wheezing of his mouth-organ more than I can say.

It is people like Larry – well-meaning, talented and utterly impossible – who make me wonder what on earth I am doing in the same business, if indeed I am in the same business. I glance sometimes at the photograph of the band I fronted briefly in a *Late Extra* programme, and marvel that the man in the white jacket could possibly have been me. (*See plate 5.*)

I cannot now remember what tune we played. I rather think it was 'On the Sunny Side of the Street' because Norman Wisdom was rather keen on it. I did not have a preference, nor of course did Humph or Larry. That left Peter Sellers, who was a rather better drummer than any of us expected, and the Duke of Bedford, who as a bass player was far worse. Just before the performance I showed him (with the aid of a chalk mark) where the note C was on the bass, and told him to pluck that and the open G string alternately. He obeyed. I must say it was exhilarating telling His Grace the Duke of Bedford what to do. It was the only time in my life I felt drunk with power, though the feeling did not last long: the sound that Norman Wisdom got out of his clarinet was enough to sober up any musician.

The series at this stage was being run by a high-powered committee of top Television House executives, all experienced in the ways of business and the boardroom, but largely innocent of entertainment experience. Their endless interference was based on the belief that while such mysteries as music and camera direction may best be left to people who understand their jargon, everyone is an expert on The Spoken Word since everyone has the gift of speech. Who can deny it? A man who can dictate a letter to his secretary is qualified to dictate an interview-scheme to a compère. It was also apparent that the executives enjoyed the boozy, star-studded parties which preceded and followed each edition of the programme, not to mention the chat-ups with our hired model girls.

Attendance at the pre-transmission green room drinks sessions was part of my job, and I can still see in my mind's eye the little knot of sycophants grouped around William Saroyan, Thomas Mitchell, Burgess Meredith or Jayne Mansfield. For my part, I usually looked around for some nervous, lonely minor contributor and had a chat with him. One week the object of my concern was a shy, good-looking young man sitting all alone in a corner, whose inclusion (I remembered from the morning's planning meeting) had been agreed to with some reluctance by our star-conscious executives, though it was conceded that he had taken some rather good photographs of the Royal children and could probably use a boost. We had a pleasant chat, Anthony Armstrong-Jones and I. Six months later he became overnight the most famous young man in the western world, and it amuses me – him too perhaps – to reflect that as he sat there contemplating his gin and tonic he already knew who would be wearing the smile at the year's end.

I wonder sometimes whether the writer Colin Wilson remembers his interview at the hands of one of our better *Late Extra* hosts.

By this time the boardroom committee was not only interfering at all levels in the show: it was even writing the questions for the interviews. This principle could not conceivably work, for the simple (if frequently overlooked) reason that an interviewer is supposed to listen to the answers he is given and frame his succeeding questions in response to what he hears. One can prepare for an interview: one cannot script it.

Except in *Late Extra*. As Colin Wilson was joined by our compère I looked down at my copy of the script, and there, inexorably typed out for our host were the nine questions which he was to put to the young author of *The Outsider*.

'Mr Wilson, good evening. You once said "I am a genius." How do you justify that remark?'

It was a pretty savage start, but Colin Wilson took it very calmly, in fact he laughed. 'Well,' he replied (in so many words), 'I didn't actually say that. What I said was that I needed somehow to try to persuade myself that I have some sort of talent in order to force myself to write to the best of my poor ability.'

The interviewer glanced down at the script he had concealed behind a wine glass on the bar, and read off the next question.

'If you are a genius, does that make the rest of us idiots?' he duly enquired. I held my breath.

'I didn't say I was a genius,' Wilson replied. 'What I said was ...'

'Speaking as a genius, Mr Wilson, can you enlighten us as to why ...' But the rest of the conversation was too painful to recall. Perhaps the committee learnt something from the experience. And then again, perhaps they were upstairs in the Green Room, checking the drinks.

* * *

My own interviews for the series were allowed to be unscripted, no doubt because I was a musician talking to musicians and media folk are rightly wary of showing their musical ignorance. (They are also terrified of musical technicalities being mentioned. 'You won't say anything about diminished fifths or anything like that, will you?' they implore, when one is about to have a friendly chat with some happy-go-lucky songwriter or drunken jazzman... As if anyone would! Yet nobody tells a football commentator not to mention the offside trap, or an art-critic not to speak of neo-classicism.)

I had learnt my interviewing early, in the hard school of jazz. As a warning there had been the cautionary tale which every new recruit was ceremonially told on arrival at the *Melody Maker*.

Long before my time, in fact in 1934, the legendary tenor sax star Coleman Hawkins had come to Britain on his first visit. The relatively few jazz addicts of those days were at fever pitch, and their anticipation was heightened when word filtered across the Atlantic that their hero had acquired a tenor saxophone which was not only silver-plated in the usual way, but had *gold-plating* inside its 'bell' or horn.

Hello! What could that strange genius be up to now? Gold-plating! – did it alter the tone in some way? Did it affect his vibrato? Speculation, as they say, was rife. So rife in fact that at great expense a *Melody Maker* reporter was dispatched to

Southampton, to waylay the master as his feet touched the gangplank.

The reporter stepped forward. 'Mr Hawkins, I represent the British jazz public. Welcome to our country. We understand you are now playing a silver-plated saxophone with a gold bell. Can you tell our readers why?'

'Sure,' replied Coleman Hawkins. 'Because it glitters when ah play.'

The moral of that (possibly fictitious) tale is that time spent talking to jazz musicians is almost always time wasted; time which could have been spent in listening to them doing something which they do far better, namely playing. The ultimate confirmation of that, so far as I personally was concerned, had taken place in 1949 in Paris, when I was the only journalist to secure an interview with the ultimate in jazz legends, Charlie Parker.

According to what his hapless manager told me at the time, Parker was giving himself six heroin injections a day. When I joined him in his apartment at the George V Hotel he must have been somewhere around Shots 3 or 4, indeed after talking to me wildly for a few minutes, he sloped off to his private bathroom to take Shot 5. Manfully I made notes, but all Parker gave me was a phoney story about how he came to be called 'Bird', followed by a stream of pseudo-poetic stuff about Europe being a beautiful woman and Paris her jewel. I managed to file something or other for my paper back home but it was a tough quarter of an hour and highly revolting into the bargain.

My reward was a confused mention in the standard biography of Charlie Parker, where I appear as an earnest American reporter who solemnly took down every word of his nonsense, while the Master played with me like a cat with a mouse. I can only say it was not like that, though I must have been the reporter concerned, since I was, I repeat, the only journalist to get him alone.

Even in those days I knew all about the 'Mister Charlie put-on', as Negro musicians referred to the harmless sport of twisting the white man's tail. It was done without real malice and – truth to tell – with considerable justification, 'whitey' having muscled in on black music and got a living out of reporting, criticising and indexing it. Jazz journalists may be useful propagandists; they also live off the efforts of others, and for that there is an unflattering word.

I do not want to imply a colour barrier in jazz. Goodness knows, there is less there than anywhere else. The days are long gone when a musician's name in a jazz catalogue would be followed by a small 'n' to indicate his race. Such Jim Crow divisions in jazz hardly survived the 1930s, though the opposite – known as Crow Jim – lingered on for considerably longer in Paris, where jazzmen, to be accepted, had to be either Black or French.

No one went round colour-testing faces when I was one of the group accompanying the great blues singer Josh White at the Decca studios in 1950. We made six or eight recordings, for which I played either piano or celeste. For one of the songs ('Like a Natural Man') I merely exhaled.

It was a work song and Josh wanted to incorporate the rhythmic sound of a man digging, the spade crushing the breath out of his lungs. At his suggestion I stood beside him at the vocal microphone, and after each line he gave me a fairly violent punch in the pit of the stomach. *'Haaar!'* I went, and the result can be heard on the record we made that afternoon, though the bruises have gone down now.

But to return to *Late Extra*. Here I was, preparing for the infinitely civilised task of conducting a TV interview with Duke Ellington.

Our conversation was completely impromptu. However Duke and I had taken the precaution of arranging one detail in advance. When I received my cue to wind up the interview, I would invite him to give us on the piano the theme of the composition which he had dedicated some time before to Princess Margaret, 'Princess Blue'.

It was my suggestion and he approved it. 'Sure, that'll be OK,' said the highly professional Duke. 'You just cue me in when you're ready for it.'

Came the programme. We talked of this and that. Duke as always was courtly, bland, interested and totally uninformative. At the appointed time, the floor manager gave me a hand cue which meant 'You have two minutes to go.' I duly turned the conversation round to 'Princess Blue'.

'To take us out, Duke,' I said, 'how about giving us just a little of it now, will you? – "Princess Blue".'

'Delighted,' Duke replied, placing his hands over the keys. But in the tiny pause that followed, both Duke Ellington and I knew that he could not remember a single note of it.

He gave me a private look under his lids which I shall always treasure, followed by the merest trace of a wink. Then he played a chord ... another chord ... a third chord ... an octave run or two. There followed as delightful a chunk of aimless Ellingtonian improvisation as one could wish to hear. After about two minutes he stopped with a flourish.

'There you are,' he announced firmly, '"Princess Blue". Dedicated to a beautiful and royal lady whom I love madly.'

It was not even in the same key as 'Princess Blue'; it was just a wodge of lovely purplish Dukish doodle. Countless jazz enthusiasts must have watched the programme; some even wrote to say how good it was to hear 'Princess Blue' again. But not one of them pointed out that anything was wrong.

* * *

Though we had a number of fine producer/directors at Associated-Rediffusion, none was more gifted than Joan Kemp-Welch. I organised and conducted the music for many of her shows, of which the most memorable was one that in the event never took place.

We were to do a half-hour programme with Paul Robeson. Joan, with her customary artistic thoroughness, had decided that I should orchestrate afresh every note of every song chosen. To this end she and I went to the Bayswater apartment where the elderly singer and his wife were living in seclusion after their stormy earlier years at the hands of politicians and press.

Paul Robeson had tremendous presence; he was a man of great dignity and sadness. But in talking about music his eyes took on a glint of light. Under Joan's advice, and with a suggestion or two from me, he chose his programme. As to the orchestrations, it was arranged that I should pick him up in my car a day or two later and drive him out to Wembley studios where he would test the studio for its acoustic response. I would take him to my home for tea, then back to my office in Television House to record privately his suggested programme. Working later with the tapes I could orchestrate the accompaniments, taking into account every pause or nuance in his performance.

And so it was that I called for them with the car, and took the Robesons to the studios, where he stood in the middle of that huge bare Studio One and sang:

Nobody knows the trouble I've seen …

– in his glorious bass voice. It was one of the most memorable and impressive single lines of song I have ever heard. Then we went to my house for tea, as arranged, and on into town for the unofficial recording.

My office was Room 319 on the third floor front. Whenever I go past it (now St Catherine's House) I look up at 'my' balcony and recall that evening. Altogether Paul Robeson recorded on my tape five songs: 'Water Boy', 'Lovers' Lane', 'Going Home', 'My Ain Folk' and 'Silent Night', with additional comments from him on their tempi and general performance.

Unfortunately it all came to nothing. A few days later he was taken ill and went to East Germany for treatment. Returning finally to America, he underwent a pacemaker operation; his wife Essie died; Robeson himself died in January 1976. My private tape recordings, on the evening of 14 March 1961, were the last ever made of that proud, incomparable voice.

18. Listen darling, they're paying royalties on our song

I was playing The Warsaw Concerto in a Birmingham radio studio when the right leg fell off the grand piano.

At the moment that the keyboard descended firmly on to my right knee I happened to have the sustaining pedal down. It stayed down, until the end of the piece, when the studio manager thrust a chair under the treble end of the piano – and about time too. Meanwhile, like the clown in *Pagliacci*, I smiled through my watering eyes and played on.

The event would hardly be worth recalling if it had not been for a letter I received two days later from a listener. 'I was sorry to note that you were guilty of over-pedalling,' he wrote testily. 'It is all the more to be regretted in an Academy-trained musician such as yourself, and sets a poor example to students.'

Such letters are more usually addressed, not to the offending broadcaster, but to the Director General of the BBC, sometimes with the appended plea that the culprit should be taken off the air once and for all. I do not think I myself have ever written a letter to an employer suggesting that a member of his staff should be fired. Suffering at the receiving end of a disagreeable broadcast seems to do strange things to listeners and viewers.

That said, however, I must add that for something over thirty-five years I have been delighted and often moved by the letters I have received from people who have heard or seen my broadcasts. Who could remain unmoved on receiving this, for instance, from an elderly radio listener in Somerset:

> Dear Mr Race,
> I feel I cannot delay any longer in sending our grateful thanks for the joy your *Invitation to Music* series gives us.
> I have been chair- and house-bound for twelve years now with osteo-arthritis (I am eighty-one). My friend here cared for me until she was eighty-three but then in one of those power-cuts she had a stroke. Her mind is badly impaired and she cannot converse, but one day to my amazement while your music hour was on she suddenly said 'Hasn't that man a nice voice?' And then another day, while you were playing Debussy's 'Gardens in the Rain' she suddenly said 'Pitter, patter, do you hear the rain?'
> Who was it said 'Music, that balm to a mind diseased'?
> This is the first and only letter I have written to anyone on the BBC and I do not find it easy to write. I do not expect an answer, as I know how little spare time you must have ...

One would have to be made of stone not to answer a letter like that. For many years I tried to reply suitably to every single letter I received, but in the end I was beaten by sheer

135

weight of numbers and by the disproportionate cost of post-age. Some broadcasters, unorganised and one might say ungrateful, never bother to reply to correspondents, though they can usually be relied upon to whip out some comic letter or other to read to a bunch of cronies in a bar.

I must admit it is tempting. Every musical broadcaster has had his collection of favourite request cards. 'Please play "In the Monster's Garden"' was an early one in my professional life, along with 'Please play "Goodbye" for my little brother who is in hospital'. I also liked 'Would you play "I'm Walking Behind You" as a surprise for my mummy?' Poor mummy.

A high percentage of correspondents feel the simple desire to say that they have enjoyed something, and their letters are always heart-warming, even those which spell one's name wrong. ('Are you any relation to the *Percy* Ross who used to cut my hair in Tripoli?') Many letter-writers want something – and why not? – whether it be the catalogue number of a record, the name of a composer, or someone to write to who sounds understanding. About one correspondent in twenty encloses a stamped addressed envelope for a reply.

My letter-box has always contained a number of unsolicited song manuscripts, though goodness knows I have never given amateur songwriters the slightest hint of encouragement. On the contrary, I have seldom missed an opportunity to dissuade them.

The first and most important point to be made about pop songs is that any fool can write one. It takes no great talent to make up a hummable tune or to put together a few doggerel lines about Love. There is an amateur songwriter in every street – sometimes I think in every house – assiduously putting together the thirty-two-bars' worth of musical and verbal platitudes which make up the common currency of Tin Pan Alley. 'The enclosed song is as good as anything in the Top Twenty,' they write in their covering letters. Exactly.

The difference between their trivial songs and the trivial songs being recorded and broadcast by the stars is that the latter were written by professional recording artists, their executives or their friends. That should come as no surprise: in a village where everyone grows roses, it is the squire's rose which wins at the Flower Show. By the same token, if any half-intelligent person can knock out a pop song in half an hour, the people with patronage are not going to turn to the unknown amateur for their supply.

Despite all this, a few amateurs do make it into the professional ranks; one or two even become full-time composers. For that fortunate few an important royalty-collecting body exists.

I served The Performing Right Society for thirteen years, first as council member and latterly as deputy chairman. The principles on which the society is based are straightforward enough and can be summarised in a single example. The moment I have written a song or a symphony a number of rights in the work exist: for example the right to perform it, to broadcast it or to make a record of it. If a publisher is involved in the work too, he joins me in sharing those various rights. I have created the song; he in his turn will exploit and publicise it. We share the proceeds on what these days is normally a fifty-fifty basis.

When a writer or publisher applies to join the P.R.S. and is accepted for membership, he assigns the right of performance in all his works. The society's control over these rights enables it to command a fair level of royalty payments on behalf of all its writer and publisher members. If a broadcasting company, concert hall or even a pub lounge wishes to perform music, it must expect to pay an appropriate royalty through the society to the creators of that music. And quite right too. Music is property: you may not use my music without permission any more than you may borrow my car, or wander about in my garden. Even a composer must live.

So it is that the Performing Right Society collects tens of millions of pounds each year from the world's music-users and distributes the money to all writers, composers and publishers involved, deducting only the bare costs of administration. Without P.R.S. and equivalent bodies, music makers could not live. They could not even know the extent to which their works were being performed.

The ultimate direction of this huge international organisation is entrusted by its members to a council of twenty-four people: twelve *writers* (the term is used to include lyricists as well as composers) and twelve music publishers. I have served on endless committees in my time and recognise the truth of the much quoted aphorism that 'a camel is a horse designed by a committee'. Nevertheless I have to say that the running of the P.R.S. Council during my years (1965–78) was as proper, as efficient, and certainly as lively, as any administrative body I have ever known.

It was hardly surprising, when one looked round that enormous boardroom table. Anyone who imagines that the serious composer inhabits a dream world has clearly never argued a point with such bright spirits as Joseph Horovitz, John Gardner or Ernest Tomlinson, just as no serious topic could be airily dismissed in the presence of the Society's distinguished president and deputy-president, Sir Lennox Berkeley and Vivian Ellis. During my time we had pop music directors of great stature and ability as well, such as Roger Greenaway, Tony Hatch and Tim Rice. Our publisher colleagues were loyal, informed and clear-headed. I repeat: it was the most efficient administrative body on which I have ever served.

I could never quite figure out why we served. What attracted us all to that gruelling work? Why would twelve busy, prosperous music giants of the music publishing industry, together with twelve successful and active composers, be prepared to donate five hours of their time, at least once a month and often once a week, to attending meetings requiring great expertise, judgment and patience, not to mention sheer stamina? Surely the music studio would have been more tempting, the office, or the golf course? Why give so much of one's life to something called The Performing Right Society?

The answer must be slightly different in each case. Some people in the musical profession are power-hungry; others are basically suspicious and want to keep an eye on every corner of the business. But the broad answer must surely be that having derived much satisfaction and profit from the profession of music, they felt they wanted to put something back. That at any rate was the reason enunciated privately to me by our chairman, Alan Frank. It was certainly my own answer.

The fact that there are an equal number of writers and publishers on the P.R.S. board is no chance arrangement. Their respective professional interests do not necessarily coincide, indeed there is no disguising the fact that a long-standing love–hate relationship exists between the actual creators of music and the publishers who act as middle men between the composer and his public.

The Performing Right Society boardroom has been the scene of many an epic battle between the forces of the writers and the publishers, ranged against one another in mutual mistrust on some divisive issue. The rafters must still be echoing to some of the exchanges between Dick James and myself, though our fights were refereed fairly, and at times skilfully defused, by our chairman Alan Frank.

My memories of those thirteen years on the P.R.S. board are preponderantly memories of goodwill, good sense and purposeful discussion, often involving complex matters of international trading and Copyright law.

Why then did I resign at the relatively early age of fifty-six? For three reasons. First, because after thirteen years' service I simply felt that it was someone else's turn. Secondly, because the Society had been under constant and unjustified attack from a disaffected member who refused to be satisfied. I was heartily sick of fighting a slippery and perpetual adversary who seemed impervious alike to the patient explanations of the board and the irritation of his fellow members expressed in general meeting.

The third reason for leaving was because I wished to do my bit to lower the average age of boardroom members. From time to time we were showing signs of becoming a gerontocracy.

In my early P.R.S. years I had watched the decline of a senior and greatly respected music publisher whose achievements with the firm of Chappells had become a legend in the profession, but who lingered on into almost total deafness and his ninety-second year.

Not for me, I decided, the covert wink, the upraised eyes behind the sheltering hand. If the time ever comes when I am heard saying to a youngster 'Go on, see if you can guess how old I am!' I hope he will reply, 'Well, you *look* over a hundred. But I suppose you must be less, or you wouldn't be asking me, would you?'

19. Tea with George Brown – and other stories

It is reported that Sir Thomas Beecham once turned round on the podium and addressed his audience in the following words:

> Ladies and gentlemen, in upwards of fifty years concert-giving before the public, it has seldom been my good fortune to find the programme correctly printed. Tonight is no exception to the rule, and therefore, with your kind permission, we will now play you the piece which you think you have just heard.

The audience must have loved it, each person thinking that the last line was a dig at his neighbour. But Sir Thomas knew his public. He knew what immense opportunities for misunderstanding music provides; the extraordinary notions of the professional life which the layman entertains.

The same is true of broadcasting. Opening a richly varied morning's mail each day, I have come to recognise each type of listener's or viewer's letter even before slitting open the envelope. Different programmes encourage different types of correspondent. It is a plain fact, which I report without comment, that a series on commercial television will bring a sudden crop of letters on scented pink notepaper, while the bulk of BBC2 correspondents seem to have custom-made writing paper with their addresses printed in illegible Gothic script. They live in houses with names like 'Heron's Creek' or 'Druggetts'.

The principal letter-begetter for any broadcaster who takes part in the series is radio's *Any Questions?*, in which topics of the day are discussed impromptu by four panellists drawn from the worlds of politics, journalism, entertainment and public life in general. As I have already indicated, letters of agreement are addressed to oneself, while letters of complaint following a contentious appearance are mostly directed to the producer, or in extreme cases to the Director General of the BBC. The normal addressee for comments on *Any Questions?* is of course the reply programme *Any Answers?*

My first *Any Questions?* was in 1963 during the spacious days of Freddie Grisewood's chairmanship. Indeed Freddie himself welcomed me to the panel with the words 'It's like waiting in the pavilion to go in to bat, isn't it?' After that first broadcast – perhaps *blooding* would be the better word – he stumbled arthritically across the platform to me in his kindly way, and whispered in my ear, 'First eleven, I'm sure. Well played.'

I never did make the first eleven though, remaining a regular twelfth man throughout fifteen years of sporadic invitations to appear, and for a while dropped to thirteenth. Perhaps I try too hard to tell the truth as I see it; perhaps I belong too obviously to no political party; perhaps I should not have turned down the BBC's offer to try for the chairmanship when Freddie Grisewood retired. Yet when my invitation arrives to take part, I look forward to the experience with a keen if nervous pleasure.

The programmes are broadcast live, completely unrehearsed and unprepared. The questions are disclosed to the panellists for the first time at the very moment the listeners hear them being asked, indeed I find it quite difficult to judge on the instant whether it is better to try to listen to the questioner or read the slip of paper being passed along the table. Some of the topics are more or less predictable, of course. In the week of the Budget there will certainly be a fiscal question. If there has been an unusually juicy court case, there may well be a question about penal sentencing. But these are not difficult to handle, if only because any reasonably intelligent participant can see them coming and has worked out the basis of his ideas on such perennially important subjects. The difficult questions are the sudden one-liners. 'Which three characters in history would you take with you to the moon?' 'Do the panellists cry often?' 'What is truth?' 'What are the qualities of a good wife?'

The greatest difficulty for me lies in knowing which way to

jump: whether to answer a given question flippantly or with deep seriousness. One's instant decision is almost bound to be wrong in the eyes of someone. Quoting the American tennis star who declared that all women should be kept 'barefoot and pregnant' will get you a delighted ripple of laughter from the audience at the Douglas Haig Memorial Hall, Upper Twittingham, but can be guaranteed to call forth a sackful of letters pointing out that marriage is a sacred compact instituted by the Almighty and 'your voice will never again be heard in my house'. On the other hand, mention the sterling wifely qualities of loyalty, understanding and godliness, and the M.P. sitting opposite you will get a howl of happy laughter by talking archly about the little woman's cooking or driving.

The most memorable part of an *Any Questions?* engagement for those taking part is always the preliminary get-together. We meet at about 5 pm at some highly recommended hotel not too many miles away from the hall in which the broadcast is to be given. David Jacobs, who is a brilliant (if occasionally waspish) chairman, takes over as host the moment the panellists arrive, and my admiration for him as a host – just like my affection for him as a person – is boundless. The teams enjoy successively conversation together, tea together, drinks together, dinner together and still more drinks together, until tensions disappear under conviviality and occasionally under what Roget's *Thesaurus* calls *temulency*, *ebriosity*, or even (God forbid) *titubancy*. Only once did I have to support a colleague as she staggered on to the platform in a state of (quoting Roget again) *grog-blossom*, but several noted colleagues on the programme have become slightly flushed, even over-fond, under the influence of the BBC's well meant, if in my opinion excessive, hospitality.

The respective techniques as host of David Jacobs and his predecessor were very different. David is all charm and efficient activity, marshalling waiters and hall-porters like an Orient Express courier. No one ever suffered an empty glass or a break in conversation when David was around. Freddie Grisewood was quiet, welcoming, utterly lovable, but occasionally he would doze for an hour by the fire as the rest of us compared journeys and sipped our sherry.

I remember once we were idly discussing what sort of

questions we might be getting later on in the evening from the good folk of Huish Episcopi (or wherever it was). Someone suggested that there might well be a question relating to the troubles in Cyprus between the Greeks and Turks. We had passed on to another topic altogether when Freddie, quietly nodding in the chair next to mine, stirred slightly and remarked under his breath:

'Damn fine fighter, Johnny Turk!'

I was fascinated. When had that expression last been used? – Surely during Freddie's own war.

Sometimes when he was feeling well Freddie would be very lively indeed, and he was usually feeling well when one of his old cronies was on the panel, notably C. A. Joyce, Bob Boothby, Lady Violet Bonham Carter or Mary Stocks. Over a hotel dinner in Cerne Abbas I shared a table with Freddie and his beloved friend Mary Stocks while they exchanged jokes which began by being a saucy blue and ended up not far short of filthy. We were being served by a young and very flushed teenage waitress who, it seemed to me, was always arriving at our table just as Mary or Freddie reached the barely repeatable punch line. Worse, perhaps, at the only other table in the room was a sedate looking middle-aged couple who could obviously hear every word being said.

I admit it, I was embarrassed. I could do nothing to spare the waitress, who fled scarlet-faced after bringing our coffee, but as our little party moved out into the lounge I felt constrained to offer some sort of explanation to the middle-aged couple. I hung back after the others.

'I feel I ought to apologise,' I began lamely. 'You see ...' Then I stopped. The man, as pure chance would have it, was Hardiman Scott, the BBC's diplomatic correspondent, enjoying a quiet weekend in the Hardy country. I fled in confusion: no doubt Mr and Mrs Hardiman Scott thought I was insane. Outside in the hotel lobby Mary Stocks was saying in her piercing voice, 'Freddie, do you remember the one about the prostitute and the curate ... ?'

During the pre-programme conversation one learns about one's fellow panellists, and even more about panellists who are not present that week. The crisp opinions offered on the subject of others in public life do not necessarily accord with party affiliations, in fact it is often quite a shock to discover that when the 'on air' sign goes on, politicians who have been affable to one another, even pally, suddenly treat each other with scorn, derision and ill-concealed malice. Could it conceivably be an act which they put on in deference to the party Central Office they telephoned that morning for guidance? Perish the thought. I can reveal, however – even if I ought not to – that the only political figure I heard treated with uniform scorn over repeated *Any Questions?* dinner tables was Anthony Wedgwood Benn. It seemed that no politician of any party could find a word of praise for him. Poor Tony, they said, poor Tony.

It was after, rather than before, one of the programmes that I enjoyed a journey with a fascinating companion.

Baroness Asquith, formerly Lady Violet Bonham Carter, was one of our team at a broadcast from Billingshurst in Sussex. I had never met her before, but her entrance into our hotel lounge had amazed me because she really seemed to be the tallest, thinnest person I had ever set eyes on. As she came through the door Freddie Grisewood rose creakily to his feet to greet his old friend. 'Oh Violet,' he said, 'isn't it too awful? Bob Boothby has married a sardine.' (Actually the lady was Sardinian.)

After the broadcast it transpired that the baroness and I were the only ones going back to London by train. I therefore escorted her to the station and secured a first class carriage, in which we sat for a memorable train journey.

It was not just what she told me, but her very presence. I repeat that I have always had a great capacity for hero (and especially heroine) worship and it has been the source of great pleasure to me over the years. During the early part of my committee work with the Performing Right Society I enlivened for myself many a tedious ten minutes by simply resting my eyes on our president, Sir Arthur Bliss, musing on the music he had composed and the people he had known, from Saint-Saëns to Thomas Hardy.

Here was I, then, sitting in a railway carriage with someone who had been a girl friend of the young Churchill and the even younger Rupert Brooke; the daughter of a Prime Minister; the confidante of great personalities from Lawrence of Arabia to Albert Schweitzer. She had even dined once, as a very small girl, with Mr Gladstone, and had commented to her nurse that

The million-pound band, or Who's that at the end of the Peer?
(Humphrey Lyttleton, the author, the Duke of Bedford, Peter
Sellers, Norman Wisdom, Larry Adler)

A pyramid of pianists. (From top: John Dankworth, Lennie Felix,
the author, Joseph Cooper, Dame Alicia Markova, Cyril Smith,
Louis Kentner, Phyllis Sellick, the Hon. Gerald Lascelles)

If you want to get ahead, get a hat (but pick one your own size). L to R: Keith Fordyce, Don Moss, Jimmy Young, the author, David Gell, Pete Murray, Alan Dell, Sam Costa, Alan Freeman, Joe Henderson

Question time at Ambridge. (L to R: 'Walter Gabriel', the author, C. A. Joyce, Michael Bowen of the BBC, 'Dan Archer', Freddie Grisewood, 'Carol Grenville', Ralph Wightman, Godfrey Baseley, Lady Barnett)

the great man was not chewing each mouthful nineteen times as she herself had been instructed to do.

The baroness sat back in her train seat and reminisced freely. Once when a young girl she had been riding in a carriage on an outing from her home at Number 10 Downing Street, and had asked her nanny who those people were who watched them go by with such strange expressions on their faces? 'You are not to worry about them,' nanny had replied reassuringly. 'They are called the Poor.' But little Violet did worry about them in later years, fortunately for Britain.

I wanted to learn as much about that life as I could, without seeming to pump the charming old lady beside me. Arrived at Victoria station, she got into my car and I drove her to her home in Bayswater. I could see that she was tired – after any *Any Questions?* everyone is – so I politely declined when she said, 'I do hope you will come in for a drink, Mr Race.' Mr Race would have given anything to accept; it was the action of a true lady to ask. But as I watched her walk very slowly into the house I knew we would never meet again, and we never did.

If anyone deserved to be in the Upper Chamber it was Lady Violet, with her concern for proper values and her natural sense of service to the community. I am a supporter of an appointed House of Lords, indeed I find its existence easier to justify than the presently constituted House of Commons. All the same, the concept of a Socialist peer has always seemed to me the weirdest of paradoxes. *Manny* Shinwell, yes; but *Lord* Shinwell? ... Lord Kier Hardie perhaps? Lord Francis of Assisi? After Lord Scanlon, all things are possible.

Almost as bizarre to my mind is the idea of an ennobled parson. Not that I would require modern clerics to undertake a vow of poverty, though there is food for thought in Malcolm Muggeridge's naughty ambition to 'conduct the risen Christ on a tour of the Vatican'. Much as I always enjoyed meeting Lord Soper on an *Any Questions?* panel, I suspect that it was services to party rather than church which led to his life peerage. In fact during one discussion I had to complain that while I was trying my hardest to answer an ethical question, he kept dragging politics in.

Donald Soper on a train would never consent to be one of your anonymous clerics who dress 'down' and try to look like a commercial traveller in order to 'meet the common chap on his own ground'. Donald would be the last person on earth to do as a certain BBC parson did, and drag the word 'bloody' into the conversation every few sentences to show how earthy and emancipated he was.

Sitting with me on the 1.10 train from King's Cross to Newark, Donald was clad, not as one might expect in Methodist grey, but in a long black priestly cassock. He might as well have carried a flashing sign reading 'Lord Soper – religion discussed here'.

Arrived at Newark, we changed to a diesel train that was to take us on to Lincoln. The platform was packed. Remembering his age I was quite worried as the crush of passengers converged on the entrance door and the infirm but game Donald Soper vanished in the struggling throng. But a few moments later we were inside, and he collapsed panting in the seat beside me.

'Strait is the gate, and narrow is the way,' commented the Rev. Dr Donald Soper.

'Donald,' I said, having known him well enough and for long enough to be permitted the liberty. 'Why do you *say* things like that?'

He laughed. 'When you're a parson, it's expected of you,' he said. 'People like their parsons to be parsonical. We must maintain the image, you know. And anyway, I have to keep in practice!'

Then he told me of the church in Chicago at which he had preached. After the service they proudly showed him the crèche that had been set up to house babies and young children while their parents were at the service. And over the door of the crèche someone had caused to be printed a text from St Paul: 'We shall not all sleep, but we shall all be changed ...'

Lord George-Brown was even more communicative on a train journey, in fact only half an hour out of Waterloo I became quite alarmed at what he seemed prepared to tell me. Of a noted writer and life peer: 'He was my own idea actually, and a bad idea as it happened.' Of the then President of the United States: 'Kennedy's all right, but he's more of a thinker than a do-er'. Of his immediate boss – George Brown was Deputy Prime Minister at the time – 'Harold and I have our ups and downs, mostly downs'. One could not help but like a man so blissfully indiscreet.

George was again a member, this time of our panel at the British Rail Works in Derby, along with Mrs Margaret Thatcher (then shadow Minister of Transport) and Sir Henry Johnson. If I had not already known who Sir Henry was, I would soon have realised: at every station we passed through from St Pancras there seemed to be groups of pin-stripe-suited men at the salute, even one or two in top hats. Sir Henry was the Chairman of British Rail. We were on the Sycophants' Special.

Dinner at the County Hotel passed uneventfully, except for a nasty moment when the affable and ever-enquiring George Brown buttonholed the waiter with the brussels sprouts and demanded 'How much do they pay you a week, brother?' Margaret Thatcher and I looked the other way: at least we had that much in common.

But it was what followed the broadcast that I remember best. There were four of us in the hired Rolls-Royce which brought us back to the hotel after the transmission had ended: Mrs Thatcher and Sir Henry in the back, the driver and myself in the front. Mrs Thatcher was doing something which hardly any broadcaster ever does: she was continuing the discussion after the red light had gone out. In fact she was quite vociferous in the back of our Rolls on the subject of certain ungrateful working folk and their desire for the easy life.

As we walked into the hotel lobby I said, genially but I suppose rather cheekily that I thought her views were rather unsuitable ones to proclaim while riding in the back seat of a chauffeur-driven Rolls-Royce.

I would not now make such a remark. But Mrs Thatcher was very nice about it. Her hand flew to her mouth. 'Of *course,*' she said. 'You're quite right. I should have remembered. *The driver!*'

Pas devant les domestiques was not quite what I had meant, but the story shows a nice touch of humility in a Conservative lady whose voice and manner might almost have been invented by the Socialist party. For the reverse – a Socialist invented by the Tories – one must turn to Clive Jenkins, with whom I shared an *Any Questions?* from Blackpool. The ebullient, somewhat weasel-faced Jenkins arrived fresh from some emergency

147

negotiation nearby with half a dozen trades union colleagues in tow, all of whom had somehow to be accommodated in the modest dining room which the B B C had hired in the expectation of a smaller party.

Over dinner it became clear that Mr Jenkins was looking for a local *cause célèbre* to espouse on the air. It turned out to be the threat to close Blackpool's Grand Theatre. But before he was able to choose sides, he had to find out the view of the local left-wingers. I listened fascinated as he probed for information. Did the theatre represent the people's entertainment against the big-money land developers? Or were the wealthy theatregoers of Blackpool holding out against the desperate need for more housing? To support, or not to support?

As soon as reassurance came that the former was nearer to the truth, Jenkins accepted an enormous dossier on the subject, and just before we went on to the stage at the Winter Gardens he deftly planted on each of us a large sticker reading 'Save the Grand Theatre'. (Some years later the Grand Theatre Blackpool was still in the news. In March 1978 a local lady resident gave the building warm praise on a B B C broadcast. 'Such a nice place,' she said, 'ought to be for Bingo.')

It will be divined that I found Clive Jenkins rather tiresome. Moreover I was dumbfounded by one of the things he said. To quote from the programme transcript:

JENKINS: I cannot understand those people who say our country is in a crisis. I don't believe that for a moment. I'm incredibly optimistic about the future of this country.
RACE: Incredibly is right. (LAUGHTER.)

Not bad for 2 August 1974.

When one of the programmes took us to Bournemouth I sat during dinner between Malcolm Muggeridge and the then Rt. Hon. Ernest Marples (later Lord Marples), feeling rather like the dormouse at the mad hatter's tea party. I had travelled down from London with Malcolm who had chided me for glancing at *Punch* on the train; a sure sign, he said, of a withered mind. He repeated for my benefit his delicious comment that when he first sat down in the editor's chair at the office of that humorous journal he was 'seized with utmost melancholy'.

There was no melancholy about Malcolm at dinner as he

systematically set about provoking Ernest Marples. It was nothing quite tangible, merely a succession of the minutest verbal pin pricks. In the end I realised from Marples' heavy breathing that he had at last got the message and was working on a counterpunch.

'Tell me, Malcolm,' he suddenly said, 'do you get much walking? You seem to be putting on a little weight.'

'Never less than five miles a day, Ernest,' replied the guru, 'sometimes ten. And you?'

'At *least* ten.'

'Ah well, you'll need more, since you're a wine drinker,' said Muggeridge.

The following morning while Malcolm, Ernest and I were being driven to the station the taxi driver suddenly said over his shoulder: 'I owe my life to one of you gentlemen'.

Yes, I thought, that will be due to one of Marples' reforms as Minister of Transport. Or could it be that reading Malcolm's killingly funny book *Tread Softly* had given our driver the will to live?

'It's you I mean, Mr Race,' he went on to my surprise. 'What you said on the radio about smoking made me pack up cigarettes and I reckon you saved my life.' I thanked him. (I had to agree, because taking my own advice had prolonged my life as well as his.)

My two companions did not seem to have noticed the conversation. But once inside the station they set off and walked at a great rate several times to the far end of the platform and back, breathing deeply as they went. I suppose they were trying to see who would tire first.

One final *Any Questions?* reminiscence takes me to a Miners' Welfare Hall in the West Riding of Yorkshire in 1969 with Lord Robens. I liked Lord Robens. It was certainly brave of him to accept an invitation to appear, since he was then Chairman of the National Coal Board and the pit closures in the district had made him far from welcome. Perhaps the presence of Honor Blackman on our panel was sufficient compensation to tempt him. Russell Braddon was also among those present.

Over dinner I wondered out loud who was staying overnight and who would be catching the night train back to town. It is an unfailing topic of harmless conversation over the *Any*

Questions? dinner table, but this time I sensed that I had somehow put a foot wrong in raising the subject. Everybody seemed to clam up; David Jacobs changed the subject with less than his customary adroitness. I took another swig of coffee and waited for David to brief me on what I had done wrong.

'It's like this,' he told me in the gents. (And now surely the story can be told.) 'Alf Robens, as Chairman of the Coal Board, has the use of a private plane, and he's going to fly us home afterwards. The only thing is, as he's a leading socialist somebody might make capital out of it if we let it be known. So we have a sort of pact not to say anything on the programme.'

I joined in the conspiracy, and sure enough a few minutes after the transmission ended there began my one and only experience of the efficiency of a nationalised industry. A Rolls was standing at the side door of our Miners' Hall. In stepped Ted Robens, David, Honor Blackman and myself. Smoothly chauffered through the night, we arrived at some aerodrome – I never did know its name – where we cruised straight through a hangar and out on to the flying field. A De Havilland Dove was waiting with engines revving.

We took off, our host passing affably among us dispensing Scotch and soda. After what felt like only a few minutes the plane landed at Luton, taxied out of the airport and straight into the car park, where another Rolls awaited us. Boarding it, we were decanted one by one at our various destinations in London. The whole thing was smooth and effortless. And when I greeted my startled wife several hours before she could possibly have expected me, I reflected that since leaving the Miners' Welfare Hall at Royston, Barnsley, I had walked exactly thirty yards.

Ernest Marples would not have approved.

20. Race against time, ha ha

Ever since my first day at school people have been cracking the
inevitable joke about my name.

'Ah, Race against time, eh?'

I laugh helplessly. I laugh until the tears run down my
cheeks. I clap the punsters on the shoulder and ask how they
managed to think up such a brilliant quip. I have to sit down
and drink a glass of water in order to recover. And through the
tumbler I have the satisfaction of seeing their beetroot red
faces.

Such people probably imagined that I would call this book
Race Against Time, but they must settle instead for a mere
chapter heading. I have to admit that there was a stage in my
life which really was something of a race: when I did seem to
be fighting the clock much of the time. I had an enormous
appetite for work, because work itself was so fascinating, and
in every sense rewarding. But any career needs examining
from time to time.

The move away from performing music and towards becoming 'a talking head' on radio and television was a calcu-
lated one on my part. Music makes a marvellous mistress but a
demanding wife – or is it the other way round? Anyway, I had
a haunting mental picture of myself at some point in the future,
silver-haired and sixty-five, still seated on that piano stool,
playing what I fondly imagined to be the popular music of the
day. There I would sit, like Queen Victoria's statue in a town
square, while the critics and reviewers searched for words like
'durable' and 'indestructible'. 'Someone really ought to tell
him,' people say to one another in those circumstances. Well
somebody did tell me. I did.

In changing my professional emphasis in that way I was
helped by something quite beyond my own control. Without

trying, indeed without even noticing it, I gathered that I had developed a pleasant speaking voice. What more logical that I should use it on the air?

I wrote and introduced many general interest programmes based on material in the BBC Sound Archives. On the musical side I introduced record programmes ranging from Radio 2's *The Jazz Scene* to the classically-orientated World Service series *Music Now*. A curious weekly discussion programme was called *We Beg to Differ*, with the Bradens, Charmian Innes, Lord Arran and Bernard Levin. ('Maybe Steve Race is the wisest of us all,' wrote his lordship cryptically, in his newspaper column.) And in 1964 the BBC's Charles Maxwell called me in, to create a questions-at-the-piano spot in his new quiz *Many a Slip*.

We were a happy crew from the start. There was Isobel Barnett, the Lady Barnett of *What's My Line?* fame; cool and cultured, but infinitely warm-hearted too. A weekend spent at Isobel's home in Leicestershire is one of the most civilised pleasures I know. But beyond that, she is one of the very first people I would go to for help and advice if I were in some sort of trouble. Wisdom, warmth and beauty make an impressive trio.

Beside Isobel during the initial *Many A Slip* years sat Eleanor Summerfield, a mite scatty but enchantingly full of life; a girl whom any man in his right mind would want to marry if the elegant Leonard Sachs had not captured her first. Later Gillian Reynolds joined the panel, bringing her quick journalist's mind and her Liverpudlian intonation which I find so attractive; the same Gillian Reynolds who cunningly lent me a show business autobiography and then when I returned it said 'Why don't you write yours?', a fact which is duly (and gratefully) recorded in the dedication of this book.

The ladies' team in *Many a Slip* was opposed at first by the duo of Richard Murdoch and Lance Percival, later to be supplanted by David Nixon and Tim Rice, both of them charming men with towering intellects: the sort of people who play chess without bothering to move the pieces.

Many a Slip was devised by Ian Messiter, who has, I suppose, the strangest job of anyone I know, being a full-time professional inventor of panel games, puzzles and quizzes. Endlessly curious, restless and energetic, Ian is the eternal schoolboy, in fact I suspect that he works quite hard at it, to the show's great benefit.

Which leaves Roy Plomley, sage and witty questionmaster, who has been in overall charge from the very first week. Everyone likes Roy Plomley, indeed it is a perpetual tribute to his courtesy and intelligence that the world's most brilliant and busy people are prepared to queue up to be shipwrecked with him and their *Desert Island Discs*, content, nay even eager to answer questions about building rafts and mud huts, when many of them would leave a party in disgust if asked to play Consequences. For myself, I have been castaway by Roy twice (1959 and 1971), taking with me the second time rather a lot of Elgar and the collected stories of Winnie the Pooh.

Although *Many a Slip* consists merely of four bright people trying to spot deliberate mistakes, either in words or (during my spot) in music, the series has been renewed again and again for two reasons. First, because we all enjoy ourselves. (Believe it or not, there are some panel games which are not enjoyed by certain participants, at least not unless they win.) Secondly, our contestants have become expert in the split-second detection of deliberate errors. Ian Messiter and Roy Plomley, for their part, and I for mine, are compelled to go to strange and devious lengths in order to smuggle even the tiniest slip past the alert ears of the foursome.

Once, when we were recording *Many a Slip* at the old BBC Playhouse Theatre, a gentleman from Swedish radio came to study our production methods. I chatted to him over a cup of tea and was explaining how the game worked when he asked me politely who Lady Barnett was.

'She's a well-known personality,' I told him. 'Very popular.'

'Yes, but what is she, please?'

'She's one of our contestants.'

'I know. But what is she? – A musician? A singer? A politician perhaps? Is she a writer of stories? Or maybe she is an actress . . .'

I did my best to explain that Isobel was not exactly any of these things, but what we in Britain call . . . well, a Personality. Then something prompted me to glance across the canteen table. I found Isobel's eyes resting gently on mine, with a look of utter Cheshire Cat delight on her beautiful face.

'Do go on!' she said. '*I* wouldn't know how to get out of it either!' No wonder I adore her.

* * *

When the ITV franchise for London was divided between two independent television contractors, some wit pointed out that while one of the companies consisted of gentlemen trying to be showmen, the other was made up of showmen trying to be gentlemen.

If the remark was quoted with more relish by the gentlemen's side, it was nevertheless the showmen who enjoyed the last laugh, since the gentlemen went out of business altogether when the franchises were re-allocated. The showmen's company soldiered on into a bright future and figured appropriately in Sir Harold Wilson's Resignation Honours List.

'Gentlemen v. Showmen' remarks could never be made about the BBC's board of governors. That huge concern, with its virtual radio monopoly and its rich potential for patronage and corruption, has to be run in the most scrupulously sober manner, its top management as far removed as possible from the day-to-day business of making programmes or even troubling about them.

Be that as it may, making programmes is what broadcasting is supposed to be about. There are times when 'the Corporation' (as BBC people of my generation tend to call it) momentarily forgets that the end-product of all its efforts is not a smooth-running organisation, but a schedule full of good programmes. There is a well-attested story that a high BBC official at a planning meeting once thumped the table in anger and cried, 'This is yet another example of programmes interfering with administration!'

The civil service mentality undoubtedly reaches right down through the BBC's structure. A BBC Head of Publicity once astonished his staff – though not anyone else who knows the Corporation – by pointing out in a pained voice that 'our job is not to create publicity, but to regulate it'. No one raised in the hard world of competitive broadcasting, in America perhaps, could ever understand how a public relations man could hold such a philosophy. Equally, those of us with experience of the BBC from the inside recognise the essential truth of the story, and might even add a few other stories like it.

The Corporation, still Reithian in outlook despite the passing of so many years, labours to keep its affairs regular, ordered and humdrum; general rather than particular; decently humane and civilised rather than personal or committed. At the highest level the BBC does not quite approve of Show Business, and would prefer to run its share of broadcasting with as little contact as possible with creative folk, well known as they are to be impulsive, undisciplined and difficult to control. Their attitude towards money is inclined to be ungentlemanly. They are 'artists', in the BBC's all-encompassing parlance, and artists must be kept at arm's length. Some of them do not realise what a privilege it is to be allowed to write or act, to play, to compose music, indeed to broadcast at all.

The compensation for all this is that while the BBC can be infuriatingly obtuse, unbending, petty and sometimes parsimonious, in its general administration it is as straight as a die. Nowhere in the world is there a broadcasting organisation that does not envy the BBC's reputation for independence and resistance to pressure. Admittedly, far too many incompetents walk its corridors. Lifelong drunks hold court in its bars. There is almost nothing that can uproot a member of the BBC staff once he has been allotted a place in the establishment. From a staff man everything is tolerated, from incompatibility to indolence; from sodomy to the last stages of alcoholism.

Only major corruption, once detected, is unceremoniously rooted out. Perhaps more of the minor kind should be investigated, especially in the areas where such things might be expected to flourish, namely popular music and TV variety. But it is difficult to draw the dividing line between a proffered handshake and an outstretched palm. As a well-wined producer once observed to me, the difference between a lunch and a crate of champagne is only ten bottles!

Having said all this I can only report that I love and admire the BBC. I honour its unique structure, its determination to pursue high standards and to foster what is good in addition to what is merely popular. On my own professional level, I can repeat the plain truth that in thirty-five years of studio work involving uncounted thousands of programmes on both radio and television, I have never offered anything resembling a bribe to any broadcasting official nor was I ever asked for one. Perhaps there are one or two producers around who might have favoured me more if I had shown signs of being 'flexible' in that respect. Perhaps a couple who vanished from my professional life are at this moment drinking their third bottle of someone else's champagne. I shall never know.

Disgruntled folk on the fringe of the entertainment scene tend to complain knowingly that 'it's a matter of who you know in that business'. Of course it is. No producer can book an artist or commission a songwriter whom he has not heard of, or whose work he cannot safely underwrite. It is therefore up to the beginner to make himself known somehow or other. And in answer to the question 'Yes, but *how*?' I reply that it can be done, in fact I did it. But not by payola, flattery or bar-propping. By being hard-working, consistent and reliable, I like to think.

One programme, one booking, leads to another. Which is no doubt how I came to be involved in *Home This Afternoon*, one of the two series that have meant most to me from the point of view of purely personal job-satisfaction.

Home This Afternoon was broadcast each weekday at 4.45 on what is now known as Radio Four. It was a magazine programme, unashamedly directed towards the housebound, the elderly, the lonely – in other words to those listeners who wanted to be cheered, entertained and mildly informed while eating their tea and toast. They did not wish to be harangued, shocked, or educated in the ways of an increasingly repellant world.

There is a theory in radio nowadays that such people should give way to their juniors by twenty years, who are politically aware, 'into Rock', and crazy about fringe theatre. I can only say that such people were not the first concern of our dedicated *Home This Afternoon* team under Jack Singleton.

In a lifetime in the communications business I have never come across a better example of the right man in the right job than the appointment of Jack Singleton as head of our afternoon magazine programme unit. His basic production staff of Anne Catchpole, Bob Gunnell and Rosemary Hart – together with the rotating compères, Ken Sykora, Polly Elwes and myself – all adored him. He in turn supported us, screened us from the petty interference which in broadcasting always threatens from above, and kept the programmes genial, warm-hearted and gently paced. Opening the programme at quarter to five each day, one felt as though one were opening the doors of a nationwide club.

Clearly there was no way that such an unsophisticated series could escape the attentions of a committee seeking the key to 'Broadcasting in the Seventies' and our programme was killed off on the very same afternoon in April 1970 as a not dissimilar 'get-you-home' series on Radio Two, *Roundabout*, to which I had also been contributing. I went to both farewell parties that night and got quite merry, which is more than our faithful listeners seem to have been at the double blow.

The series which took the place of *Home This Afternoon* for me began the very next week and is the subject of a later chapter. Meanwhile I have warm memories of the H.T.A. (as we called it) team, and its faithful residue of listeners, some of whom still enquire wanly if the programme is ever coming back. Some of my happiest recollections are of the occasions when we took the show 'on the road', visiting halls and theatres in various provincial areas in order to meet in person the listeners whom we were trying to serve.

On one such visit we found ourselves at a small theatre in Brighton. As host, I was seated with the various contributors at a long table on the stage apron facing the audience. Our producer, concerned that the somewhat elderly audience might not be able to hear what was being said without the maximum aid from amplification, insisted that every one of us should speak into what broadcasters call a lip-mike: a hand-held microphone fitted to a metal frame which is pressed against the mouth and which ensures that the speaker's lips and the microphone are almost touching. It so happened that one of my guests that afternoon was Dame Sybil Thorndyke and I was most apprehensive as to what that formidable old trouper would make of it when she learnt of our producer's decision to impose hand-mikes on us. In her long lifetime on the stage, no theatregoer could ever have complained that he had missed a word Dame Sybil uttered. I myself had sat in the back row of the gallery and been almost deafened by what she probably regarded merely as an aside.

Just before the programme began I proffered the monstrous mike with its superstructure of struts and metal grills. 'The producer would like you to use this . . .' I began, without much hope.

Dame Sybil eyed it with amazement and disgust. 'What's this?' she enquired. '*GAS?*'

In fairness to that superb professional I should add that the story does not quite end there. Dame Sybil, having made her point, quietly took the offending implement from me and used it throughout the broadcast with the greatest of expertise.

* * *

I was responsible for dozens, indeed hundreds, of casual radio programmes during those busy years. Glancing through old engagement diaries I see the programme titles, though many of them mean nothing to me now. But the heart still sinks at diary entries which read 'Eartha Kitt, Carlton Tower 11.30', or 'Alfred Hitchcock, Dorchester 2 pm', because going out to their hotels interviewing world-class celebrities was always one of my unfavourite activities.

For a start I do not much like interviewing, any more than I relish being interviewed. The questions always seem to involve either a mere recapping of the subject's life, in which case a glance at a few press clippings would have done just as well, or the questions are self-consciously challenging, which between strangers can be something of an impertinence. I can honestly claim that I have never asked anybody – though plenty of interviewers have asked me – to list some of the 'amusing incidents that have happened to you during your life'. It is the ultimate interviewer's cop-out.

A major problem when taking a portable tape recorder to interview the very great in their hotels is that they are never there, or if there, never up, or if up, hungover. After an hour spent sitting on the edge of a settee in the Savoy Hotel foyer, I am ready to blow my stack, and am certainly in no fit state to fawn on some sleepy film actress or corseted male pop singer. But in general it seems true that the bigger they are the nicer they are, and I have to admit that interviewing David Niven was a pure joy, because that delightful man did not sit back to be quizzed, but immediately set out to entertain *me*, and through me the listeners. The fact that part of our resulting tape was, as Lord Reith would have put it, 'hardly suitable for broadcasting', did nothing to lessen the pleasure of the occasion as far as I was concerned: rather the contrary, since the tape did not need editing ... merely suppressing.

I should not fail to mention the 1964–5 late-night radio series *Through Till Two*, during which Jimmy Young and I made modest history by hosting Britain's first *almost* phone-in. I have to say *almost* because although our listeners were invited to phone in to the BBC for the first time, their voices were not heard on the air. The calls were taken by an army of telephone operators, who noted the record requests and handed them on to Gramophone Library clerks. They in turn fished the discs out of the library shelves, sometimes in a matter of seconds, then rushed them into the studio where Jimmy or I would read the scrawled messages and cue in the music.

Jimmy handled the 10 p.m. to midnight part of the programme, I then took over until 2 a.m. but there was about a quarter of an hour's overlap period during which we compèred the show jointly.

After one of Jimmy's handovers to me he was ticked off by the then Assistant Head of Gramophone Programmes, alias A.H.G.P.

'I noticed last night that you said to Steve Race "I've kept the seat warm for you". Have I got that right?'

'Yes.'

'Well, you might remember that we don't encourage that sort of talk in the BBC, will you?'

That anecdote does not appear in Jimmy's breezy auto-biography, perhaps because it slipped his memory, or maybe because when Jimmy wrote his book the H.G.P. to whom A.H.G.P. was A.H. was still very much around. (The BBC habit of referring to people under their job initials is hard to shake off.) What does appear in Jimmy's book is a very fair summary of what it felt like to do *Through Till Two*. Through the glass window that divided the studio from the control cubicle, wrote Jim:

> I could see the producer's head bobbing around among other heads and slips of paper being chucked around like confetti while Yours Truly sat solitary and somewhat in the dark as to what the hell was going on. I had a key I could press down that would let my voice be heard in the bustle of the other room and I would ask

frantically 'What's coming up next, Geoff?' He'd say, 'We haven't sorted it out yet, I'll let you know.' Then a body would hurtle through a door into my room and fling pieces of paper down and say something like 'the record is Nat Cole singing "Lazy Days of Summer" and it's coming up in about thirty seconds.' And the red light would flash on, signalling me on the air and Jim lad was on his own, with scraps of paper everywhere and the job of inventing something to say forthwith . . .

For Jim lad substitute Steve lad, or (who knows? J.Y.'s success may be catching!) S.R.

During the run of *Through Till Two* I was taken ill, and Jimmy Young took over the whole four-hour stint. I was therefore not around when the then Head of Light Entertainment – H.L.E. to his intimate friends – came back from a visit to America. He had crossed the Atlantic on a fact-finding mission, one of the questions exercising him being whether or not it would be possible for the BBC to mount a programme in which the public phoned in instant requests. The very concept was regarded with ponderous clicking of tongues in Broadcasting House circles.

He came back to announce that he had looked into the idea and found that for certain practical reasons it was quite impracticable for the Corporation to handle such a thing. Presumably someone had to tell him that Jimmy Young and Steve Race had been doing exactly that with unqualified success for the entire six weeks of his absence. I do not know how he took it, but not long afterwards he left the BBC and became an authority on wine.

I hope we didn't drive him to it.

21. Sweet as the moment when the bank account went pop

It must have been the most profitable part of my life. It was certainly the most bizarre.

They are known in the profession as 'Jingles', because in their simplest form they are jingly little tunes that stick in the public's mind after one hearing. For example:

Murraymints, Murraymints, too good to hurry-mints

– as an earlier generation of television viewers sang to one another. While to quote a composition which has brought me more money than Beethoven made from his Ninth Symphony, Birds Eye Peas are –

Sweet as the moment when the pod went pop.

There has been a jingle industry in Britain since well before the Second World War. Which of us, growing up in those years, did not singalong with our radios –

We are the Ovaltinies, happy girls and boys?

– warming the sentimental hearts of the admen concerned, though truth-to-tell they probably preferred the more hard-selling –

Hurrah for Beetox, what a delightful smell!

After the war, the Continent-based commercial radio stations underwent something of an eclipse, at which point cinema advertising took over. Then in 1955, the market opened wide with the advent of independent television. The smart composer moved in.

That must have included me, because over the first ten years of ITV, I composed, conducted and supervised the recording of several hundred jingles. Not all of them were jolly little tunes; some were moody string orchestra backgrounds ('Dawn Glow makes you lovelier all over') while others were mercifully free of sung lyrics, for example my score for Birds Eye Skinless Cod. (It is not listed among my major works.)

The sequence of events leading up to the recording of a TV commercial was in principle always the same and always somewhat fantastic. The maker of some product would agree to spend several thousand pounds of his money on making (say) a thirty-second film. The advertising agency which had captured his account would prepare elaborate scripts and drawings outlining the sort of film they recommended; a production company would be called in to do the actual film-making; the resulting half minute of persuasion would then be shown to the client, who approved it for exhibition. In due course it would appear in airtime booked by the agency on behalf of their client. You and I viewing in our homes would be influenced by the film, either consciously or subconsciously, and sales would soar. 'These Slimbix biscuits,' you and I would observe to our wives, 'really are slim biscuits with the crispest bite, are they not, my love?' And she would smile knowingly, just like those wives and mothers on the telly.

That was what happened in principle. In point of fact there were a thousand hazards lying in wait for those of us who created the nation's TV commercials.

From my point of view it would all begin with a phone call from a young advertising agency account executive whose name seemed to be Colin, Roger or Derek. Having made an appointment he would appear in my office in Television House, Kingsway. Colin, Roger or Derek was blond, wavy-haired, twenty-nine years old and as eager as a young evangelist, which indeed was exactly what he was.

'This is going to be a really hard hitting thirty-seconder,' he would predict, handing me a projected script which I could see at a glance contained enough spoken material for a full minute providing the announcer took no time out for breathing.

'It's a bit over-written,' I would point out.

'I know. But the client is very difficult. He wants all those selling points mentioned.'

At the foot of the sheet of paper there would be a sung jingle, with words by the same copywriter who had drafted the hard-sell sales talk. Since he tended to be a master of prose rather than of verse, his brainchild would read something like this:

(SUNG) Every mum's delighted,
Father is crazy about it too.
Brothers and sisters have no more blisters:
'Cos *Cornex* spells good news for your toes too!
(ANNOUNCER) In the handy kingsize pack from your druggist.
ORCHESTRA: CHORD.

'We'll have to pare this down, you know.'

'OK, we'll set up a meeting with the client. Can you give me a rough costing?'

Ah! The only sensible way of quoting one's charges for a TV commercial was to think of a number, double it to be on the safe side, add a hundred pounds for eventualities, then bring it up to the nearest two hundred and fifty.

'About seven-fifty, I should think.'

'Oh that'll be all right. Can you record it next week? How about Friday morning, ten till twelve? First hour music, second hour commentary.'

And so it was arranged. But first there would be the meeting at the agency, which would be attended by the client (Mr Cornex, as it were), together with three or four account executives of varying importance, the scriptwriter, a layout expert, someone from the film production company and one or two senior men with steel-grey hair who were called Creative Directors.

'Derek tells me that Colin feels we should have urgent exciting music right throughout the narration. Do you agree, Roger?'

'If you do, JD.' (This is no surprise to me at all. There comes a stage in most commercials when its creators lose their confidence and try to flog their jaded enthusiasm with what the trade calls 'music under'.)

163

'Colin, what is our current viewer through-put personnel rating, cost-effective wise?'

'About seven point eight, JD, but rising fast of course.'

At this point someone gets out a large chart, which he spreads out on the boardroom table. We crowd around and study it, while Roger (or perhaps Derek) points to the various headings:

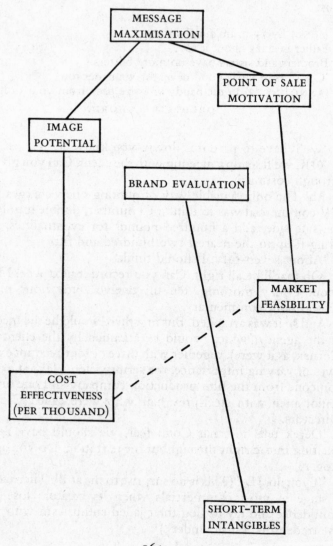

After a few minutes of scrutiny, the chart has done its work. Someone suggests that as it is 11.45 it must be time for a drink. In column of route, the client leading, we walk round to the pub.

The young account executive who came to my office falls in step beside me.

'Client seems happy,' he observes, with a hunted look. 'I guess we can cut down that narration on the session. See you then.'

'Will the client be coming?'

'Thank God, no. He's got a breakfast conference in Manila that morning and won't be back till evening.'

* * *

On the recording session the vocal group is having trouble singing 'Cornex spells good news'. It sounds like 'Corn expels good news'. We try Take Thirty-seven. It is no better.

Then suddenly they get it right, but not so the announcer, who tells us to buy Cornex 'in the pandy kingsize hack', then breaks down in hysterical laughter. Even after a glass of water and some face straightening we cannot get the laugh out of his voice; it sounds as though the very idea of Cornex amuses him. Less amusing is the fact that our studio time is running out.

'Take thirty-eight,' I intone. 'And please sober up in the studio. This is serious work we're doing.' But I know I lie.

* * *

Those sessions are so far away now that I may have embroidered them slightly in the recollecting. What I do know is that I spent hour after hour at the plate-glass offices of firms with names like Foote Colne & Belding, Colman Prentice & Varley, Alan Brady & Marsh, Young & Rubicam, and for all I know, Athos Porthos & Aramis, gazing at charts and listening to people who were quite capable of saying, without a trace of a smile, 'Let's run it up the flagpole and see if anyone salutes!' I created music designed to sell products from cocoa to brassières. I set the artistic scene for that imperishable line 'Just spray and iron with Reddistarch'; I helped to set Callard and Bowser's Juicy Jellies on the road to national acclaim. Oxo, Batchelor's Soups, Mobil, Alka-Selzer, Walpamur, Stork, Drambuie, Fairy Soap, Ryvita, Lyril: all have one thing in common. All of them used my music at one time or another, a fact for which my bank manager and I are eternally grateful.

Ah yes, Lyril – now *there* was a story. Lyril was a new kind of soap, new because it contained Paso. (Anagram, right?) It was new in other ways too. For example it left no scum round the handbasin, even when washing one's hands after a day's work in an oily garage. Better still, it came in the cosmetic range of toilet soaps and smelt like the sort of thing you might find in Brigitte Bardot's boudoir. No doubt about it, the future for Lyril was set fair.

The curious name of this marvel, according to rumour, had been devised by one of those newfangled machines called a Computer. The basic vocabularies of seventeen different languages had been fed in, the computer had been told to cough up a new word which would be acceptable in all seventeen, and the thing had come up with

LYRIL

Odd, I always thought, that anything so logical as a computer should offer a word in which the same sound was represented by two quite different letters, I and Y. No matter: Lyril was all set to conquer the world, or at least that part of it that washed its hands with toilet soap.

Science having played its part in the development of Paso, it was now up to the world of business to make its vital contribution. That contribution, according to my information, was an advertising appropriation of two million pounds.

That was just for the launch. Later, when unexpected difficulties arose, the two million pounds was said to have been increased to three million. I received a good part of it myself, thanks to successive changes of advertising policy, endless re-recordings, and a blind reluctance on the part of any of the top executives to be present at the music recording sessions where changes in instrumentation or musical emphasis could be made on the spot.

The sales pitch was clear and emphatic:

'Get that lovely, lively Lyril feeling ...'

– ran the first line of my jingle, and I followed it with a welter of singing strings that made Mantovani's Orchestra sound like a café trio. Proudly the agency people bore my tape back to the top brains of the Lyril campaign.

166

'Great,' they said. But one of them added, 'I rather thought we might have some horns.'

That was all it needed. Back to the drawing-board. My next Lyril score had the sound of a thousand violins *plus* a soaring counter-melody on four French horns.

The top people were thrilled with it. 'Superb,' they said. 'But this is a launch, a new boon to mankind, a revolution. Where's the brass? – The Fanfare?'

Where indeed? I rescored my Lyril theme for swooning strings, soaring horns, stinging brass, pulsating rhythm and excited narrator, plus the seductive girl singer who had served us loyally throughout.

'Fantastic!' the committee reported. 'Out of this world. Just one thing: the accompaniment's great. But wouldn't it sound better sung by a vocal group? After all the product is for men as well as women. Mustn't forget that!'

As we assembled for the next wickedly expensive recording session I asked the account executive why in the name of all that was wonderful the committee could not come along to the studio and make their comments in person, where I could make immediate adjustments in accordance with their every whim. I do not think he replied: perhaps the answer was that we were still only at the start of that third million. Two million down and one to go.

I must say the final mixed music track for Lyril fairly made one's hair stand on end. At any rate it was over-dubbed into countless European languages, while the leading smart society photographer of the day was dispatched to New York for a few weeks, to take stills of any good-looking girls he happened to come across in the street, the kind who might be of the type to use Lyril in their Fifth Avenue pads.

The reader must be wondering by now why he has not seen Lyril on sale in the shops recently. I never did get the answer direct from the horse's mouth. But word got around that there was a technical problem with the product itself. Nothing wrong with the advertising campaign, you understand: that was one of the most successful ever launched, a classic of cost-effective, message-maximised, image-motivated, sales potential feasibility. No, what was wrong was that when you had washed your hands with Lyril and placed the wet cake of soap at the side of your handbasin, it went on disintegrating while you were out at work. Any sane person wants to experience 'that lovely, lively Lyril feeling'. But not everyone wants to have a piece of soggy soap slide down his plughole.

The same firm master-minded the Birds Eye Peas campaign. I remember being unenthusiastic when I first read the suggested tag line 'Sweet as the moment when the pod went pop', but as the royalties rolled in I have become artistically reconciled to it through the years.

The only time in my jingle career that I uttered a squawk of actual moral protest was when called in to provide music for advertising a fruit sweet which I had better call 'Fruitipops', though that was not quite its name.

Most television viewers do not realise that for technical reasons the *sound* of every commercial they see begins one second after the picture is seen. In order to cover this curious mute moment, all kinds of devices are called into play, a typically cunning one being the start of a commercial made by the Beverley Sisters in which they began with their backs to the camera, then spun round and started to sing. Similarly at the end of an advertising film the music runs out slightly before the picture does, while the product is held visually in what the trade calls a 'freeze frame'. This is particularly noticeable in the last commercial shown in a sequence, when the freeze frame is sometimes held for quite a long time before the end of the natural break and the resumption of ordinary programmes.

I could not understand why in the half-minute commercial I was invited to make for Fruitipops, the sound track should last, not for the customary twenty-eight and a half seconds, but for twenty-three. Then the truth came out. Fruitipops, despite its inviting flavours of lemon, tangerine, orange, lime and greengage, *contained no fruit of any kind*. Citric acid, yes; picric acrid, formic acid, formaldehyde, potassium trisulphate and for all I knew, arsenic, but no fruit. Those last few seconds on the film had been reserved for the addition of an announcer's voice, which would reassure the consuming millions who might be worried about the risk of contracting appendicitis after eating those orange or lemon goodies.

'And remember,' he said, in his most comforting voice, 'remember, there are absolutely no pips in Fruitipops.'

Too right.

22. The missing minim: a three-pipe problem

The fact that the ethics of the Fruitipops campaign bothered me was a clear legacy from my chapel days. Though its dogma no longer has any place in my life, I am grateful to Methodism for many of the basic social views I still hold, for example that the only possible way to run our world is through mutual honesty and truth.

Growing up, it comes as a shock to find that human beings are not as trustworthy as one always thought; they can be cruel, deceitful and dishonest. It is a depressing discovery and some of us never recover from it. But later, with luck, comes a second realisation: that most people are basically decent after all and that the best course is to trust them.

That is where I now stand on the matter. It seems hardly worth the effort to try to run one's life on the misanthropic assumption that nobody can be trusted an inch. Better to be conned occasionally than to spend three score years and ten counting one's fingers after every handshake.

The dubious ethics of the Fruitipops campaign could perhaps best be described as sub-honest. My misgivings were obvious to the client concerned and I was quietly dropped from their books, a fact about which I have no complaints. As I keep telling myself, no one will ever thank you for proving them wrong. It is good advice I give myself, though I seldom listen. Correcting what one sees as the faults of others is a luxury, and all luxuries have to be paid for.

In between bouts of ad-men's music therefore, it was a relief to be involved in music of a slightly more reputable kind; music such as the poet Crabbe must have had in mind when he wrote:

I used to prefer the simple ballad. But now, by often hearing more *scientific* music, began to like it best.

'Scientific music' is a good expression, certainly preferable to 'serious' music, 'concert' music or even 'good' music, all of which suggest unpleasant corollaries, while the term 'classical' music should not strictly speaking be applied to the late-romantic music which its users often mean. Whatever else Liszt's 'Liebestraum' may be, it is not classical.

I often hear people claim that there are 'only two kinds of music, good and bad'. The distinction sounds all very well until one points out that the same applied equally to eggs, parasols, politicians and pepper pots.

There are, however, in a special sense, three kinds of music. At the very top there is music as fine as its creator can make it; music which is as inevitable as the sunrise, complete and unchangeable. Its composer – Beethoven perhaps, or Bach – is quite unaffected by considerations of performance or public taste. The music exists within him; it must be born, after which it simply *is*.

At the opposite end of the scale there is music which is created in order to sell. Such music is aimed at the lowest common denominator of public taste, nothing being allowed through which might cause a moment's uncertainty in the listener or lose the chance of a single sale. Much of this music is immensely enjoyable, as indeed it is intended to be.

In the middle, between those two extremes, is music which the composer and performer combine to make as good as they possibly can, while still remaining within the bounds of the likeable and even the saleable. All my life I have tried to make music of this kind, while only very rarely aspiring (or descending as the case may be) to the other categories by way of a day excursion. It is perhaps significant that the only time I decided deliberately to write *down* to the public and produce something musically juvenile for the musically juvenile listener, the resulting record put me in the pop charts for thirteen weeks ('The Pied Piper'). For the rest of my composing activities I always aimed as high as I dared ... and missed the pop charts.

The exigencies of musical life did not always make it easy to keep one's standards up. In the mid 1960s, during a lull in TV bookings at the new Rediffusion studio complex in Wembley, two American teams moved in, to make programmes for their own market. Peter Knight was invited to handle the music for *The Bing Crosby Show*; I was chosen to compose and direct the music for a television drama trilogy called *Three Roads to Rome*, starring Deborah Kerr.

My three American bosses were Fred Coe (television adviser to President Kennedy), Arthur Penn (who has become one of Hollywood's major directors, following his *Bonnie and Clyde*), and the then little known Bo Goldman, who was my music co-ordinator for the Deborah Kerr plays, but has since made his mark as a movie scriptwriter (*One Flew over the Cuckoo's Nest*).

The technique they required of their composer was hair-raising. I would go to the rehearsal-room sessions, where I became familiar with the plot and the general delivery of Deborah Kerr and the other members of the cast. I would discuss with the producers the scenes which seemed to call for musical underscoring. I might even compose a theme or two to be played over on the piano for their broad approval. What I could not do was put pen to paper, in the sense of writing the orchestrations or planning strict musical section lengths; not until the actors' performances were down on videotape and capable of being timed.

In one sense we were simply using the cinema technique. Where our plan differed was that whereas a film composer has a month or six weeks in which to write his scores to fit the film's measurements, I had to be present at the day's filming, then go home, compose and score overnight the appropriate music for those scenes which had been completed. I had only one weekend between the last scene being shot and my first conductor's downbeat at the Monday morning orchestral session.

I made it, because I had to. Working in the enormous Wembley Studio Five, the art director had constructed elaborate sets, which fitted inside one another like layers of an onion. As Deborah Kerr and the others completed a given scene to the satisfaction of Fred Coe and Arthur Penn, the inner layer of scenery was stripped away, and the next scene in the schedule – not necessarily the next in the play's sequence – was rehearsed and immediately put on tape. I sat all day at a table at the back of the producer's box with a mountain of score paper, a stopwatch and a bottle of something designed to keep me awake. The moment filming was over for the day, I would go home with my precious final timings, switch to black coffee, and score the required orchestral music far into the night.

It was hair-raising, though not too much so for me to notice how magnificent Deborah Kerr was being. That gentle person and consummate artist looked as fresh after a killing week as she had looked on the Monday morning. And she was still giving every bit as subtle a performance.

'I don't know how you do it,' I babbled to her on the Saturday night. 'Honestly, neither do I,' she said, looking at me rather closely. Then she added kindly, 'I think we could both use a quiet weekend!'

About that time, working closely as I was with Sir John Barbirolli at Associated-Rediffusion, it was decided that a concert programme similar to 'This is Your Life, Sir John' should be secretly arranged as one of the concert evenings at the Buxton Music Festival. The then General Manager of the Hallé Orchestra, Ken Crickmore, would somehow ensure Barbirolli's presence, while the Hallé, under its deputy conductor, would play various key pieces associated with his life. My contribution was to write for the orchestra a fifteen-minute set of variations on a favourite theme of Sir John's, which might reflect the influence of some of his favourite composers.

I called the piece 'Variations on a Smoky Theme' for the very good reason that Sir John's 'favourite theme' turned out to be Jerome Kern's 'Smoke Gets in Your Eyes'. I cannot say the tune particularly lent itself to variation treatment, though when later Sir John conducted it himself he was kind enough to suggest that I had done a creditable job.

I conducted the first performance myself at Buxton. It was then played at the Manchester Proms under George Weldon. Subsequent performances were given under Maurice Handford, Marcus Dods and Maurice Miles. When Sir John Barbirolli himself conducted the score at the Bexhill Festival, he announced it in these words:

I suppose everyone has a skeleton in their cupboard and mine is the passion I've had for this lovely tune for many years. My old friend Steve Race – not so old, he's much younger than I am – has written this set of variations which enable me, with a certain decency, at last to indulge myself and conduct this lovely tune. It's the most extraordinarily witty, ingenious work that he's written, and he's used many of the composers that he knows I like.

Needless to say, it was a highly flattered Steve Race who sat back in his seat in the front row of the circle at the De la Warr Pavilion to listen to the definitive version of his Barbirolli variations given by the man who had inspired them.

But something quite awful happened. Throughout the performance Sir John had manifestly been enjoying himself, luxuriating in the romantic parts, grinning to his beloved Hallé musicians at the various light-hearted allusions. Then at the *fermata* before the final grandiose statement of the tune, he gave a sort of twitch; it was not a downbeat but a kind of convulsion of anticipation. At least that was what I took it to be, and so did most of the orchestra. But the violins, who happened to have the main theme at that point, took it to be some sort of downbeat, with the result that they started the final section two whole beats before anyone else.

Chaos ensued. Nothing harmonised with anything else; every member of the orchestra played his part with the stern consciousness of rectitude so characteristic of the Hallé musician. Sir John conducted the *fortissimo* mish-mash with his eyes closed in a transport of delight, while I sat in my seat with my head buried in my hands. To be fair to Sir John, it would not have been an easy matter to resolve. Perhaps after a bar or so he should just have stopped the orchestra and gone back to that last double bar.

The audience applauded loud and long. (Had not Sir John Barbirolli himself swept round with a satisfied smile and compelled the composer to take a bow?) We then repaired to the green room for those post-performance drinks and compliments which Sir John so enjoyed, and usually merited. On this occasion I went with trepidation, not knowing what I would say to him until he had said something to me. Laugh it off? Sympathise?

I need not have worried. 'Wasn't it splendid?' enthused Sir John. 'Marvellous ... Marvellous. We must do it again as soon as possible.' Not one word about the chaotic final page.

Did he know? It was unthinkable that he had not noticed;

equally unthinkable that so generous a man as Sir John would fail to give me a broad wink and a quick word of regret when it was so obviously called for. Much later I asked the man most likely to know: his greatest admirer, friend and biographer, Michael Kennedy. 'On the whole,' said Michael, 'I think he was enjoying himself so much that he just didn't notice.'

I rather hope that was it. And now Sir John has gone and we shall never know for sure. As for 'Smoke Gets in Your Eyes', needless to say I never hear it without thinking of him. And on the odd occasions since when I have conducted the piece myself, I have made certain that I gave the violins at that point the clearest, most unequivocal downbeat ever seen in the history of music.

23. How I joined the Bloomsbury Group, or very nearly anyway

During 1957, 1958 and 1960 I spent a good deal of time in the United States of America.

A week or two before the first visit I met the charming, generous Ben Lyon in one of the Television House lifts. 'I'm going to your old hometown next month,' I incautiously told him. Within the hour, a file of carbon letters was sent round to my office; letters written by the kindly Ben to some of his old associates in Hollywood, introducing me as a friend of his and asking them to look after me. 'Dear Daryl . . . My dear Selznick . . . Jack, you old devil, it seems a long time since you founded Warners . . . Cecil, my old buddy . . . Dear Hal . . .'

I tried waving one of the letters around on arrival in the Celluloid City but I got such a stupendous brush-off from

Miss Moneypenny in the outer office that my pride would not allow me to take the matter any further. In any case, I needed a few days' quiet in order to recover from the horrors of New York.

I am not one of those people who come to life in New York, finding stimulation in its human bustle, its teeming anthill, its vast melting pot and other clichés. When I think of New York it is not the New York of Broadway musicals and Cadillacs on Fifth Avenue, but the New York of midtown Manhattan streets where a man in a dirty shirt is waiting on the kerb to hurl insults at a passing truck driver; the streets where you could be born, set fire to yourself or die, right there on the sidewalk, without anyone pausing to ask if you were feeling all right. They might take your picture, they would not take your pulse.

Strictly speaking I was there to study television and musical matters rather than New York city itself. One morning I went to a studio just off Broadway to see a show called *Strike it Rich*, a kind of quiz show for the chronically disabled, at which the contestant with the biggest ulcer got the biggest mink coat. The only healthy person in the studio was the compère, a young man who combined deep compassion with a cold ruthlessness. I marvelled at the speed with which he could reduce someone to tears, and the even greater speed with which he could get them off the screen when the floor manager gave him a time cue. He was indeed a master; in manner something of a cross between Liberace and Captain Bligh.

One of his contestants was a rather shaky old gentleman with a nasty-sounding disease about which our compère grew quite excited in his deeply compassionate way. After giving the old chap a dishwasher – or perhaps it was a trip to Europe or a Fabergé egg – the young host was just getting rid of him when the contestant said 'May I tell the viewers something?'

'Sure-sure.'

'Friends,' said the old man, squaring up fearlessly to the camera and transfixing with his eye the correct lens on the turret, 'It's Sunday School Week. *Send your kids* to Sunday School.'

It was an unremarkable moment in the eternity of tatty daytime American television but it stuck in my mind as an example of the spirit which has made the American people great. No nation could ever be vanquished as long as its geriatric citizens know unerringly which camera lens to look into; when the eyes of a sick old man of eighty still light up at the chance, for five short seconds, to become a salesman.

As the audience filed out of the studio I was button-holed by a likeable young American executive in an Ivy League suit, who asked me if I could spare half an hour to serve on a television research panel. I explained that I was a foreigner, but he seemed to think that was unimportant, so I joined seven or eight other people and was driven in a fast car to CBS headquarters. There we were handed over to a researcher.

'In front of each of you,' we were told, as we sat at a big table before a large projection screen, 'is a green button and a red button. We shall now show you a pilot programme, which has been made for test purposes and may or may not become the basis of a series, in accordance with your verdict. As long as you are enjoying the programme, keep the green button pressed. If you are not enjoying it, press the red button. Green for good; red for bad.'

I wanted to know what would happen if one felt like pressing the two buttons simultaneously or not pressing either for a while, but that sort of subtlety is lost on a New York researcher once he is in orbit. He shot me the sort of look that Paul Revere would have given John Gilpin.

The play they showed us had been adapted from a story by O'Henry. It was brilliantly done, and I kept the green button firmly down almost the whole way through, in fact I only released it to change thumbs.

After the lights went on again our researcher came back into the room. 'I've been monitoring your reactions on the "taste-meter",' he told us sneakily, 'and you didn't like it, of course. Well, one of you did, but he's not an American. Thank you for your co-operation, ladies and gentlemen. I can tell you now, that show will never take the air.'

As we left they gave each of us a cigarette lighter to mark the company's sincere gratitude. But the researcher caught my arm: 'Let me ask you, why did you like that show?'

I told him I thought it was intelligent, literate and beautifully photographed: a programme the English television would be proud to show.

'Well ... yes,' he said. 'But you see, we have things figured

With Paul McCartney and John Lennon at the recording of 'All You Need is Love', Abbey Road Studios

With the Many a Slip *team in 1966: Eleanor Summerfield, Lady Barnett, Richard Murdoch and David Nixon*

My Music – *my teams. Ian Wallace, Denis Norden, Frank Muir and John Amis.*

differently here. As far as we're concerned, the newspapers are for information, the radio is for companionship, and television is only for entertainment.'

That over-simplified philosophy is one which has not so far been adopted by those who control the media in Britain. I hope it never will.

Driving on my own down through New Mexico some three weeks later, I was feeling rather sorry for myself. I was hot, sated with travel, bored with the tedium of long-distance American driving, and just plain homesick. Late one stifling afternoon I turned into a small New Mexico town which seemed to be made up of adobe houses, found my way to the town square, parked my car and looked round for somewhere to stay the night.

The entrance to the hotel turned out to be the waiting area for the bus station, and I perked up a little when I saw the line of Pueblo Indian women in their ponchos and black pigtails, some of them holding chickens and one of them with a small but resentful pig.

The hotel seemed all right. I felt better, though still a million miles from home. A pleasant Greek clerk handled my reservation and pointed up the staircase to where I would find my room. Taking my suitcase I started to mount the stairs, then came face to face with a handwritten notice:

> TO THE D. H. LAWRENCE
> EXHIBITION

D. H. Lawrence? Here in New Mexico?

Then finally it dawned on me, tired as I was from driving and somewhat disorientated by homesickness. Of course! – I was in Taos. This was Lawrence's promised land – *Rananim* – which he had found in the 1920s and where he had unsuccessfully tried to persuade his Bloomsbury friends to join him in setting up an artists' commune. Here in Taos, Lawrence had lived his stormy life with Frieda. They had been joined by that odd girl who followed him out from England ... What was her name? No doubt it would come back to me. In my mind's eye I could see her face in those snapshots taken at Garsington Manor with Yeats, Eliot, Lytton Strachey and Carrington.

The exhibition adjoining the Hotel de Taos turned out to be of Lawrence's so-called erotic pictures, first shown in 1929 at the Warren Gallery in London but abruptly withdrawn from the public gaze following a police raid. I found them colourful and moderately interesting, but sexually about as stimulating as a production of *H.M.S. Pinafore*.

I was joined in the exhibition room by the Greek reception clerk, who turned out to be the hotel's owner and an Anglophile. He insisted on my joining him for dinner, after which he drove me out to visit a nearby Indian village. ('That cinecamera? You pay five dollar.')

The following morning I was preparing to leave Taos and drive on to Arizona and the Grand Canyon. When I went to say goodbye to him the hotelier asked if on my way out of town I would care to see an exhibition of paintings by an elderly lady artist of his acquaintance.

'Matter of fact I called her while you were having breakfast,' he told me, 'and she's very keen to meet you. She was born in England and likes to meet any English person who comes to Taos.'

I still had not realised. 'All right,' I said.

When I reached the long adobe studio-cum-gallery I found waiting for me a deaf, elderly lady, trailing a tiny dog on the end of an enormously long chain. Large and corpulent, she showed every sign of being an eccentric. She stepped forward as I got out of the car, grasped my hand and boomed in an English upper-class accent 'How do you do, Mr Race. I'm Dorothy Brett.'

Of course! – *Brett*. The Hon. Dorothy Brett. It all flooded back to me from the Bloomsbury Group's books about one another. Dorothy Brett, daughter of Viscount Esher, had been brought up on the edge of Windsor Park. As a child her playmates were Edward VIII and George VI. Queen Mary supervised her dancing lessons; Kaiser Wilhelm once chatted to her after a hunt. Then on being discovered by Lady Ottoline Morrell, she became an accepted part of the stimulating, bitchy artistic world of Bertrand Russell, Virginia Woolf and Augustus John, until the Lawrence animal magic worked on her and in 1924 she set off in his footsteps to Taos, taking a studio at Los Piños. Frieda Lawrence always maintained that while pretending to paint, Brett was merely watching her platonic

178

hero down at his *hacienda*. It was Dorothy Brett who did the picture of D. H. Lawrence which hangs now in the National Portrait Gallery. And here was that self-same Brett – 'that Slade crophead' as Virginia Woolf called her; the deaf painter in Aldous Huxley's *Crome Yellow* – pointing her deaf-aid at me and asking me what I thought of her paintings.

What did I think of them? To tell the truth, not much. They represented scenes from Pueblo legends and rituals; small naïve figures tumbling from huge rocks, braves carrying off squaws across distant hills. The canvases were certainly large, but that had been a characteristic of Dorothy Brett's work, even in her Garsington days, when, according to the biography of Lady Ottoline Morrell, Brett was:

– having trouble fitting all of Ottoline onto the canvas. So, rather than start the portrait again, she tacked on a few feet of extra canvas, making the picture over nine feet high and necessitating the use of a stepladder, which Brett climbed up and down ...

That had been the day Siegfried Sassoon was shown in for the first time, and Ottoline – Lytton Strachey's 'daughter of a thousand earls' – had added him to her stable of young lions. Dorothy Brett's portrait was not a success. Clive Bell called it 'Brett's Colossus' and Lady Ottoline observed of it 'you've made me look like a prostitute'.

No one looked like a prostitute in those sprawling landscapes which the very same Brett was now describing to me as we walked round her gallery at Taos. The awful thought occurred to me that she had imagined I might buy one, though I could hardly have got it into the car, let alone flown it back with me to London.

She was not the sort of lady to be deterred by difficulties. Her *penchant* for abduction had proved that. Having decided that Lady Ottoline's daughter was unhappy at her convent, she sent the girl a rope ladder in a parcel. She also enclosed a plan of escape, under which Brett was to wait outside in a car with engine running. (The nuns intercepted the parcel and the plan had to be abandoned.) Many years later, after D. H. Lawrence's death, Brett was involved in a preposterous plot to steal his urn from its chapel and scatter the sacred Lawrentian ashes over a nearby ranch. In the event, the relics were mixed with sand and cement and became a sturdy immovable altar in the chapel at Taos. In her later years, Brett conceived a tremendous passion for the conductor Stokowski, but I gather there was no report of any attempted kidnapping in his case.

Dorothy Brett was seventy-five when I met her. She was to live on into her nineties, in fact when she died at the age of ninety-three she had become one of the only three true Bloomsburyites surviving. (The other two were Duncan Grant and David Garnett.) I remember she asked me about both of them. It was quite embarrassing as she reeled off name after name like a walking Burke's Peerage, craving news of the Asquiths, the Sitwells or the 'Bertie' Russells, none of whom were any part of my social background but were so obviously a part of hers.

Most of all she asked me about places. Did Gower Street look the same, she wondered? Had Bedford Square survived the blitz? Had I ever been to Charleston Manor? I found myself growing quite fond of the strange lady with her thirst for news of 'home'. I wish now that I had somehow managed to buy and transport home one of her massive Indian canvases. But I disengaged myself somehow, patted her rat-like little dog, and promised to relay her greetings to Duncan Grant if I ever ran into him.

As I shook hands with her and got into the car to drive off, Brett said to me, with a hint of sadness but still with the brisk pride of a Viscount's daughter: 'I often think I might go back. But then, I don't suppose I'm much remembered now.'

24. Interlude

In October 1964 my mother died. Through all my growing years she had surrounded me with a great tenderness, tempered by an understanding of how we differed, enlivened by a sense of humour that exactly mirrored my own. She was the best person I have ever known and the greatest friend: small wonder that to this day I miss her, often seeming to hear her voice, constantly wanting to share with her a funny story, a good book, or just an ingenious crossword clue. In addition to giving me life itself, she gave me sensitivity, a respect for truth and loyalty, and what she liked to call our 'funny bump'. In return I gave her . . . what? Sleepless nights, no doubt. But also my love and admiration for more than half her lifetime, so I hope the debt was honoured in some degree. She made me, not in any sense what I am – whatever that may be – but essentially *who* I am. While I live, so does she, through the ways of my mind and the memories that lie in my heart.

The answer to grief lies in work, as she knew for herself, and I had plenty of work to do. There was *Jazz 625*, a series which helped to launch the BBC's second television channel, for which I was the host, interviewing legendary jazzmen like Muddy Waters (fabulous name!), Henry Allen and Pee Wee Russell, as well as Woody Herman, Erroll Garner, Dave Brubeck and other current favourites on the international jazz circuit.

With Brubeck I had a special relationship, having won his attention some years before by announcing in a newspaper article that I had been studying his work and had come to the conclusion that I had undervalued it at first hearing. This simple act of public recantation so amazed Dave – the butt as he was of a hundred self-important jazz critics – that a close correspondence developed between us and I stayed at his home when visiting San Francisco.

We drifted apart somewhat later on, when I grew tired of the rut into which his quartet seemed to me to have settled. But I was interested, as recently as May 1978, when I watched Dave being interviewed on a BBC-TV chat-show from Birmingham, to hear him tell the interviewer:

> At first only two people understood what I was trying to achieve, and stood up and defended. There was one black music critic, a doctor, who said 'Brubeck's on the right track'. The other person that spoke up is a fellow named Steve Race, English critic. He said we'd shot an arrow that would hit a new mark.

I do not recall using that exact expression, though I do plead guilty to having promoted Brubeck's music as hard as I could in the days when it was fashionable for knowledgeable jazz folk to knock it. I thought he was on to something: now we know he was.

One of the *Jazz 625* groups I introduced from the stage of the Television Theatre was led by the trombonist J. J. Johnson and featured the amazing Sonny Stitt. Stitt was more amazing musically than intellectually, as was proved by something that happened at the start of the programme.

We began, dramatically, with an empty stage. I entered and with a brief biographical sentence or two brought on J. J. Johnson. The audience applauded. I then did the same for Stitt – applause. The pianist – applause. The bassist – applause. The drummer – applause. 'Now the group is complete,' I said, and was going on to announce the first piece when Sonny Stitt turned to J. J. Johnson and said in a loud voice: 'He didn't introduce you.'

If the brilliant Stitt was inclined to be thick, the no less brilliant Roland Kirk had a vengeful streak, as I discovered to my cost.

Kirk – or 'Rahsaan' Roland Kirk, as he liked to call himself – was booked for an opening season at Ronnie Scott's old jazz club in Gerrard Street. Kirk would arrive on stage with armfuls of saxophones and flutes, some of which he managed to play simultaneously, while slung round his shoulders were various hooters and horns on which he would occasionally blow a resounding *whoop*! It was great fun and a good deal of it was great jazz. But those adjuncts seemed to me to be in danger of cheapening his music slightly. At all events, on the first of his London visits I described him in a magazine as 'the Charlie Cairoli of jazz', Cairoli being a well-known multi-instrumentalist who worked mainly on the variety stage and who like Kirk had mastered the curious technique of blowing two saxophones and a clarinet simultaneously.

'There's a Mr Roland Kirk on the phone for you,' said my secretary one afternoon.

'Hello.'

'Man, what's this about you calling me a circus performer?'

I was non-plussed for a moment. Then I cottoned on. 'No,' I told him, 'I never called you that. What I said was ...' But it was no use. Someone at Ronnie Scott's Club had told him that Charlie Cairoli was a circus performer, *ergo* I had said the same. Circus performer ... Insult ... Ring the man up to complain.

A few evenings later I went along to the club to hear Kirk in person. Unfortunately I was seen going in and some kind pudding-stirrer, perhaps Ronnie himself, told Kirk that I was in the audience. After a couple of numbers he grasped the microphone and began a diatribe about critics who can criticise but cannot play, instancing one in America who, when called upon to show his worth, turned out to be the world's worst pianist. The implication was obvious. I could feel Kirk's hot breath on me across all of ten rows as he called out:

'Brother Race, are you there? Come up and show us how to play the piano, man.'

As a last attempt to pacify him I called back, 'I'm up here, brother Kirk. But I'd rather listen to Brother Tracey, if it's all the same to you.' Stan Tracey was in his accompanying group.

It was not all the same to him, he wanted his pound and a half of flesh. He kept on taunting me and in the end I had to get to my feet and join him on the tiny bandstand, while the kindly but bemused audience gave me a patter of welcoming applause. Stan Tracey gave up his place at the keyboard and I sat down, experiencing a curious mixture of irritation at being singled out, apprehension at how my rusty jazz playing would hold up, and excitement at being about to play alongside a truly outstanding jazz musician.

'What do you want to play?' demanded Roland Kirk.

I was still in pacifying mood. 'Something slow,' I replied, adding in an undertone, 'remember I'm only a critic.'

'"These Foolish Things", E flat,' announced Kirk, and kicked off four fairly slow beats with his foot. Picking up the tempo he had set, I improvised an introduction of some sort, whereupon Kirk came in with the first chorus, but *at exactly twice the tempo*. Aha – so, it's to be war, I thought.

It is not for me to say how I fared. From where I sat my performance seemed all right. I was more involved than I could have wished in trying to establish which of the piano notes were working and which were missing. ('Try to avoid that octave there,' Stan Tracey hissed helpfully in my ear, pointing to the most often-used octave on the whole keyboard.) After something like seven minutes our performance ended in what I noted was quite respectable applause. At least there were no boos. 'Thank you,' I said, making to leave the platform. 'A pleasure to play with you, Roland.'

But 'Rahsaan' Kirk was not satisfied. He caught me by the arm in a vice-like grip and pulled me towards him at the mike. 'Well, Brother Race,' he enquired nastily in a form of question that has always struck me as being more or less unanswerable, 'What do you know?'

The fool, I thought suddenly. *He may be a fantastic player, but words are my business, not his.*

'I'll tell you what I know,' I replied. 'I know that Ronnie Scott ought to buy a new piano. This one is falling apart.'

'Maybe Brother Scott can't afford a new piano.' (The 'brother' business was beginning to irritate me.)

'At the price that Brother Scott charges for a glass of red wine,' I said, 'he can afford a whole new club.'

The audience laughed and that was when Kirk let go of my arm. Under his breath he sent me on my way with two words, and I noticed that they were the same two words of dismissal which Ike Hatch had used when firing me from his Cuba Club all those years before. (By an extraordinary coincidence, I think both events took place in the very same basement in Gerrard Street.) I went back to my place and listened to the rest of the set, still admiring Roland Kirk's fine playing, but with a new respect for the way in which Stan Tracey was dodging that missing octave. Then I left. Two ———— offs are enough for one basement.

A month later, Ronnie Scott bought a new grand piano. I like to think I had something to do with that. Though at the same time he put up the price of a glass of red wine.

* * *

I was becoming disenchanted with jazz, almost bored by it, and it was a surfeit of live performances in clubs and concerts which was to blame. The tradition that every member of a jazz group should enjoy a protracted solo in every number had led to interminable solos on the double bass which I was finding increasingly unbearable. Even worse were the drum solos, always the closing piece at a jazz concert, during which the rest of the band would firmly leave the stage (sometimes to play cards in the wings) while the demented drummer would hit everything in sight for some minutes, before summoning his colleagues back with a pre-arranged and unvarying triplet figure. A final *fortissimo* chord ... Applause ... Curtain.

After one seemingly endless farrago of drum-battering, I told myself that I had better things to do with my life and swore that I would never sit through another. I never have. The sabbatical which I began that day has extended into the present, and I now enjoy playing myself an occasional jazz record as a personal treat, though being careful to wander off to pour myself a drink if the bassist shows signs of having pretensions as a soloist.

In any case there was more than enough to occupy my time fully in other fields of music, what with conducting, arranging, composing, writing reviews and organising recording sessions. In fact I remember thinking, as I went to bed on the night of 13 April 1965, what a lovely full life I was enjoying. The next day was going to be an unusually busy one: the sort of day to remember in future years.

I was right about that.

PART FOUR

25. *Into extra time*

My bed in the Middlesex Hospital was cool, clean and welcoming. It resembled a womb, I reflected contentedly, snuggling down between the sheets, while my heart worked out its new underground system and some of the prettiest nurses in London hovered around in their provocatively belted uniforms.

But the trouble with life in the womb is that one has to be delivered before long. How was the big professional world outside going to respond to my return, now that I had hit the coronary headlines and worried everyone in sight? I remembered what the blind pianist George Shearing had told me: that the night club owners of America were delighted to hear that he had formed a successful sextet, but none of them wanted to employ him because he might fall off the bandstand and sue them for a billion dollars. Was I now a potential faller-off of bandstands?

The question of my return to the broadcasting business occupied me a good deal, and when I got back from a convalescent cruise to the West Indies with Clair and Nicola, I discovered that similar thoughts had been in the minds of others. Two or three people, notably in Broadcasting House, were clearly worried that I might have a second attack and were determined that if so I was not going to have it on one of their programmes. They may have thought they were protecting me from myself; I suspect they were protecting themselves from me.

One man to whom I shall always be grateful was the BBC producer John Powell for whom I had written and presented many archive-based programmes, and who now offered me the chance to compose and conduct original music for some important Radio Three drama productions, among them Sir

Ralph Richardson's *Cyrano de Bergerac* and Paul Daneman's *Richard the Third*, together with John Arden's play *Ironhand* and a stage version of *Twelfth Night*. The loyal Jack Singleton took me back on *Home This Afternoon*. A little later I teamed up with Alan Owen, one of the best music producers the BBC has ever had, to host the daily orchestral series *Invitation to Music*. As the holiday replacement for the unwanted Radio Four schools programmes, our series eventually died a political death when the education slots were hived off elsewhere. But by then I had rebuilt as much as I needed of my former freelance work.

One interesting new departure was a commercial television series for ATV on Sunday evenings, in which we traced the history of English church music over five centuries, the examples being sung by a group called The New English Singers. Their conductor was the brilliant organist Simon Preston, while standing in the semi-anonymous ranks of that *ad hoc* choir were now-recognised soloists like Ian Partridge and Michael Rippon, not to mention Alastair Thompson of the Kings Singers.

The ATV series was networked at seven o'clock on Sunday evenings, quite a good slot, particularly if one happened to be followed by something special. One week we were indeed followed by something special: the Royal Command Variety Performance. From 7 to 7.25 pm I compèred our choral programme, whereupon the world's greatest stars took over. Subsequently the audience research people estimated that although only five hundred thousand people had seen me say 'Good evening', nineteen million or more had seen me say 'Goodnight'. For some weeks afterwards people kept coming up to me and saying 'I saw you on television. Let's see now, what was it you were doing?'

'I was saying Goodnight,' I told them.

* * *

Just as there is a special tie which may be worn by people who have been rescued after parachuting into the sea, or another for those who have been plucked from a burning building by a passing pelican, so there ought to be a club-tie for people who have survived a heart attack. What stories we could tell one another! – Repeatedly.

188

We would agree, for example, that no outsider ever describes what one has suffered as a *minor* heart attack. 'I hear you had a *serious* heart attack,' they say, or even *massive*, but when you tell them that on the contrary it was quite a small one they are not really listening. They prefer it to have been massive. Sometimes their deeply solicitous faces reflect not so much their concern for you as their apprehensions for themselves. Worried about their own coronary future, they are eager to check your symptoms against theirs. One particularly well known television conductor (who incidentally took over a highly profitable series from me when I went into hospital) wore an expression so woebegone whenever we met that I came to the conclusion that his conscience had somehow been touched as well as his compassion. As I feared, it was not long before his turn came for the coronary ward.

The least welcome surviving legacy of my 1965 heart attack is the way total strangers come up to me even now, with an almost prurient concern across their faces. 'I hear you've been ill,' they say, or, 'I read that you've had rather a bad time. I do hope you're all right now.'

They try to avoid identifying my 'bad time', as if the word 'heart' were four letters long instead of five. Though kindly meant, I find their solicitude rather tiresome after so many happy and active years. Sometimes I even affect not to know what they are talking about.

'Me?' I say. 'Ill? I don't think so . . .' (I search my memory.) 'Oh, you mean that heart attack I had? Good heavens, that was fourteen years ago. I thought you were talking about a touch of 'flu I had last month. I'd forgotten all about the heart attack.'

Not true. I *would* perhaps have forgotten all about it if kind friends and kinder strangers would allow me to do so. The fact is that I had my coronary at just the right age. I survived it; I obeyed its clear warning. I slowed down just a little, lost over a stone in weight, gave up smoking and set about living my second life with as much relish as the first.

I was lucky in having the perfect secretary, Roslyn Georgiades, to look after things at the office end. At home I had the ideal next-door neighbour in the one-and-only Benny Green, who with his wife Toni had been very helpful to Clair while I was in hospital. Come to that, I had occasionally been helpful to Benny, who would sometimes drop round at eleven at night, hurl himself exhausted into a chair and say, 'Tell me another five thousand words on Ella Fitzgerald!' Poor Benny, slaving over a hot typewriter as all journalists must, and confronted with his fifth Fitzgerald souvenir programme, had run out of things to say after the four thousandth word. When Toni and Benny moved out to the country, life in our road became less exacting, I must admit, and far less fun.

Benny's unannounced visits were always a joy. But what I needed above all was a new consuming professional interest. It came within the year, under the ready-made title of *My Music*.

One morning there was a phone call from Tony Shryane, a BBC producer in Birmingham whom I knew personally only slightly, though of course I knew his reputation through *The Archers* and the panel game he had devised, *My Word*.

'We're thinking of trying out a musical version of *My Word*, to be known, hardly surprisingly, as *My Music*,' said Tony. 'Would you like to be the chairman?'

I said I thought I might. 'Who would the panellists be?'

'Frank Muir, Denis Norden, Ian Wallace and David Franklin.'

I said I *would* like to be chairman.

We met in the BBC studio in Lower Regent Street on 31 July 1966 to make a test recording. It went well, in fact that trial programme was eventually transmitted as it stood, the first edition of our brand new series.

'What is the meaning of *La Donna è Mobile*?' I asked Denis Norden that first evening.

'*La Donna è Mobile* is Italian,' Denis replied, 'for "The bird's got a motor bike."' Somehow his reply set the pattern. If I may be allowed a platitude, we have never looked back.

Immediately after the recording I put up a modest black when I went to join Frank, Denis, Ian and David in the tiny artists' room, almost under the stairs at the BBC's Lower Regent Street studio. Not realising that Frank and Denis were in conversation, I went bouncing up and said something like 'Well, that seemed OK...' Then I stopped and added, fool that I was, 'Oh I'm sorry Frank. I didn't realise you were in the middle of one of your stories.' A slight *frisson* chilled the air in the room as I spoke the fateful words 'one of your stories'.

Many times since that evening I have seen the glance that passed between them, though never again, thank goodness, have I been its cause. Neither Frank nor Denis is blessed with the ability to suffer fools gladly. For a moment that had meant me, and their eyes had enquired silently, 'What have we got here? What on earth have we let ourselves in for?'

But it was a passing moment and of course I imagined it, did I not? Moreover there was work to be done. Our pilot programme had become the first of a series; many further questions must be worked out in association with Edward J. Mason (though on Ted's death I took over the whole of the question-compiling myself). I had to get to know my producers Tony Shryane and Stan Stancliffe. More important, I had to get to know the musical knowledge, range and tastes of my contestants.

'What is a sitar?' I asked Frank a week or two later.

'I don't know what a sitar is,' he replied. 'But a baby sitar is something you get in for the evening when you and your wife want to go to the pictures.'

'Can you describe an *entrechat*?' I asked David Franklin, who replied, 'An *entrechat* is when a chap rises in the air and twiddles. If he's still twiddling when he hits the ground again, he's in dead trouble.'

It turned out that Ian Wallace was a masterly raconteur, and this, coupled with his hilarious experiences on the opera stage, led to some of the really golden moments of our *My Music* programmes. David Franklin's schoolmasterly manner made him an ideal partner for Frank, while Ian's partner Denis made great play with his own supposed musical ignorance, though in fact his knowledge of early films and shows is encyclopedic. Denis remembers songs which everyone else has either forgotten or decided not to notice in the first place.

Odd impromptu gems stick in an admiring question-master's mind. Frank characterised Denis's singing as sounding 'like a moorhen with its leg caught', an inspired choice of bird, I always thought. Denis, musing on the tune 'Chopsticks', pointed out the interesting fact (if fact it is) that in China 'Chopsticks' is known as 'Knife and Fork'. Asked to think up a suitable signature tune for a fishmonger, they came up with 'Whale Meat Again', 'Salmon Chanted Evening', 'There's a Plaice for Us', and the three-star 'Whale Kipper Whelk-ome in the Hillsides'. Puns are not banned in *My Music*.

For several years our team remained unchanged, though

temporary indisposition brought in five casual guests: Lionel Hale, Barry Took, Michael Flanders, Owen Brannigan and Alfred Marks. Our basically happy family relationship was enlivened by the fact, well known in the profession but perhaps not outside it, that David Franklin and I did not get on together. He thought me an arrogant upstart; I found him pompous and condescending. It was not really a happy working arrangement and though we both tried loyally to like one another and work together in harmony, we constantly rubbed each other up the wrong way. Sometimes Ian acted as intermediary, having worked alongside David in their Glyndebourne days and therefore understanding something of his temperament.

When David's brilliant radio essay *Cambridge Revisited* won him the equivalent of an Oscar, I was thrilled for him. 'When David comes in,' I said to my producers Tony and Stan, 'don't forget to congratulate him. He'll be so pleased.' At that very moment David appeared at the far entrance door of the stalls.

'David – ' I began. But he interrupted me.

'Well,' he said aggressively, as he strode towards us down the theatre aisle. 'Aren't you going to congratulate me?'

The morning after one of our *My Music* recordings David suffered a stroke in a London hotel bedroom. All thoughts of irritation or rivalry far from my mind, I rang the hospital the moment I heard about it, sent him my love (which was as genuine as my exasperation, if not stronger) and wished him a speedy recovery. After a week or two I was able to go and see him, finding him slightly slowed down and somewhat sorry for himself, but otherwise very much the same drily witty David of old. He told me a story that was characteristic of him. A young nurse had come to his bedside that first day he was admitted at University College Hospital.

'We've just had a get-well-soon message for you from a Mr Steve Race,' she had said. 'Would that be *the* Mr Steve Race?'

'Naturally,' replied David instantly, 'since I am *the* David Franklin.'

I laughed at that and told him a story or two about my own days in hospital, embroidering the tales slightly in an attempt to cheer him up. I think we both knew that he would never be back on the programme, but one kept up the cheerful pretence of his complete recovery.

As I finished a barely repeatable story about my stay in the nearby Middlesex Hospital, David reached out a hand and placed it on mine. I remember his words exactly.

'Dear Steve,' he said. 'Dear Steve. You're doing me good.'

It was one of the truly touching moments of my life, and I confess that my eyes filled with sudden tears. I remembered it a few months later when he died, and again at the star-studded Memorial Service in All Souls, Langham Place, where Lord Soper spoke so highly of him, and which David – bless his pompous old soul – would so much have enjoyed, could he have known about it.

But the show must go on, as performers are always telling one another. David Franklin's death had left an empty chair next to Frank's.

Pause a moment, gentle reader – and I promise not to call you that again – pause a while and speculate on what a formidable hill John Amis had to climb when he sat down in David Franklin's chair and looked across at me to receive his first *My Music* question. He was taking the place of a man much loved, much respected, much mourned. He was sitting next to one of the wittiest men on earth, with whom he would have to work out some sort of a light-hearted relationship.

Yet within a mere half hour John had established his own personality, his own brand of quick wit, and not least his own high tenor voice, so complementary as it turned out to the rich bass-baritone of Ian Wallace opposite him. I shall never get over my admiration for John during his trial period. Nor, I think, will he forget the way in which Frank guided him into a co-relationship which happily still flourishes.

Mention of John's and Ian's songs in the programme leads to the question I am most often asked, namely 'Are the final songs in *My Music* rehearsed?'

The plain answer is that they are not rehearsed, but they *are* planned. After all, it would be unthinkable for the show to end on a song that Ian Wallace could not recall.

STEVE: 'Finally, Ian, give us a chorus of "Carry me back to Green Pastures".'
IAN: 'I'm sorry, Steve, I can't remember how it goes.'
STEVE: 'Well that's the end of *My Music* for another week …'

No, such an anti-climax just is not conceivable. So it is necessary to find out in advance which songs the contestants can remember, and then offer them in that final round which I call, deliberately, 'the party-piece'. Yes, the final songs are indeed planned. But for spontaneity's sake, they are not, I repeat, rehearsed. No doubt they would be better musically if they were. But they would be much less fun.

Having written the questions for hundreds of editions of *My Music*, I have learnt a lot about the questionmaster's craft – or *art*, as I think I would call it on reflection. His art is an instinctive thing, as all art must be, but his craft is to enable his panellists to show off their memory for musical facts, as well as their ingenuity when they cannot remember. That is what the chairman is paid to do; that is why the series flourishes, given a cast as brilliant as mine. As Ian expressed my side of things so crisply in his autobiography:

> Don't make the questions too hard, accept witty answers as well as correct ones, allow everyone to gag and reminisce to their hearts' content, and realize that the least important aspect of the whole thing is who wins or loses.

One of the ever-present problems, not only for me as question-setter and chairman but for the panellists as well, is that our programmes are eventually heard in every English speaking country of the world, thanks to the BBC Transcription Service. The key word is 'eventually', some stations transmitting the shows years after they were recorded. We have to ensure that nothing exclusively parochial is mentioned, still less the date of the recording implied. Any reference to 'last year's So-and-So Centenary', or a comment on the recent results achieved by Ian's beloved Arsenal, would bring a sharp cry of pain from Stan Stancliffe, whose job it is to watch over the programmes' exportability and prepare them for world consumption.

In recent years *My Music* has been seen on BBC-2 television as well as heard on radio, thus giving me the privilege of working under three producers as opposed to my former two, and everyone else's one. I can offer no finer tribute to the three gentlemen concerned – Douglas Hespe (TV), Tony Shryane (domestic radio) and Stan Stancliffe (world outlets) – than to say that their professional expertise is equalled by their geniality. One has known producers who could not get on with a pet goldfish. My three are a joy to work with, and *My Music* would be infinitely less of a pleasure to do if any of them were absent.

After all these years of preparing and recording the programmes I have learnt a lot about my four colleagues on the stage. I have also learnt a good deal that I did not know before about music itself. For instance I have heard from Frank Muir what the leader of an orchestra does.

STEVE: 'Frank, what does the leader of an orchestra do?'
FRANK: 'Well for a start he gets a bit more money than the others. Also he sits beside the driver on the coach. And he gets first crack at the lady harpist.'

From Denis Norden I learnt the meaning of an Italian musical expression *tempo comodo*, which in my innocence I thought meant 'take at a convenient speed'. It is not so.

STEVE: 'Denis, can you explain *Tempo comodo*?'
DENIS: (*thinking hard*). 'Well now, *tempo* is Italian for time. *Comodo* ... Ah yes. A *comodo* is a bedside cupboard. So *tempo comodo* is about half past three in the morning.'

Gentlemen, I salute you. I don't know how you do it. But it's my enviable job to make sure you do.

26. *Annie Arstim just exactly*

I am not sure who it was that invented the lady known on the third floor of Broadcasting House as Annie Arstim. I only know that her name is enshrined in a million News and Current Affairs programmes. 'We sent our reporter along to talk to Mr Smith, *annie arstim* just exactly how serious was the allegation ...'

For some reason radio reporters always go *along* to interview people, never round. No reporter ever asks directly about something, he asks *just exactly how serious* it is thought to be. In fact a *Times* diarist some years ago invented a mate for Annie Arstim whose name was Justow Serious.

No broadcaster takes a deliberate pleasure in perpetuating such mindless expressions. The trouble is that topical magazine programmes of the *World at One* school are compiled against the clock. This is especially true of the links between items, the cues into the interview tapes which the reporters have brought back for slotting into the day's programme. The anchor man, who provides the listeners' anchor to the various items but who is himself anchored to the presenter's chair in an airless, windowless studio, is so busy conducting individual interviews of his own and keeping the whole show linked, that he scarcely has time to do more than rough out a paragraph or two between items. Annie Arstim and Justow Serious are born at moments of stress a few minutes before transmission. Happy is the man who at such moments can keep not only his sanity but the integrity of his verbal style and the purity of his syntax.

I know something about this at first hand. From 1970 for two memorable, indeed unforgettable years, I sat opposite the daddy-of-them-all when it came to news presentation, William Hardcastle. First of all for two weeks out of three, then later week and week about, he and I sat face to face across a studio table in the heart of Broadcasting House, jointly presenting the five o'clock weekday programme *PM*.

Bill Hardcastle was a legend, in Fleet Street as well as in Portland Place. Uniquely in top journalism he had enjoyed three careers, first as Washington correspondent of the *Daily Mail*, and subsequently as editor, then, when his newspaper career came to an abrupt end, as presenter of *The World at One* and co-presenter of *PM*. At a time when any other deposed editor would have become reconciled to spending the rest of his life on the scrapheap, Bill became a radio star.

He ate, drank, slept and breathed journalism, carrying in his mind a fathomless memory-bank of world facts. It was said that when someone told him that there had been a *coup d'état* in – let us say – San Jobango, he instantly retorted that he wasn't surprised, since at the last elections President Nemo had only polled 51½ per cent of the votes with his Agrarian Reform Party.

On another occasion, the producer had gone into Bill's studio during a momentary lull in *The World at One*, to tell him that 'some nut is on the phone with a plan for Great Britain'.

'Sounds promising,' said Bill. 'Put him on.'

Thirty seconds later he was saying on the air, 'I understand, Mr Pobjoy, that you have a plan for Great Britain.'

'No, Mr Hardcastle, not Great Britain. *The* Great Britain. I think she should be towed further up the Bristol Channel and opened to the public at Chepstow.'

'Hardly,' said Bill, not one whit disconcerted. 'With her draft you'd never get her past the Summerleaze mud flats' (or some such comment).

At such moments Bill Hardcastle was the Reuter-trained man *par excellence*. His dedication to radio was unbelievable. Having driven each morning from the Surrey cottage where he lived alone, he would arrive at Broadcasting House at 8 am, read all the morning papers, dispatch young reporters with their tape recorders in all directions, tackle a half-dozen major interviews with everyone from Cabinet ministers to film stars, introduce *The World at One*, take most of an hour off for lunch, then repeat the process for *PM*, winding up the day with several drinks and much conversation, leaving the West End finally at about 7 pm. On the way home he would sometimes stop the car and call in at his friend Peter Black's house for a swim. Then to bed and up next morning for another eight o'clock start.

The man was amazing. He was also physically immense; a great overflowing mass of flesh, with a chronic smoker's cough and dreadful breathing problems which increased as the taxing week wore on and culminated in stentorian wheezing which worried the listeners, though scarcely as much as it worried the rest of us. When the whole unit gave up smoking for an agreed month's trial, Bill's resolve lasted exactly half an hour.

When I reported for duty on my first *PM* I found Bill and the production staff in a side office having their lunch. I noticed that his lunch seemed to consist of an apple which he had peeled and then covered with salt, while in his left hand he held

197

a neat tumblerful of whisky. A good deal more from the same bottle went the same way after the programme.

Not that he was drunk. Emphatically he was not, but he was a man who needed constant stimulus, physically, mentally and socially. I have never met an intelligent man with less small talk. Bill at a party was conviviality itself, but he could no more talk about the weather than could the spiritual ancestor whom he rather liked to resemble, Doctor Johnson. He once told me that finding himself next to Groucho Marx at some Washington cocktail party, Bill had racked his brains for something worth saying to such a man. He began to extol the brilliance of S. J. Perelman, until he noticed the whites of Groucho's eyes. It had not been a good idea. The weather would have been safer.

Bill's Washington days still hung about him like a malaria bug and he was the only person since the war had ended whom I ever heard refer to someone as being 'hep'. (*Hip* – yes, *hep* – no.) When some tasty item of news was about to be covered, Bill could always be relied upon to observe to me enthusiastically 'That'll get 'em into the tent', while letters of complaint (of which there was a constant flood) drew from him the aphorism 'Every knock's a boost'. Often he would talk like a character out of *The Front Page*, reminding himself if time was running short that we were due to 'hit the streets' at five o'clock. And for two years, as each broadcast ended and the red cue-light went out, he pushed his chair back a few inches and observed to me, 'Ah well – another day, another dollar.'

The listeners' complaints centred mainly on the problem of Bill's microphone delivery, which was mangled to the point of incomprehensibility. Rushing at his material like a bull at a gate, he would stumble, pick himself up, stumble again, and finally emerge at the bottom of the paragraph, though one could never be sure how much the listeners had learnt from his references to *presdentialection* or *parlmenty dmoxy*. Once, after a more than usually gruelling afternoon, he began his opening announcement, not with his usual 'This is William Hardcastle', but with the words 'This is William Whitelaw ... I mean Hardcastle'.

Equable, about his own mistakes at any rate, Bill did not object to being lightly twitted about such things. The reason, I soon discovered, was that he did not really care about the listeners at all. The programme – yes. The *programme* was all-important; it was the insatiable god that must be served. The listeners however were invisible people; unreal and unknown, except for the nuts who wrote letters.

Though he insisted on seeing all the letters, their contents did not seem to affect him in any way, other than to reinforce his view about the sort of people who write letters to editors. Many of Bill's views were of the instant, computerised variety. Musicians, as he often enjoyed telling me, were in the main drug addicts. Clergymen were secret collectors of erotica. Boxers were punch-drunk. Dog owners were people who fed their pets on buttered toast. Women required to be classified according to their bust measurements, or at the very least by age and colour of hair. 'Blonde thirty-five-year-old attractive Mrs Robinson said today ...'

Habits died hard with Bill Hardcastle. He would indulge in strange verbal fancies, some of them persisted in for the same reason that the little boy sneezed in *Alice*. The great mystery was the name 'Antony', spelt as in the musician Antony Hopkins, which he invariably pronounced An*TH*ony with a *TH*. It transpired that when a little boy at school he had known an Anthony, and saw no reason to change the habit of a lifetime. Similarly, when the unhappy Mrs Linda Desramault was in the news with what he called her *tug-of-love* case, Bill never failed to pronounce her name *Dezz-ramo*. A pained BBC pronunciation unit pointed out repeatedly that if the first syllable was to be anglicised, so should the rest: *Dezz-* can logically only be followed by *-ramorlt*. But *Dezzramorlt* was clearly more than Bill could manage. Would he say *Day-ramo*, then? No, he would not.

The head of our *PM* section was a charming and cultured man, a brilliant biographer, but administratively speaking someone over whom William Hardcastle had long ago achieved total domination. The gentle Andrew Boyle would wander into the studio where Bill and I sat, wait until the microphone was switched off after we had completed some live link or other, then during a three or four minute insert tape he would discuss the framework of the next ten minutes.

'Bill,' he would begin, 'I thought we might put the book review in next, then the Peter Hain interview, then Steve's

199

piece about the last night of the Proms. That'll bring us to the half-way headlines. We could drop the British Rail discussion, don't you think?'

'No I don't,' Bill would say. 'Put the discussion on now, then Peter Hain, then Steve's piece. Drop the book review.'

'Oh, all right.' Off Andrew would go, to reappear in view some seconds later behind the glass panel of the cubicle where his lips could be seen moving as he explained Bill's new running-order to the staff. 'Nice man, no idea of news sense,' Bill would observe to me.

I learnt a lot about news values from sitting opposite Bill Hardcastle. I also learnt that without the supply of newspapers to raid in the morning, *World at One* and *PM* were in danger of being more or less non-existent, since the B B C was unable to maintain a nationwide network of 'stringers' (local correspondents) whose local stories were the best source of interview material. When there was a Fleet Street strike, our programme almost died of starvation.

I learnt a little about the remorseless drive of the journalist when he glimpses a story, as for example when the Rt Hon John Davies M.P. made what was clearly an unguarded remark about the Common Market and it seemed to me that our programme went out of its way to draw the maximum amount of embarrassment from the incident. I should add that so far as I could see there was no political bias in this, though few of our complaining listeners seemed to understand the point. We were neither to the left nor to the right. But we were journalists, and journalists have a vested interest in trouble. That was why a three-way studio discussion between Bill and two people holding differing views was never referred to by the department as a discussion or a conversation; it was always known hopefully as 'the punch-up', however cool and friendly its participants.

In human terms I found William Hardcastle to be a fascinating mixture of the soft and the hard. Certainly it was true that if he liked someone they were in, and if he disliked them they were out. I suspect that he actually enjoyed power over others, that appetite for control over other people's lives which I have always found impossible to comprehend. But he liked me, and being liked is a powerful persuader. He had a quick, irreverent sense of humour, and he would take a delight in giving me the lowdown on some great political figure slightly before the studio door had closed on that worthy's retreating figure.

I enjoyed the pleasure of his close company for two years. Then, for reasons which I never understood, he turned against me. Race was suddenly on his way out: it was a toss up which would come first, my resignation or my dismissal. My departure was being hastened by a characteristic manoeuvre: Bill had taken it into his head to mispronounce my name whenever he had to say it on the air. In vain Andrew Boyle asked him not to do it. *Stevie* Race I had to be, or on one occasion *Steven Rah-chay*. It was clearly time to go.

The letter conveying Bill's decision came, as it should have done, from the official head of our department. All the same, I was interested to note that Andrew's letter began:

Dear Steve,
It has been decided (and I must say I agree) ...

When the time came, I was fascinated to see what would happen during the convivial drinks session which followed my very last *PM*. The convention was that Andrew Boyle would give a brief, light-hearted speech of thanks and farewell. I waited, whisky in hand, while we all chatted brightly. Then Andrew called for order.

'As you all know,' he began, 'we shall be losing Steve after today. It falls to me to ...'

At that moment one of the secretaries called 'You're wanted on the phone, Andrew.' He was gone for several minutes and the normal level of conversation resumed.

When he came back he had evidently forgotten that he had been making a speech. Nothing more was said, and at seven o'clock I went home, saying goodbye all round, with a special word of thanks to Andrew and Bill, who shook me warmly by the hand and wished me all the best. I had learnt a lot from them; I liked them both.

As they used to say in Washington, another day another dollar.

27. Full circle

Because of the BBC's closely guarded monopoly of sound broadcasting there was no rival programme in News and Current Affairs to which I could transfer.

And a good thing too. I had already spent far too long away from music. I celebrated my return to crotchets and quavers with *Invitation to Music* (a series which helped to launch the brilliant King's Singers), *My Music* and *Many a Slip*, plus a weekly show for the British Forces Broadcasting Service and a long-running series of music programmes on the BBC World Service.

There was television work as well, notably a recurring series for Thames Television called *There Goes that Song Again*, an easygoing, conversational quiz in which my guests ranged from Cleo Laine and John Dankworth to Vera Lynn and Ann Shelton, with Roy Castle and Lionel Blair for good measure, even extending to the legendary Hollywood songwriters Johnny Mercer, Sammy Cahn and Arthur Schwartz. Lovely guests, all of them – and many others besides – though my most memorable guest turned out to be Diana Dors.

Di, as everyone calls her, had formerly been one of the sexiest things seen in films: she was the fiery filly of the fifties, the sexpot of the sixties. Now, in the 1970s, she had filled out a notch or two and was well on the way to being the all-time Red-Hot Momma. The new Diana Dors was – how should one put it? – comfortable, ample. 'There's enough to go round,' as she herself says.

So there sat Di, facing me across the piano, shrouded in a great voluminous gown which my mother would probably have called a dust-sheet. The quiz questions were of course unrehearsed, but each guest sang a chorus of some old favourite as a kind of cabaret turn. Di had elected to sing 'My Funny Valentine'.

The studio had an easy, rehearsal feeling about it; any moment someone was going to call out 'OK, back at 4.30 everyone.' I was enjoying accompanying Diana Dors' pleasantly stylish singing.

'Your looks are laughable,
Unphotographable—'
sang Di.

And then she broke into mad hysterics.

I was staggered for a moment, until I realised that my guest was simply suffering from an uncontrollable fit of the giggles. She was shaking with laughter and pointing to the monitor screen that stood beside her close-up camera.

'Good God!' said Diana Dors. 'I'm sorry, Steve, but I've just seen myself on the screen and I couldn't carry on. What a sight!'

Soon after that we broke for tea. Later on, for safety's sake, I seem to recall that we substituted a different song, lest my guest should suffer another bout of self-mockery. For my part I could only put my arms half round her and hug the girl in admiration. Is there another woman on earth with an international reputation for glamour who could catch sight of her face in a monitor screen and collapse with laughter? I doubt it. If there is one thing I love it is a star who doesn't fancy herself.

That particular TV series was an unusually relaxed one all round, because its producer too had his feet on the ground. David Clark is about as far from telly producer's megalomania as anyone could be, a fact for which his artists are ever grateful. He also has a winning way with an audience, cheerfully handling what is known in the business as the 'warm-up'. When David took on that chore for my show it was a relief, because I am not by nature a person who revels in the opportunity to get pally with the visiting coach parties. In this respect I am not a snob, merely a misfit. I fully realise that crowds are made up of people; I simply prefer people to crowds, and friends to people. As a result of that admission it may be claimed that I have spent all these years in the wrong business, and it is certainly true that the ideal audience for me is an unseen one. In a word, I am no Thespian, no actor laddie, no showman; just someone who enjoys communicating to receptive people the pleasure he finds in words and in music.

The BBC Midlands TV series *Major Minor* is very much

my 'scene'. After extensive regional heats, nine young boy or girl pianists are invited to the Birmingham studio to compete for an attractively-designed award. They play their party pieces – Beethoven, Chopin or very often Shostakovitch – and undergo tests in quick study and improvisation, while my job is to compère the programmes, trying at the same time to make sure the youngsters are relaxed and happy. Just one half-hour spent in their company, as the show's deviser – Derek Smith – will testify, is enough to allay all one's fears about the up-and-coming generation which they represent. Musically, personally, they would cheer up the most jaundiced observer of the modern scene.

* * *

Programme after programme, show after show, script after script, journey after journey: did the man never sleep?

Yes, I slept. I even rested, read books, went for walks and spent precious hours with my family doing whatever families do when simply being together.

Nicola was growing up. Clair's response to my absorbing professional life, inevitably, had been to create an equally absorbing alternative life of her own. Starting with one family dog (who actually had been a birthday present for me) she became a lover of Afghan hounds at a time when there were relatively few in the country, then a breeder of them, a judge at championship dog shows, and eventually a world authority, writing a regular weekly column, and adjudicating at major canine events as far away from home as the Californian coast. Her super champion, Rifka's Musqat D'rar, won an unbeliev- able twenty Challenge Certificates under different judges at championship shows: in other words Musqat was technically a champion more than six times over, a record which for many years no exhibitor was able to equal, despite the enormous increase in the popularity of Afghans and the number of shows for which they qualified.

One morning I woke up to find Clair reading a letter, tears of happiness on her cheeks. 'It's come,' she said.

'It' was the invitation to judge Afghans at Crufts; the realisa- tion of her dearest dream, as I well knew. I put my arms round her and said it was wonderful news. It would call for great expertise and total integrity, both of them qualities which she had in abundance. 'You'll do it so well,' I told her, with pride.

But Clair's crowning moment at Crufts never came. She died, at the age of only forty-six, after a brief but magnificently brave fight against cancer. For half her life she had battled against rheumatoid arthritis while her poor fingers and hands inexorably closed in a grip of swollen pain. Then came the cruellest blow of all. When I broke to her the news that no one else in the world could, she walked into the bathroom, wept quietly for a minute or two, then washed her face and came out, to resume her life quietly and bravely for the very few weeks she had left. I have never known such courage, and can only long for its equal when my time comes.

I kept Clair's beloved Afghans for as long as possible. Friends put me under tremendous personal pressure to show Rifka's Musqat D'rar for one last time, thereby turning her twenty challenge certificates into twenty-one and making her a seven-times champion, but I would not put the judge in such an appalling position. I never showed the dog again, though she lived on happily at home for some time.

The following year when Crufts Show came round, the very one which Clair was to have judged, I presented in her memory a bronze trophy in the shape of an Afghan, the model for which had been moulded by an American friend whom she loved. Each year the Clair Race Afghan Trophy is still presented at Crufts. It acts I hope as a perpetual reminder of a pioneer worker in the breed, someone whom I would often find at home standing at a window watching those lovely animals as they played or simply posed, in their innocent, proud, incomparable way.

'Just look at them,' she would say. 'They must be the most beautiful creatures in the world.'

28. Our speaker, Mr Er, is known to you all

We are here in the world for others as well as for ourselves. So one tries to serve, offering help with committee work here, support for a good cause there. Merely an unexpected letter can bring enormous pleasure to someone; a fact which I learnt from the singer Benny Lee, who writes sudden little fan letters to people in the profession, as the whim takes him. It is an extraordinarily nice thing to do and it sets up surprise pockets of sunshine over many a grey breakfast table. I have tried to emulate Benny's example over the years, and was only once to my knowledge misunderstood, when a light orchestral conductor told a mutual friend, 'I've had a sort of fan letter from Steve Race. Is he sending me up?' No, Frank, just complimenting you.

I repeat: we are here in the world for one another as well as for ourselves, though it is not always easy to tell who comes off best, donor or recipient. One of the most enjoyable unpaid jobs I do is serving on the Council of the Albert Hall, or to give it its fine sounding title, The Royal Albert Hall of Arts and Sciences. We the Council meet monthly to administer the affairs of what was derisively known in its early years as 'the Kensington mausoleum', though Queen Victoria was nearer the mark when she looked at its ponderous façade and said 'It is like the British Constitution'. It is indeed, and not unlike Victoria herself in design. I love every brick of the place, being somewhat addicted to Victoriana anyway, and I never go through its portly portals without remembering the brilliant people and strange scenes the hall has witnessed, from Wagner and Verdi to Billie Holiday and Billie-Jean King; from the suffragette meeting at which someone boomed 'Votes for

Women!' through an organ pipe, to the annual progresses of weepy Miss Worlds as they receive their homage.

It would not occur to any of us on the Albert Hall Council to require payment for our services (though the provision of an excellent lunch does sweeten a long agenda). There are some things one simply does for love.

And others out of a sense of duty. These are the sporadic speaking engagements one undertakes here and there; the functions attended (as a friend of mine so graphically put it) by 'ladies with corrugated hair'. Some are a pleasure to do, others are frankly not. And one can usually judge how things will go from the welcome.

'For my sins I am the chairman of the executive committee,' he says advancing towards you. When any man says 'for my sins' you know he is about to show off. ('For my sins I received the OBE last year ...') That evening, when the audience is assembled, the chairman stands up and calls for silence.

'Our speaker tonight is well known to all of us. Among other things, he has ...' His eye drops to the piece of paper he holds, on which his secretary has that afternoon copied down a few biographical facts from *Who's Who*. For some reason the facts are always out of date, or at best mistyped. 'We all know Mr Race from *Face the Music* with Lady Eleanor Barnett and Denis Muir. His programme *There's Many a Slip* with Roy Plumtree ...' On he lurches, generous, well-meaning and wrong.

At least he is usually on the visiting speaker's side. A few chairmen are perceptibly jealous, and this seems to apply particularly when one's chairman is a clergyman. Some of the clergy do not like the idea of the laity speaking in public, regarding us as amateurs who lack the proper qualifications. Their words of welcome to 'our visiting speaker tonight' can show a want of enthusiasm bordering on the uncharitable. I would not mind a pound, as the saying goes, for every clergyman who has introduced me to his flock with the words 'Of course, I myself have never seen or heard any of Mr Race's programmes. But I understand that he has a great following –' (among folk like you). A similar air of professional rivalry can be detected in the welcome offered sometimes by headmasters. I suppose it must be difficult to spend all day with one's educational or spiritual inferiors and then change attitude completely for the evening's guest.

So church and school speaking engagements can present something of a problem and are not always the gratifying experience which charitable work ought to be. Nevertheless one tries to do one's bit for worthy causes. I draw the line only at Garden Fêtes – not my scene – and Bazaars. Bazaars, Sales of Work, or 'Fayres' as they used to be called in my Methodist youth, are a lot of fun to arrange and they involve much hard work. But very often they simply do not merit a hundred-mile round trip on the part of a guest opener, who may find himself on arrival talking to thirty ladies, five children and a dog, all of whom would rather be having tea than listening to a speech. The only part of the bazaar opening that anyone cares about comes after the speeches, anyway, when the guest speaker tours the various stalls, buying damson jam and upholstered dress-hangers. No, I don't open bazaars if I can possibly avoid it. And the kitchen cupboard is full of damson jam.

* * *

In recent years I have done a certain amount of purely professional public speaking in small theatres and community halls, giving a one-man entertainment (illustrated with music on cassette) which I have tended to call *An Evening with Steve Race* since that is exactly what it is. Perhaps *Musician at Large* would be a better title.

Better still might be *Steve Race draws himself up to his full height*, since people meeting me for the first time always seem amazed at how tall I am. 'But I thought you were a short man!' they exclaim, running their eyes up and down my 72 inches. I am neither tall nor short, and for some reason the conversation always irritates me slightly.

I enjoy the contact with a small audience, providing it is fairly intimate. I like to meet 'my kind' of people, and they are my kind for the very good reason that they have taken the trouble to come and hear me in the flesh. All we broadcasters should make some attempt to meet the people whom we assault so freely with our chatter and our opinions. It is too easy to spend a comfortable lifetime pouring one's views into a microphone or a camera, never hearing the cries of 'rubbish!'

or 'get orf!' at the listeners' end; never feeling the sting of the boot hurled furiously at the TV set.

Towards the end of the evening I usually include an impromptu question-and-answer session and enjoy the stimulus of not knowing what the questions are likely to be.

Not *always* knowing, that is. I have to admit that some questions seem inevitable, whether one is in Bude, Bradford or Banff. 'Are the songs in *My Music* rehearsed?' 'How do you react to Rock music?' 'What do you think of people who jazz up the classics?'

The question I was least prepared for came one night from the very back of the hall.

'Why the beard?' a voice enquired.

'I beg your pardon?'

'I said why the beard?'

On the spur of the moment I replied 'Having brought it with me I thought it was a shame not to let you see it.' But the experience reminded me what an extraordinarily traumatic effect my growing a beard seemed to have had on otherwise quite kindly people.

My beard was born, as most men's beards are, on holiday. Only a man knows how boring and uncomfortable it is to scrape the same old face every morning without even an anaesthetic. So I grew my Majorcan beard.

It itched, though not for long. On my return home I regarded myself in the mirror, turned my head from side to side, put on my now-necessary reading glasses, and decided that the beard could stay, at any rate for a while. There seemed a good chance that it might cover up whatever monstrous changes were to go on underneath in the years to come.

Two years later on a whim I shaved it off, took one look at what was revealed and hurriedly grew it again. Meanwhile the letters from television viewers took on an almost menacing character. Well brought up ladies who would never dream of commenting on the cut of one's suit felt impelled to attack the cut of my beard. 'Take it off, it's horrible!' they wrote, using capital letters or red ink. I was astonished to find the effect that a chinful of Santa Claus-type hairs could do to an otherwise reticent correspondent. No wonder those American producers, wanting to shock society at large, had called their show simply *Hair*.

I dug my heels in. I rather liked the beard myself. And after all, it was my own face.

But the best reason for keeping the beard, truth to tell, was because my wife liked it. My new wife: my understanding, loyal, lively-minded Lonny. She liked the beard. In fact she rather thought she loved it. So it stayed.

I had known Lonny Mather a long time. During my busiest radio years she had been one of the outstanding studio managers in Broadcasting House, the sort of person whom one was always glad to find allocated to a programme. She and I worked together on series after series, and I had come to rely on her natural ear for music as well as on her gift for creating a good atmosphere in the studio. Not all studio staffs realise that strong personal characteristics, not to say neuroses, can cast a blight on a programme, eating into the broadcaster and affecting everyone present. In broadcasting work, hang-ups must be left outside the door.

Much of the S.M.'s job is highly technical, and I stand dumbfounded before their expertise. But the success of any broadcast depends in the end on the creation of a relaxed, purposeful atmosphere, and in that Lonny was an expert as in the engineering and artistic aspects of her job.

After she left the control panel to become a producer in the BBC Gramophone Department, coping with the demands of multiple international cable circuits for *World-wide Family Favourites*, I used to drop into her studio sometimes simply to admire her steady coolness.

That quality is now employed in a more domestic setting. It may not be easy being my wife, as women readers will already have decided for themselves. Like most men, I want to be the master, while retaining the right occasionally to be the child. The perfect wife is steady enough to be an unwavering support, yet pliable enough to respond to her partner's moods as they change.

To being moody, neither Lonny nor I need plead guilty. Nor I think are we dull. But a basic steadiness on both sides is a recipe for a durable marriage, and we are happy in one another's company with everything to share and everything to talk about, just as if we were meeting for the first time.

I have noticed that women are better at some things than at

others. To put it more directly – though goodness knows one must be careful! – there are some things that women do not do quite so well as men. It has been my joy to discover that Lonny not merely does the expected things well – cooking, homemaking – but the unexpected things too. For example, she is one of the rare women who can navigate, even to the extent of reading a map which happens to be lying at 180° to the direction of travel. She is a first class driver herself, even sometimes when I am at the wheel. She can add up a column of figures in the time it takes me to write down:

$$
\begin{array}{r}
17+ \\
12 \\
3 \\
\hline
\\
\hline
\end{array}
$$

Her knowledge of wines placed her among the finalists in a national newspaper's wine competition (though I admit that I make the better cup of tea). Best of all, she is compassionate, genuine and utterly un-neurotic, bringing happiness to our home and order to our V.A.T. returns. Her existence is a constant reminder, not that I need it, that I am the most fortunate of men.

Which leads me to the final chapter.

29. *Autumn leaves, as we all must*

It was a purely chance happening, hundreds of miles from home, in fact behind the Iron Curtain, that brought a kind of self-realisation and set me on course for the mode of life I am now enjoying.

I had been invited to be a guest of the Czech government at

the Prague International Festival of Jazz, joining the panel of judges for a composing competition and generally commenting on the concerts for press and radio.

I flew over to Prague on the same plane as John Dankworth and Cleo Laine, in fact it turned out that we were staying at the same hotel in Wenceslas Square. On arrival I was immediately swept up into a cosmopolitan crowd of jazz writers and critics. For two or three days I saw little of my English colleagues and practically nothing of the city of Prague, shuttling endlessly from committee room to concert hall and from concert hall to all-night jazz session.

On the Saturday I rebelled, announcing firmly that I was going off on my own to look at the Prague I had always longed to see: the Prague of the première of *Don Giovanni*, of Smetana and of Kafka's diaries. Off I duly went, for a memorable morning's sightseeing, ending up at the Charles Bridge over the Vltava.

It was a much refreshed Steve Race who walked into the hotel lobby that afternoon, to find a little knot of people looking thoroughly unhappy. At the centre of them was an ashen-faced John Dankworth. Just as I sauntered up to them, John was saying 'What on earth are we going to do? If only we could find an accomp ...'

That was the moment I chose to arrive. It was like a scene from a bad backstage movie. I stood there, while Cleo put her arm round me, something which no flesh-and-blood man could resist, whatever the ultimate cost to his sightseeing plans. I thought I could guess what was coming, and I was right.

John and Cleo had gone off an hour before for a rehearsal with the Czech pianist who was to accompany Cleo in her Festival appearance that evening. He had proved to be a magnificent jazz player, indeed he is known as such throughout the world. Unfortunately he was a poor sight reader. Cleo's music is difficult to read; consequently there was a complete collapse in the rehearsal. John, Cleo, their bassist and drummer had trailed back to the hotel disconsolate. And at that moment in had breezed, guidebook in hand, that well-known scholar of Czech history, Steve Race. 'If only we could find an accompanist ...' John was saying.

Clearly I was it. All the same, it was something of a

challenge. For years I had not played jazz in the improvisatory sense, and certainly not at the Dankworth level. I was rusty and out of practice simply as a piano player. Moreover like the hero of *The Prisoner of Zenda* I was emotionally unprepared for my new role. Just about the only thing I knew I could do for sure was actually read Cleo's music. 'That's all you need to do,' said John, lying bravely.

After the briefest of backstage rehearsals we went on the stage that night at the great Lucerna Hall, packed to the doors with fans, musicians and critics. 'Some of us think it very courageous of you to go on and play, after being an adjudicator last night,' commented one of the Czech organisers, in well-meaning encouragement. I could have done without that remark.

Our quartet (complete with John) looked very small on the huge platform. The piano seemed a long way away from Cleo, who stood downstage with her back to me, acknowledging the initial welcome from the audience. The keyboard had a strangely unfamiliar appearance and for a second I wondered which was middle C. Then John beat in Cleo's opening song and we were away.

From my point of view things went quite well, as I know from the LP record that was subsequently released in Czechoslovakia. But what mattered was not the pianist's performance. What mattered was Cleo Laine's reception.

They adored her. The place erupted. From the depths of that cavernous hall came wave after wave of applause, cheers and love. In a ridiculous sort of way, I was part of it. John motioned to the accompanying group and we stood up, just as another wave of love hit the platform.

I could scarcely take it in. I had shared in modest applause before, all my life in fact, some of it directed at me individually. But this was the ultimate; this was the mountain peak. I drank in great draughts of Cleo's acclaim, and as I did so I knew with a curious sudden detachment that I was experiencing an important moment. A professional door was firmly, finally closing behind me. Or would it be more proper to say a curtain lowering? Anyway it was happening – and I did not mind a bit.

Never for a moment had I aspired to that sort of adulation. On and on it went. Such receptions are the meat and drink, the be-all-and-end-all of the Show-Business compulsion. The cheers and even tears of an audience are the drug to which many of my colleagues are deeply addicted; they are the reward for a lifetime of scruffy rehearsal rooms, cracked teacups and broken marriages. It would be hard to blame the victims of such an addiction, after once accepting even a moment's fix of one's own.

I loved it for Cleo, but it just wasn't my scene. I knew that as soon as I could I was going to move away from that glorious, heady, blood-tingling, chromium-plated atmosphere. Not in order to leave the entertainment profession, still less to give up working in the communications field, compulsive persuader that I am. Just to get out of show-biz; show-biz as spelt with a 'z'. I was turning aside from the goal which has to be the target of every performer; the shedding of the last veil, the ultimate act of surrender to an adoring public. It simply was not in me to make that self-sacrifice.

I left the stage, said goodnight to John and Cleo, and walked back through the anonymous streets to bed, happy, exhausted and determined.

The realisation of my somewhat reluctant part in the comedy-drama that is show-business came to me that night in Prague as I have tried to describe it. But the chance to act on it had to wait for the right moment. Only at the beginning of 1976 did I make the deliberate, symbolic act of moving from the town into the country. Lonny and I had both been looking forward keenly to the change, and here we were at last, living in a house set between a beechwood and a wheatfield, watching a heron wheel away from our own garden; seeing a stoat cross the lawn; hoping the nuthatches might nest. How marvellous to know that instead of feeling one ought to have a second telephone line installed, a single one seemed rather more than enough.

Here at home there is much to be done: so many pieces of music still to be heard, books to be read, trees to be patted affectionately on the trunk when nobody is looking. 'No, I'm afraid I can't lunch with your directors in the city today. I have to stay at home and count the bees on my *hebe salicifolia*.'

I had not retired. What I had done was reallocate my time, reconsider it. I had *re-evaluated my priorities*, as my old friends in

214

the advertising agency world would have put it. Run your engagement diary up the flagpole, Steve, and see if you feel inclined to salute. Up to a point, Lord Copper.

All my professional life I had seen workoholic colleagues suffering from advanced cases of the freelance disease, a condition which manifests itself in the compulsive cry, 'My God, it's June, and I've got nothing in the diary after September. I'm ruined!' – Except that the chap isn't ruined of course, he is merely undergoing a familiar occupational neurosis. Come September he will have plenty of work . . . (And nothing in the diary after the following March.)

It is true that the successful freelance has to ensure that there is an enormous amount of work constantly coming in. On the other hand, he can easily suffer from the compulsion to accept any and every tiny, time-consuming engagement that is offered, whether or not it might be worth doing from the financial, or indeed any other, point of view.

From the new position on top of my personal flagpole I was able to take a bird's-eye view of my freelance existence. I found that quite a lot of what I was doing was aesthetically unrewarding and even economically pointless. I am constantly amazed at colleagues who seem prepared to work for derisory fees, merely for the pleasure of being asked. In that respect there is a crying need for a Guild of Freelance Broadcasters, though I doubt if it would command the necessary loyalty.

The acid test of my personal new-found freedom came quite soon after we moved to Great Missenden. I had been doing the occasional review of popular concerts for a leading daily paper. Physically it involves a taxing procedure, whereby one rushes out from the hall as the last chords of music are dying away, finds a call-box somewhere and telephones to Fleet Street one's on-the-spot review for the following morning's editions.

When Frank Sinatra came to the Albert Hall, I covered his first night's concert and duly phoned in my story to the *Daily* ——————.

They liked it. So incidentally did Frank Sinatra, though no one could accuse him of being a man with a natural affection for journalists. A few weeks after my review appeared, I received the following letter from his home in North Formosa Avenue, Hollywood:

Dear Steve,

Sorry for being so tardy but no sooner than I returned to the States for some Palm Springs sun, I received an SOS from Las Vegas.

Thanks for making my visit to London so very memorable.

Cordially,

Frank Sinatra

It was gratifying to get such a letter from a great star whose performance I had tried to review justly, though on second reading I realised that almost exactly the same letter would have done for someone who had murdered his act. They too would have made his London visit 'very memorable'.

More to the point was the newspaper's reaction, which was to invite me to lunch at the Ivy Restaurant to meet the editor and features editor. In the event the editor was not able to come, being involved at the time in fighting a major lawsuit. But the features editor came, and asked me to contribute a regular column – monthly, weekly, whenever – about more or less anything musical at a salary (I gathered) to be determined by sticking a pin in a ready reckoner.

I can still see the expression of disbelief on his face when I anticipated the discussion of terms by saying thanks, but no anyway. It was indeed a great honour to be asked. I would have enjoyed doing it – who wouldn't? But I simply did not want to be tied down to such a schedule – such a treadmill.

I went back home and patted the trunks of a few of my trees. Various radio and TV offers came, and were accepted or not according to impulse, and I am well aware that some of them left behind me a residue of producers and booking clerks who felt that Steve Race had suddenly given way to delusions of grandeur. Not a bit of it: I had finally decided to get the relationship right between what one needs to do, ought to do and wants to do; in other words, between work, duty and pleasure. Much of the time the three overlap, at any rate in a life as fortunate as mine. But not always.

The very realisation that offers of freelance work can be politely, gratefully declined is quite a heady experience.

But then ... On a Friday evening in the incomparable Chiltern autumn, when the bell-ringers are practising jerkily at the church across the valley and their sound filters through the great beech trees of Angling Spring Wood, I sit on my terrace with a glass of something Aunt Lena would not have recognised, and it occurs to me how little I now care whether my secretary has remembered to book a fourth trombonist for the Oxo commercial, or whether 'Lay Down Your Arms' is black-listed for *Music While You Work*.

Perhaps I should resume composing, which I must admit to having neglected in recent years. I have in fact made a start, with an album of four miniature cantatas dedicated to the school in our village, and published as *The Day of the Donkey and other Songs of Praise for juniors*.

Time at last to edit those Victorian diaries and tell the extraordinary story of my grandfather, a shilling-a-day Weardale lead miner who travelled half round the world under sail in 1873 and became an honoured citizen of China, a place he could barely even have spelt when he first felt the call to be a missionary there. Time to make up a round of *My Music* questions about Ringo, Ravel or *Rio Rita*. Time to stroll over to Atkins Wood and mull over the new series of *Music Now* for the BBC World Service.

Time to walk down to the village, buy a day return ticket to Marylebone – why did I want to *drive* everywhere in the old days? – and gaze once again at Botticelli's *Mystic Nativity*, the ivory diptychs in the Courtauld, or that superb Cuyp at Kenwood. Time to go to one of Christie's Old Master sales and catch the auctioneer's eye at four hundred pounds, safe in the knowledge that the charming little Constable landscape will end up someone else's property at forty thousand.

In the past few years I have been spending as much time at art galleries as at concerts. That made it a double pleasure to be invited by the trustees of the National Gallery to advise them on whether there was material in the gallery's collection for some sort of a long-playing record.

There was. I sifted through the whole National Gallery collection of two thousand pictures and then proposed a final list of eleven which showed either noted musicians, or music being performed, though of necessity in silence. With the help of colleagues from my *alma mater*, the Royal Academy of Music, I realised in terms of sound the music which otherwise one could only 'see', in canvases ranging from the Piero della Francesca *Nativity* to Degas' *Ballet Dancers*. The research had to be scrupulously correct as to date, place, instrumentation, language and even dialect. It was a great challenge, and it necessitated close liaison with the head of National Gallery publications, Gordon Booth.

One day I rang up with a small but urgent problem. 'Could you send someone to see whether the angels in the Piero della Francesca are playing their lutes with plectra or merely with their fingers?' I asked. 'We want to get it absolutely right on the record.'

'I'll go and have a look myself,' said Gordon, 'it's only just round the corner.' I waited for a minute or so, then heard Gordon's voice back on the line. 'My, are you in trouble!' he said. '*No strings!*' They had disappeared some centuries ago, thanks to a zealous picture cleaner. (On the record we duly gave the angels back their lute strings.)

A similar LP for Glasgow Art Gallery provided music for some eleven of the pictures in that fine collection too. By that time the National Gallery in London had done so well with our first record that they were asking for another. *Portraits and Music* duly took its place in the Gallery shop alongside *Music in Pictures*.

My personal taste in pictures tends to be classical, representational. I do not knock the man who sells a pile of bricks to the Tate Gallery; I simply do not bother to go and look at it. On the other hand I do not hold the view that fine painting expired, as some people seem to think great music expired, round about the year 1912. So it was quite exciting to get a letter from a contemporary artist whom I much admired, asking if he could paint my portrait for an exhibition to be held at the National Theatre on the South Bank in the summer of 1978.

John Bratby called his exhibition *The Individual in an Egalitarian Society*. 'I have conceived the idea of making a pictorial record for posterity of persons who have marked their era,' wrote Bratby, in his foreword to the exhibition catalogue. 'I have invited high achievers, individuals, persons of originality and persons with dynamic qualities.

'A society not based on the individual is a society that is not desirable ... Most of the people I have painted in this series could not live in such a society.'

Well that much at any rate was true of me, so perhaps in a modest way I qualified among the 'high achievers and persons with dynamic qualities', if only because, like them, I could not contemplate life as an ant. As Ant Number 1334498 in the R.A.F. I had not been a conspicuous success.

I went to John Bratby's studio wondering how we would get on with one another, but I need not have worried. As one of Britain's leading portrait painters he knows how to make a subject feel at ease: we seemed to be old friends from the start. I glanced at the waiting canvas on his easel, blank in the main, but with blobs of colour placed round the outside in readiness. As I watched he squeezed out an extra blodge of green and black, presumably in honour of my green and black striped shirt. I sat down to be painted.

We talked. Or rather, *I* talked. There is something of the confessional in having one's face studied and painted; so much so that after half an hour I looked wildly round to see whether a tape recorder might be taking down my unguarded blether for an amazed posterity. Then later, towards the end of the session, Bratby was called away to the telephone, leaving me sitting on my chair while my almost-completed likeness rested invitingly on its easel, just out of my view. I remember thinking that his sitters must be divided into those who would, and those who would not, peek. Which was I?

I did not peek. Eventually the artist returned and finished the portrait, melding what remained of the reserves of colour into an abstract background. Then he turned the portrait round and placed it about eight feet away from me in a good light.

'That's it,' he said. 'That's how I see you.'

Wondering which of us was the more nervous, I looked at myself, full-face, in that pitiless pose made famous by a succession of Convict 99s. John Bratby was watching me. He had made me look rather younger, I thought; that is no fault in a portrait painter, though he might have been less truthful about my ears! He had emphasised strongly the slight pear-shape of my face. But the eyes ... *The eyes*! I remembered how some time before he had dipped his blunt, stubby brush into the black paint and gone 'blob – blob' on the canvas. That must have been the moment at which he did the eyes, and they were dead right. He had got me.

'You've got me,' I said.

After the National Theatre exhibition was over I bought the painting, of course – who wouldn't? It hangs opposite me in my study as I type these words. I could hardly subject my family or guests to it in the living quarters of the house, but for the sitter it is different. For me the portrait is a source of constant ...

Constant *what*? – Pleasure? 'That's me, by Bratby.' Yes, I suppose so. I show it to guests now and then. But whatever others may see in it, for myself I see the reflection of those key moments I have tried to describe in this book, together with a few others which no autobiographer can be expected to reveal. The feeling of being discovered, almost of being found out, is a strange one, though not quite so disconcerting as I had feared when I agreed to have the portrait made. Perhaps only the artist himself can read its total message.

Let me then take stock. Behind the overlaid experiences of life I see the face of a happy, fulfilled man, and that is as it should be. I have loved and been loved. I have had a daughter. I have swum in the Caribbean and seen the sunlit Alps from above the clouds. I have watched Manchester United win the European Cup, heard Count Basie's Orchestra, and played Scrabble with friends. I have visited the *Uffizi*, read *Middlemarch*, heard the slow movement of Elgar's Violin Concerto, and owned a spinney of silver birch trees. I have opened my eyes each morning on a world that seems good and exciting.

As Ira Gershwin said, nice work if you can get it. But as he was also careful to add–

Who could ask for anything more?

Index

223